Twinkle Toes and the Riddle of the Lake
a story for the young & young at heart

by Susan Peterson Gateley

illustrated by Pat Cooper

Susan Peterson Gateley

Twinkle Toes and the Riddle of the Lake

published by Ariel Associates/Whiskey Hill Press

12025 Delling Road Wolcott NY 14590

printed in the United States of America

ISBN 978-0-9646149-1-8

Library of Congress Control Number 2009900890

Schools and groups may order this book at special quantity discounts for bulk

purchases. Contact the publisher at the address above.

www.silverwaters.com

www.riddleofthelake.com

Acknowledgments

I had a lot of help from fellow writers, friends and professionals with this project. I also received encouragement from family and friends. Dr. James Haynes, Brockport, Dr. Peter Hodson of Queens U, Helen Domske of Sea Grant, Dr. Paul Bowser, Cornell, Alicia Perez-Fuentetaja, Buffalo State, and Ryan LaFlamme of Toronto Lake keepers helped with fact checking. Please note any errors and opinions contained herein are strictly the responsibility and accomplishment of the author! Anna Liese Bopp of the Sodus Central School District was a huge help and a big thank you to Dr. Jeffrey Freedman also. As always, so my husband Chris gave invaluable support and assistance and I thank Pat the artist for her patience and extra effort in helping me tell Twink's story.

This modest work is dedicated to Dusty, Twinkle Toes, Miss Piggy and all those other companion animals who give us so much and ask us for so little.

Table of Contents

1. Twinkle Toes is Taken Aback..3
2. Twinkle Toes sets sail..14
3. Twink Under Bare Poles...24
4. Twinkle Toes and Dusty Have a Gam With an Old Salt.................35
5. Reuban Outwits the Great Cat of Winter.....................................47
6. Twink Stands a Watch..55
7. A Blue Water Voyager's Tale...66
8. Twink Suffers A Knockdown..76
9. Twink Hauls Her Wind And Lays A New Course..........................87
10. Twink Picks Up A Pilot In Main Duck.......................................100
11. Twink Presses On..114
12. Twink Braces Up and Hauls Her Wind.......................................127
13. Twink Seeks Safe Harbor..133
   Sid's and Richard's List...141
   Websites...144
   Glossary...145
   Part Two: Skipper Sue's Notebook...149
   Pictures from Real Life...224

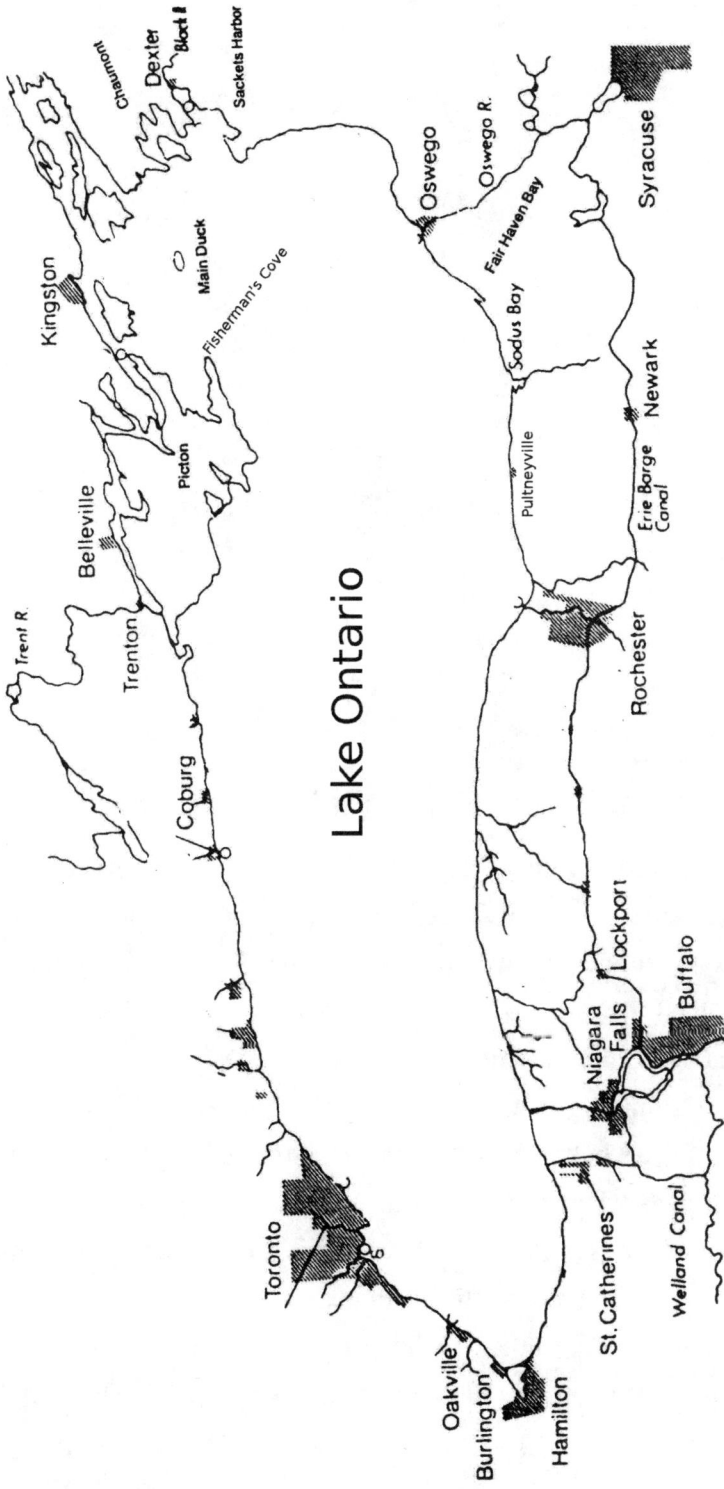

Lake Ontario

Chaumont
Dexter
Block I
Sackets Harbor
Kingston
Main Duck
Fisherman's Cove
Oswego
Oswego R.
Fair Haven Bay
Syracuse
Sodus Bay
Newark
Belleville
Picton
Pultneyville
Erie Barge Canal
Trent R.
Trenton
Rochester
Coburg
Lockport
Buffalo
Niagara Falls
St. Catherines
Welland Canal
Toronto
Oakville
Burlington
Hamilton

2

1. Twinkle Toes is Taken Aback

"Here kitty kitty kitty..." the call sounded among the trees and across the garden where Twinkle Toes was sunbathing. Too late for lunch, and too early for supper- now what does Skipper Sue want? Twink yawned and stretched. It was so pleasant lying here on the warm soft dirt beside the string beans. Let it wait.

It was summer, the finest time of the year. Twink was a sun lover, and no time was better than June in her mind. June, with its sun-flooded lazy long days when a cat could lie on the porch or watch Skipper Sue hoe the peas while the wild bees buzzed and hummed among the dandelions in the yard was the absolute best.

And there was so much to do. Like check that rabbit nest by the lettuce to see if any more baby bunnies had appeared. Twink had been thinking she should do that today-- right after her morning nap and her

3

lunch time snooze but definitely before dinner time.

"Twink-eee. Where are you? Kitty kitty!" Twink sighed. Humans are such a pain, always nagging about something. She yawned and stretched again, and with thoughts of tender juicy baby bunnies still on her mind, she thought well, maybe it's about food. I probably should go check. She gave her face and whiskers a quick tidy-up and then set off at a trot heading up the hill for the back door. Here, Skipper Sue picked her up and carried her into the house.

Uh oh, thought Twink. This isn't food. It could be a trip to the vet or the boat, and they're both bad. Then she saw the cat carrier. Oh no! Twink stiffened her legs and began to protest, but before she could even get a word out, Skipper Sue had stuffed her in where she found herself tangled up with her mother, Dusty, and her revolting cousin, Miss Piggy.

Twink was furious. "I had plans!" She snarled.

"Well," said her mother, "better make new ones."

"Is it the boat?"

"I'm afraid so-for two weeks too!"

Piggy began to whimper from somewhere underfoot. "Oh no. Oh help. I can't do it. I'm going to die!"

"Stop whining," snarled Twink.

Dusty sighed, "Leave her alone, if she's whining at least she isn't puking."

"I hate the boat," shouted Twink. "Let me out of here!"

At that point, the cat carrier began to move. Skipper Sue was taking them out to the garage. They were doomed. As Skipper Sue carried their prison to the car and placed it on the back seat, the three cats all raised their voices in wails of protest. "No! Not the lake. Not sailing. I'm going to be sick. I'm going to be sick now! Why can't we stay home? Please let us stay here. I want out out out."

"It's no use," said Dusty with a sigh as the car engine started. "We're going. We'll just have to make the best of it. We've survived the boat before. It's not really that bad."

Twink slapped Piggy on the head to shut her up, and braced herself against the back of the carrier and sulked. Twink hated sudden changes in her routine. Skipper Sue often told her that she was a grump. Well, what was so bad about that- I'm crabby and I'm proud, she thought. And sailing definitely makes me crabby.

Sailing was one of her least favorite things. She didn't get sea sick like Piggy, but she despised Skipper Sue's boat the *Ariel*. The *Ariel* was small for one thing, only 23 feet long. Skipper Sue liked it because she could sail the *Ariel* alone, but living in a space the size of a small closet with Dusty, Piggy, and Skipper Sue would test the patience of any self respecting cat. And they had never gone off on the boat for more than a day or two. The *Ariel* was also old and slow. Even Skipper Sue admitted that *Ariel* was fat. It was made of wood, and it leaked, and the water sloshing around under the floor boards made Twink nervous. It was going to be a long two weeks. If they survived.

Skipper Sue kept her boat docked in a small harbor located in the village of Pultneyville on Lake Ontario. The harbor had been dug out from a wide spot in Salmon Creek about fifty years ago and now was packed with sailboats. Most of them had shiny white plastic hulls and clattery metal masts. Plump little *Ariel* with her old fashioned wooden mast and plain gray painted hull stood out in sharp contrast among the mostly much bigger newer yachts.

On a weekday evening the dock was quiet and peaceful tucked in on the creek bank under several big willow trees, so after carrying all the one gallon water jugs, cat food, cat litter, box for the cat litter, cat carrier, and other supplies aboard, Skipper Sue let the crew have shore leave. Dusty strolled off to a nearby picnic table, jumped up and started washing.

Dusty was small and rather drab with her mottled gray and buff fur, but she always kept herself tidy. Her color rather than her personal grooming had inspired her name. Piggy sat on *Ariel's* cabin top ready to bolt back below if something dangerous came along. Twink stalked ashore and joined her mother on the picnic table.

She watched Dusty working at her bath and envied her. Nothing bothered Dusty. Twink knew that underneath her mother's well mannered exterior there was a core of steel. She remembered Oswego when they had been on the boat last summer. They had been at anchor and during the night Dusty had jumped off and swum all the way to shore. She had been so fed up with sailing she couldn't stand it for another night. Yet, she never said a cross word after Skipper Sue had hunted her down on shore and carried her back to the boat in the dinghy. She just shrugged and went along with it.

"Two weeks. I can't do it. I won't do it."

"Yes, you will," said her mother calmly as she washed up behind her ears. "You don't have any choice unless you plan to walk back to Wolcott."

The only thing Twink liked less than sailing right then was the idea of walking for days through fields and forests filled with foxes, dogs, coyotes, owls, and hawks, all of them very hungry. Then Twink would be the hunted rather than the hunter. She didn't care for that idea at all.

"Why so long? We've never gone more than a day or two before."

Miss Piggy had crept off the boat as they talked. She slunk over to join them and jumped up on the table. Twink glowered at her.

"Who asked you up here?"

Piggy was considerably bigger than Twink, even if she was a fraidy cat. Twink despised Miss Piggy and usually called her The Fat Furball. Piggy drew herself up and glared back. "I know why we're going for

6

two weeks. Skipper Sue told me."

"Ok, smarty cat. Why?"

"She's looking for something. We have to go to Canada."

Like all cats, Twink had plenty of curiosity. She wondered where's Canada? What is Skipper Sue after there? Is she hunting for food? Sunken treasure?

"What's she looking for?"

"Stories. She's writing a book."

Twink raised her front paw for a quick wash to give herself time to think. She nibbled delicately at a toe while considering Piggy's information. This sounded bad. It takes a long time to write a book, and a book needs a lot of stories to fill it up. It was even possible that they might even end up taking more than one cruise.

"Where's Canada?" asked Twink.

"It's on the other side of the lake."

Twink stopped washing and stared at Piggy, her eyes big and round. "We have to go across the lake to the other side? The lake's huge! It's fifty miles across -we won't be able to see land for hours and hours in this poky boat. We might get lost. There's storms and waves out there and monster fish. And eagles that eat cats. We could die out there."

"That's where she said we have to go to get the stories," answered Piggy.

"What kind of stories is she looking for?" asked Dusty who up to now had been sitting quietly gazing at the darkening harbor.

"They have to be about the lake. She said we're going to Kingston to find them."

Dusty said, "So if we get to Canada and she finds enough stories then we can go home?"

"Yep," said Piggy. She then twisted around and started tidying up her tail. Piggy was very proud of her big fluffy tail. It had dark rings on it almost like a raccoon's tail. It was, in Twink's opinion, the only good feature Piggy had. Piggy wore a shaggy brown coat with tabby markings very unlike Twink's sleek short haired black and white fur. She looked a little unkept next to Twink who always had her black suit with snow white feet and white chest and tummy spotless and in perfect order. Twink looked like Sylvester the cat who was never able to outsmart the bird in the old Tweety Bird cartoons. Piggy said she was about as dumb as Sylvester, too, but she wouldn't dare say it out loud. Twink had lightning in both those white paws of hers.

"No wonder you're always sea sick on the boat with those hair balls of yours."

Piggy hissed back, "Mind your own business."

While Twink and Piggy wrangled, Dusty sat as still as a little gray stone cat statue gazing off across the harbor. She was clearly deep in thought. Then she said, "Hey, Twink. I wonder if the stories have to all be from Canada? Maybe we could find some stories from this side of the lake. Then we wouldn't have to sail across all that water. If we help Skipper Sue find some stories here, we'd get home faster, too, wouldn't we?"

Twinkle Toes was the best hunter of the trio. If anyone could find a story, she could. "I bet I could find lots of stories right here in this harbor. But how can I tell them to Skipper Sue? She only knows about six words of cat language."

Piggy put the finishing touches on her tail, carefully smoothing the last long hairs into place and then said with a smirk, "I know a way to tell them to her."

Twink glared at her. "How are you going to do that?"

"Skipper Sue brought her laptop computer along. I've watched her work it. She pushes that mouse around and paws at the keys to make words. I know the button to make it light up. I could put some notes and stories in it."

Twink had seen Piggy play with things. She was always fishing under the sofa or catching drips at the faucet with her paws. Piggy could play handball too. She could stand up on her back legs and bat a paper wad right back with a swat of her front paw after Skipper Sue tossed it to her. She was tall enough when she stood up like that to reach the kitchen screen door handle and pull it down. And she had figured out how to wake Skipper Sue up at breakfast time by batting at a wind chime that hung in the bedroom window to make it clang and tinkle. Piggy was pretty smart, no doubt about it, (though no way was she as smart as Twink) and she was pretty good with her paws, too.

"If I get some stories, you'll put them in that lap top thing?"

"I'll do anything to get us home," said Piggy.

"That sounds good to me. The quicker we're off the *Ariel* the better I'll like it even if I do have to work with you. I'll do it. Come on, Mom, lets go find a story."

Dusty said, "Well, it's certainly worth a try. I sure don't want to go across that big lake if we don't have to. I wish we knew what kind of stories Skipper Sue is looking for though."

Twink agreed with all her heart about not crossing the lake. "Well, let's get at it," she said. "There must be something around here interesting." Without waiting for her mother, she leaped down from the table and stalked off along the creek alone. She'd find a story for Skipper Sue's stupid book if it took all night.

In the fading light of dusk the birds and insects of the day had quieted. A bat was swooping and zigzagging overhead in pursuit of mosquitoes, and several crickets were tuning up for an evening of music. The peaceful harbor water mirrored the rose colored sunset sky above. Twink felt perfectly safe here on shore a few yards from the *Ariel*. Then she saw something moving on land near the boat. It was brown and furry and looked like a rat only a lot bigger. It was eating clover. Twink approached cautiously and stopped several feet away. "Hey!" she said. "Hey you. What are you doing by our boat?"

The strange animal looked up and fixed a pair of shrewd brown eyes on her. Twink noticed the creature had a jaw full of large strong teeth, and that it did not seem to be the least bit frightened of her.

Better go easy here, she thought. Some good manners might be in order. She said, "My name's Twinkle Toes and that's my boat there."

"I'm Mattie. My hole is in the bank right behind your boat. I eat here all the time, and I've never seen you here before."

"Are you a rat? Skipper Sue doesn't want any rats on her boat."

Mattie drew herself upon her haunches and looked at Twink sternly. "No, I am most definitely not a rat. I am a muskrat. I mostly live in the water. See my tail?"

She lifted her scaly black tail out of the grass. Twink could see that it looked like the blade of a paddle held at a right angle to the water surface.

"My family has lived in this harbor for generations. We were here when sailing ships carried cargo to Canada from Pultneyville. My ancestors watched Captain Throop smuggle runaway slaves to Canada. Why, they saw--"

Twink heard 'Canada' and thought hey, whoa, that's where we're supposed to find stories. Maybe there's one right here. She interrupted, "Who was Captain Throop?"

"Horatio Nelson Throop was the most famous lake captain in Pultneyville. He was a hero and an inventor. He invented a screw propeller that made cargo boats faster and safer. He had one made for a boat about the size of your boat there. But even though it worked perfectly, he never made a dime off it. Some say it was the greatest sea faring invention of the nineteenth century. But a Swede named Ericsson got the American patent and the right to make propellers for ships here before Throop did. He also took hundreds of slaves across the lake on his ships to Canada where they could be free. It was part of a secret organization that formed before the Civil War to help runaway slaves, the Underground Railroad."

Twink thought, this is definitely sounding like a story for Skipper Sue's book, and Mattie seems to be quite the chatterbox. Maybe I'll stick around. Twink settled down into the grass and tucked her paws in under her chest and said, "I'd like to hear more about Captain Throop and the runaway slaves going to Canada."

"Well then, let me finish this nice clover patch, and I'll tell you a tale."

And so she did; (you can read Mattie's tale in Skipper Sue's note book).

When Mattie had concluded her story about Captain Throop and the slaves, Twink asked, "Does anyone know what became of the runaways after they got to Canada?"

Mattie reached for a sweet white clover blossom to munch on and then answered, "One of the slaves who went to Canada had a son who became a famous engineer. His name was Elijah McCoy, and his inventions made steam ship and rail travel safer. Another runaway slave wrote a book about his experiences. A very famous American author named Harriet Beecher Stowe read it and used it in her own story called *Uncle Tom's Cabin*. Some say her book made people in the north so angry about slavery that they started the Civil War. Other slave descendants in Canada became lawyers or explorers or doctors. And the muskrat that saved those runaways was my great great great grandmother Martha. That's how I know it happened. If you look up there," she added, "you can see the pole star that the runaways followed north to reach Pultneyville."

Twink thanked Mattie and walked slowly back to the *Ariel*. Back aboard, she gazed up into the night sky and thought about Mattie's story. Captain Throop had acted a lot like a cat. He did what he thought was right, not what somebody else said he should do when he helped the slaves run away to Canada. Sometimes you might even have to break a law if it's a bad law. She admired the slaves for "stealing" themselves from their owners to make a dangerous journey to a far and foreign land, trusting their lives to complete strangers along the way. It took courage to win freedom and to keep it, too.

Throop didn't have to help them either. It would have been safer for him to look the other way, or he could have turned the runaways in and collected the reward. But what would those other people who had hidden the slaves and guided them north have thought? They had risked their own farms and businesses by breaking the law to help the fugitives. And what about the important work done by the freed slaves and their descendants in Canada? Some of it had saved lives, or made other people rich. One person's actions could make a difference. Throop and the other Underground Railroad helpers had changed the world.

Well, thought Twink, there's one story. It didn't have much about Canada in it, but I'll tell it to Piggy anyway. If we could stay here for a few more days, I know I could get more stories. Twink dreaded the thought of crossing the lake. Skipper Sue was no master mariner with the ability and experience of Captain Throop, and the *Ariel* was awfully small and old to be going out there all alone. As Twink turned to go below for the night she thought, it would be 'way safer and smarter to stay right here in this harbor. This business of depending on the wind to go places with a boat is crazy. I should jump ship and run away myself.

2. Twinkle Toes sets sail

Twink had no chance to jump ship the next day. Right after breakfast, Skipper Sue got busy taking the sail cover off, checking the engine oil, and stowing the little boat called a dinghy that they carried along on *Ariel's* deck. She gathered Twink and Dusty up in her arms and set them down inside the cabin on the single small bed there. Piggy was already huddled on the bed, a lump of pure misery trying to make herself as small as possible. Clearly, like it or not, they were headed for Canada.

Skipper Sue closed the door saying, "You'll be safe down below."

The two cats settled in on the bunk beside Piggy. Then with a horrid grinding noise the engine started. It made a terrible clatter and roar. Piggy hissed and laid her ears back and fluffed up her tail.

"Calm down stupid-it's a motor, not a monster. It makes the boat go," said Twink.

"It stinks!" said Piggy.

She retreated up to the front of the boat and climbed up onto a pile of heavy rope stored there. After a moment Dusty joined her. Twink decided why not, maybe it would help to get as far away from that racket as possible, and she also climbed up into the little storage compartment in the very front of the *Ariel* where the boat's sides came together at the bow to create a wedge shaped space.

They heard footsteps on deck, then the boat began to move. This isn't so bad, it's no worse than a car, thought Twink. But after a little while the boat began moving more. It swayed from side to side and rose and fell. Occasionally it lurched suddenly or came down with a thump.

Piggy moaned, "Ooh, Great Bast, please save me."

14

"Don't you dare," snarled Twink. But it was too late. Piggy was hurling again- all over the coils of rope.

The boat tipped abruptly and before Twink could stop herself she slid into Piggy and Piggy's slop as the boat made a scary new noise, a sort of banging and rumbling as it fell onto its side. Water sloshed and gurgled nearby, and Piggy wailed, "We're going to die."

Dusty moaned and then deposited her breakfast on top of Piggy who was so sick she didn't even move.

"I will not get sick!" thought Twink to herself as she dug her claws in and climbed over the rope and back up to the high side of the compartment. Then the engine stopped. The only sound was of water sloshing and occasionally hitting against the side of the boat with a crash as they swooped up and dropped down. Twink was getting dizzy. And the smell of Dusty's breakfast and Piggy's puke now lying underfoot was getting to her.

This is bad. We must be about to sink she thought. Twink crawled out of the little space seeking the slightly better air of the cabin. It was positively sweet after the stink of cat barf in the stuffy little compartment. She staggered back to the cabin door and peered out through the screen at Skipper Sue.

"Hey, Twink. We're sailing now. Pretty nice huh?"

"I want to go home! Now!" Twink yelled.

Skipper Sue ignored her.

"Pleeeese," wailed Twink.

"You hang on. We'll be in Sodus Bay in a couple hours at this rate. Then you can come up on deck."

It was the longest morning Twink had ever lived through. And one of the worst. After what seemed like a year, the boat stopped lurching and rolling and crashing and slamming and bouncing and bucking around. The motor started again, and then everything got quieter and steadier underfoot.

After Skipper Sue did some more stomping around overhead, she turned the motor off and opened the cabin door and called out, "Ok, you guys can come up now."

Twink emerged cautiously. Dusty followed and last came Piggy looking very shaky and still a bit green. Skipper Sue picked her up and cuddled her.

"Oh Piggy, I'm so sorry about your tummy. You'll feel better soon. You'll get your sea legs. I promise."

Twink, crouched on the top of the engine box, glared at Piggy. What about me, she thought. I feel as miserable as that hairy lump of lard. Skipper Sue always fussed over Piggy.

"Come on Twink," said Dusty. "Let's go forward."

Skipper Sue had set a dish of cat food and a water dish out up on the fore deck so they could eat dinner whenever they wanted. Right now Twink wasn't very interested in dinner. No way had she been sea sick, but her stomach did feel a trifle funny still. She looked around at all the water and at the distant shore and thought about going back to the cockpit where she felt safer. Then she followed her mother forward. Dusty ate a few bites of food and then settled down for a wash with her back snug against the side of the cabin. Twink also began to tidy up. Taking a bath always made things better. It helped a cat feel a little more at home. Suddenly something swooped past her. She crouched down in alarm. Whatever this thing was it was huge-- way bigger than a cat.

The thing landed on the fore deck. It was a gray and white bird with cold yellow eyes and a sharp bill. And it was eating their cat food.

Twink glared at it and hissed, "What are you doing on my boat?"

To her surprise the fierce eyed stranger answered politely, "I'm eatin' this good grub that nobody here seems to fancy."

Twink studied the stranger. He was an attractive fellow with a sleek gray back, clean white breast and head and powerful black tipped wings. Even as they spoke, she saw his far seeing gaze was ranging over the bay around them, and as she looked more closely she noted he was clearly no spring chicken, for his webbed feet were ragged and his head was snow white.

"Be you skipper of this good little ship?" asked the bird.

"No, I am not." snarled Twink. "I hate this boat. And that's our food you're eating."

"I'm pretty well down on my marks with a full cargo. Help yourself."

The big bird raised a powerful pair of long narrow wings and with a graceful little hop lifted up on to the *Ariel's* bow railing. He settled his wings and gazed down at her. When a motorboat wake came along and rocked the boat, he balanced against the roll with the ease of an old sailor.

"I'm Harry. Harry Herring Gull. And you?"

Twink glowered up at Harry envying his ability to lift himself off the deck. He could go anywhere he wanted with those wings.

"I'm Twinkle Toes."

"Pleased to meet you. You're new around here. I haven't seen you before on Sodus Bay. Have you been voyaging for long?"

"It's our first day. We set out from Pultneyville and we're going to Canada tomorrow."

"You'll like Canada. It's got grand big cities and harbors, and good garbage dumps there, too."

"I'd rather go home."

"Home? You are home. Your ship is your home. You're a mariner now. And this Great Lake is a great place to be under sail."

"What's so great about it?"

"It's big for one thing. They don't call it a Great Lake for nothing. It's nearly 200 hundred miles long and over a hundred fathoms deep, and from here you can sail almost a thousand miles through four more lakes west to the city of Duluth in Minnesota where they have *real* winters."

Harry spread his wings in a gesture of enthusiasm. "Why, it's got ten thousand miles of shore to explore."

"Water's wet. Anything more than what's in my dish is too much."

Harry beamed down at her. "Ah, my grumpy friend. Just wait 'til you've seen the other side. Toronto is Canada's biggest city. It's got the biggest gull colony on the lake, too-- over 20,000 birds. You know it's a good place if gulls harbor there. Lots of stuff to see, and picnics and food galore in the parks on the islands. Aye, the lake's got mirages that turn ships upside down and islands that appear and vanish. And sunsets over the water are the best. Our sunsets have so many colors that the humans haven't even named 'em all."

Twink glowered up at the gull so at ease on his perch above her. "I don't see colors like you do. I'm a cat. But the disappearing islands sound interesting. That could be a story for Skipper Sue's book."

"If it's stories you be wanting, lay a course for Main Duck Island. You'll find plenty of 'em there."

"Stories about a duck? Who cares about a duck from Maine?" says Twink.

Harry threw his head back and laughed, a loud raucous laugh. "It's the biggest of a group of islands called The Ducks so it's the 'Main' Duck. It's got a good snug harbor. And lots of stories-- shipwrecks, smugglers, castaways, and a fool human lubber who went crazy looking for buried treasure."

"Treasure? Now that's got potential," said Twink."Where is this place?"

"It ain't that easy to get to. It's farther out in the lake than any other island. And there's reefs and rocks around it. More than forty ships have wrecked on it or sunk near it. You got to keep a weather eye out if you steer for Main Duck. But it's worth it. Yes sir, I tell you friend Twinkle Toes, I've flown over the rocky Maine Coast and the sandy shores of the Carolinas and over lots of salt water in between, and our sailing and our stories here on the Lakes are every bit as good as those of the sea."

Twink scowled. "Hmph, that's not what Skipper Sue says. She thinks salt water is the only place to sail. And I think all water is nasty."

"Old Ocean is the mother of us all. But they call the Great Lakes inland seas for good reason. No place on earth has more freshwater to sail upon as what we got here. But you need to keep a good watch. This lake will make twenty foot waves when the Wind Witch of November gets riled and mean. She's got a quick temper, too. In a half hour she can kick up six footers. Your ship will take care of her crew but only if you tend to her."

"That's Skipper Sue's job, not mine," said Twink. "The less I have to do with the *Ariel* the better I like it."

"You're part of her crew now, mate, like it or not. Keep a sharp lookout on deck and aloft. If you see a line coming adrift or gear not stowed proper bristol fashion, help your skipper and tell her about it. Watch the sky for dirty weather, too. It's a big job to keep a sailing vessel all ship shape. You got to stay prepared for whatever comes along or it's Davy Jones Locker for you all. It takes the whole crew to do it. But-hey, adventure, freedom, new places, aye, there's that and more. It's worth it."

Twink looked away from the bird so content up there on his perch. Dusty, who had joined her to listen, was still gazing up at Harry. Twink said, "He's kind of bossy isn't he?"

"Maybe, but he's obviously been around. He's seen a lot more of the lake than we have, and I don't think he misses much either. It might pay to listen to him."

However, the food dish was now calling to Twink. She looked back up at Harry. "I'm going to eat now, but I wouldn't mind hearing more about that island sometime."

"I fancy we'll cross tacks again before long. For now, I'll be shoving off. Fair winds." With that Harry spread his wings and lifted off from the bow rail and swept away skimming over the water with enviable speed.

It was growing dark when Twink went below and joined Skipper Sue and Piggy already snuggled together in the bunk. As she dozed off, she wondered why her mother hadn't come down to bed, too. Then she dreamed of water formed into long blue ridges that *Ariel* was sailing over. The *Ariel* lifted and fell, swooping up like a bird, then down again. Ahead Twink saw a brilliant flash of light shining then going dark, just over the sharp blue line of the horizon ahead. It was a beacon, marking something important. We must go there, she thought. I know I'll find a story there.

Then she was flying like a gull with Harry gliding alongside her a few feet away. Below lay a barren parched flat plain across which clouds of dust blew. "That was once a great lake as big as ours. People sucked all the water away and used it to grow cotton," Harry called out. Then he banked sharply off. Twink tilted her body and felt the wind carry her. She moved her tail like a rudder to steer as she floated along. Is this what it feels like to be a sailboat with wind in its sails? she wondered.

She lifted up following behind Harry as he led her over a city surrounded by flat barren desert lands. They soared above a cluster of tall buildings covered with gleaming glass and polished metal that shone like silver. She saw fountains and a huge pool of water in a cement basin with a man poling a slender black boat in it. "Las Vegas," Harry called. "All the water here comes from someplace else. Soon they'll run out, and they'll be wanting our water."

He swooped away and dove through a cloud. She followed, the wind whistling past her ears and emerged into clear air over another city on a coast. Harry dropped down to just a few feet over the buildings and flew slowly. She followed seeing flat roofs and parking lots and roads with big puddles from a recent rain. She also saw water rushing down gutters and streets. A film of oil and gas colored the water surface with irridescent rainbow colors. Harry skimmed lower over the city's waterfront where brown oily runoff with bits of plastic trash gushed from a big pipe into the harbor. A dark stain spread through the clear green depths.

"No one knows what's in that slop. But I can tell you, it ain't good," Harry called out.

A cry jolted her awake.

"Help!"

Twink sprang across the cabin to the stairs with a single leap. A second leap took her up onto the deck where she saw her mother struggling in the water near *Ariel's* stern.

"Twink," Dusty gasped. "Wake up Skipper Sue. Hurry."

Twink bounded back down into the cabin and jumped onto the bunk landing on Skipper Sue's stomach.

"Oomf, What the-"

Twink meowed loudly right in Skipper Sue's face. "Mother's drowning- help!"

Skipper Sue pushed her off and then seeing only two cats present said, "Where's Dusty?"

Twink wailed again, "Help! Cat overboard!"

Skipper Sue was no match for a cat when it came to intellectual firepower, but she seemed to be getting the idea. She scrambled up the ladder in her pajamas and went immediately to the stern where she could see Dusty was treading water furiously too out of breath to even mew. Skipper Sue dropped to her stomach on *Ariel's* deck and reached down and managed to grab Dusty. She got one hand on her but lost her grip on the slippery wet cat. Dusty went under. As Skipper Sue gasped, Twink yowled "She's there!"

A small gray cat head popped up again, almost out of reach as the boat swung at anchor. Skipper Sue hooked her feet under the tight cleated line that controlled the mainsail and leaned out as far as she could off the boat. This time she got both hands on Dusty. She hauled the soaking cat on deck and dropped her there. Dusty crouched gasping for breath with water running off her, looking bedraggled and miserable. Her fur was plastered to her skin. Twink came up to her and gave her a lick as Skipper Sue went below for a towel.

"What happened?"

"I was trying to get into that little boat Skipper Sue uses to go ashore. I thought maybe I could get to land. But I missed. I guess I used one life up."

Skipper Sue came back with the towel and began rubbing Dusty dry. Twink moved off to the stern and glared down at the dark surface of the bay. Harry hadn't said anything about how ready the Lake was to eat you. It had nearly swallowed Dusty down without a trace. She shivered as she looked down into the hungry black water below.

3. Twink Under Bare Poles

The next morning after Skipper Sue opened the cabin door, Twink hurried up on deck. Before her the bay lay calm, all seemed peaceful, and Harry was nowhere to be seen. She stretched and yawned and sat down with a sigh. The air tickled her ears softly on this early summer day, and Twink looked with longing at the steep slope of nearby Thornton Point. Dozens of brightly colored birds flitted about in the bright sunshine. A scarlet tanager perched on the top of a tall oak, a gleaming gold and black oriole flashed by, and several yellow warblers darted along the brushy shore. They whistled and chirped, and one sang a song like the repeated chime of a small silver bell. Twink's mouth watered at the sight of all the tender little appetizers flying around a few yards away.

She looked away and growled, "I wish I were home."

Dusty who had joined her said, "Well then, keep hunting for stories. We're going to need a bunch of them to fill up the book."

The cabin door opened and the *Ariel*'s captain came up into the cockpit. "Time to raise anchor and get under way," she said as she picked up Piggy from her sunny seat and set her down on the galley counter just inside the door. "You too," she told Dusty and Twink. Both cats slunk down into the dark cabin, reluctant to repeat yesterday's experience.

But to Twink's surprise, their second day of sailing wasn't nearly as bad as their first. The wind was gentle, and the lake was quite flat. After a few minutes of motor noise, Skipper Sue shut the engine off and hauled up the *Ariel*'s sails. Then she opened the door and called, "You guys can come up here if you'll stay in the cockpit."

Twinkle Toes was again the first cat on deck. She climbed onto a seat and peered over the wooden railing around the cockpit to stare at what lay before her. An ocean of blue and silver water surrounded her glittering in the sun and stretching away as far as the eye could see-- more water than Twink had ever thought could exist in all the world. At least on this side of the boat, there was no land in sight anywhere. Oh, Great Bast, save me, Twink murmured. The other times Skipper Sue had taken them sailing hadn't been like this. They'd been able to see shore, at least. This endless landless shifting liquid was the biggest thing Twink had ever seen. Would a monster wave rise up and swallow their whole boat?

As she watched the lake, a shadow fell upon the cockpit. She looked up and saw a gray and white bird with long narrow strong wings gliding overhead against the blue sky. It looked down and she recognized Harry. He called out, "I told you- it's a Great Lake!"

Twink sat up as straight as she could. She didn't want Harry to see that she was scared of Lake Ontario. And really, with the mild wind and sun warm on her back it wasn't that bad. The *Ariel* felt steady and solid underfoot, the waves were small, and as long as she stayed in the cockpit Twink felt somewhat safe. Miss Piggy did not share her feelings. She stayed put in the cabin huddled on Skipper Sue's bed. Dusty did come creeping cautiously out into the sunlight. She chose to climb into Skipper Sue's lap and study the lake from that viewpoint.

Skipper Sue was sitting on a wooden bench steering the *Ariel* with a stick attached to the rudder. She told the cats, "We're going to Kingston. It's the oldest city on the lake. It used to be French, and if they hadn't lost a battle at Oswego during one of their wars with England, we'd be living in Quebec instead of New York State today. There's a special lecture there on Friday at the museum that I want to go to. A famous author is reading from his new book, and I want to talk to him about my Lake Ontario book. Maybe he'll give me some ideas on what to put in it."

Skipper Sue looked off towards the green trees and rolling hills of the distant shore. "A lot has happened here. People have been sailing the lake for over three hundred years. When the first Europeans got here, they thought this was part of the ocean and that they could sail all the way to China on the Lakes. They called them sweet water seas. Later on, Lake Ontario was the gateway to the west especially after the Erie Canal made a water road for grain and lumber from here to go down to the coast."

With the sun warm on her black fur, Twinkle Toes was almost happy. She watched the shore slip by as the water whispered softly against the side of the *Ariel*. The boat's gentle rocking movement made her sleepy, and she was just about to take a catnap when Skipper Sue stood up saying, "This looks like a good place to stop for lunch."

They had sailed in close to shore and as Twink watched, Skipper Sue dropped the sails and went up to the front of the boat to lower the anchor. After things settled down, Twink jumped up on the cabin top to see where they were.

A few hundred feet away stood a high bluff of eroding brown clay. Runoff had cut deep gullies into its face, chiseling it into sunlit ridges and shadowed gullies. A thick forest of beach and maple and dark hemlock trees stood atop it. Some of the trees clung to the very edge of the bluff and were leaning out over the lake as if they were trying to take one last look at the water before they fell in. Twink saw that a number of trees had already toppled over the edge and were slowly sliding down onto the beach. The Lake was eating the trees, just as it had tried to swallow up Dusty.

Yet even as the lake gnawed away at the land, the wild shore before her was filled with life. Hundreds of small birds darted in and out of the nest holes they had dug in the clay cliff. High overhead a fish hawk soared, and a kingfisher with his brown belt and white front swooped past carrying a minnow in his beak. In the clear green water beside the *Ariel*, Twink saw a school of hundreds of small silver fish hanging in the boat's shadow.

Harry glided past and settled on the water next to them. "Nice place isn't it?

Twink, studying the pretty pebble beach and the piles of bleached silver driftwood on it, sniffed the air and smelled the rich woodsy land before her. "How can I get off this boat? I want to go ashore!"

Twinkle Toes turned and stared up at Skipper Sue as hard as she could trying to tell her there were Stories there. Wonderful Stories for her book. Right there on that beach. Probably enough to fill that stupid book right up. "Just let me go ashore and I'll find them," she meowed at *Ariel's* captain.

Alas, Skipper Sue showed no sign of launching the little boat carried on the *Ariel's* afterdeck that she used to get to shore. She simply sat and chewed on her sandwich and gazed at the green forest and sunlit stony beach. What was wrong with her? thought Twink. Stupid lazy human, sitting there grinding away on her food like an old cow. A whole world was waiting to be explored. Twink jumped down from the cabin top onto the seat beside Skipper Sue and cried, "Please take me to shore. Pleeease!"

Skipper Sue looked down at her and then followed Twink's gaze and studied the sun-washed beach and the cool green forest behind it. "It does look nice. Want to go ashore with the dinghy, Twink?"

Twink could hardly believe her ears. Skipper Sue had actually paid attention to her. Now that was a first. She got right at it, too. She untied the little boat on deck, shoved it into the water, and rummaged around in the cockpit locker for her life jacket and the oars. She picked up Twink and set her in the dinghy and climbed down to join her. A few minutes later the boat bottom was grinding against the rounded beach stones as Skipper Sue pulled it up on shore.

"Don't go too far," she cautioned Twink, and she walked off down the stony beach towards the outlet of a little creek. Twink followed, looking around. The dark shadowed forest and the raw eroded face of the bluff frowned down upon her, and she felt small and exposed there on the shore next to the endless expanse of water. But the lake swished softly among the pebbles, and except for the rattle of the stones under Skipper Sue's feet and the chitter of the swallows overhead, the beach was peaceful and quiet. Twink peered at the line of driftwood and wrack cast up by the lake at the top of the beach. She saw a broken bright yellow plastic hat like those that workers wore on construction sites, and a very weather beaten work boot. Had the lake eaten some people? she wondered. A bit further on, more trash lay tumbled and tangled among the driftwood. She carefully examined and sniffed at several white plastic spoons, an old bait cup, two fishing lures, a broken Frisbee, and a piece of a sign that said "Toronto" on it. A few yards away Skipper Sue bent and picked up something. It was an odd-shaped piece of plastic.

"This is definitely a piece of a boat," said Skipper Sue.

She dropped it, and the piece landed with a loud clatter on the stones. Skipper Sue looked very serious as she gazed out at the now quiet lake where *Ariel* was resting peacefully at anchor. Twink continued on alone prowling along the crest of the beach watching the quick darting spiders and pausing to admire a broken clamshell. The inside gleamed with the luster of pearl. She saw Skipper Sue nearby pondering a blue plastic trash barrel with Buffalo City Parks stenciled on it. Then as she climbed over a log she found the dead fish.

It was a big fish, about twice as long as a cat and with a long drawn out slender tail. It was dull brown and looked quite fresh as its staring eye was still clear, and it didn't smell at all. Twink studied it seeing a mouth full of very sharp teeth. The fish had powerful jaws and a single whisker on its chin, and Twink thought it wasn't something she'd want to ever run into alive and in the water. Skipper Sue came over to look.

"That's kinda weird. It's a burbot, Twink. I've never seen one of those before. I wonder what killed it? People don't fish for those things. Something odd must have happened to it."

Twink didn't like it. The big dead fish gave her the creeps. Overhead in the forest, a crow called with a harsh loud voice. It sounded like a warning to her.

"If we're going to cross to Kingston today, we probably ought to get back to the boat, Twink," said Skipper Sue as she headed down the beach back to the dinghy. Twink followed close at her heels. Back aboard the *Ariel*, Skipper Sue dragged the dinghy up out of the water and stowed it on *Ariel*'s after deck and lashed it down carefully. She then hauled up the sails, and walked to the bow where she pulled up the anchor. Soon the *Ariel* was gliding along again, heading out into the lake with the wind behind her. Twink looked back and watched the land fade into the haze astern. The beach had been interesting. It would have been nice to explore a bit more. She wondered about the fish. Then she sighed. So much for finding any stories there. Next stop Canada-- more than fifty miles and ten hours sailing away or so Skipper Sue said. She suspected it was going to be a very long day. She settled down on the cockpit seat and tried to sleep.

An hour later, the land formed a distant dim blue line on the horizon behind them. Dusty joined Twink on the cockpit seat where she was sitting beside Skipper Sue. "What do you think of that?"she asked with a flick of her tail.

Twink looked where Dusty had pointed with her tail tip. The clear sky of a half hour ago to the west had vanished behind a very dark cloud about the size of Mount Everest. And it was growing bigger by the moment.

Twink flattened her ears and growled, "I think it's going to get wet."

Like all animals, she was weather wise. Right now she knew there was trouble a-coming. Skipper Sue heard Twink growl. She looked aft.

"Uh oh," she said. "I think we'd better shorten sail."

The cats jumped down onto the cockpit floor and watched as Skipper Sue climbed around on the *Ariel* doing things with the ropes and sails. When she was finished, the biggest sail, the one Twink by now had figured out was called 'The Main', was folded and tied down to the boom, while the front sail had been unhanked and replaced by a much smaller one. As Skipper Sue worked, the black cloud had continued to grow. It now covered the sun, and the three cats heard clearly the frequent grumble of distant thunder. Miss Piggy said, "I feel prickly." Twink felt it, too, her fur was picking up some sort of electrical energy. It made her tense and jumpy. Something was coming. Something bad.

Skipper Sue looked at the cats now huddled on the cockpit floor. "You guys better go below."

Predictably she picked up Piggy first and shoved her down into the cabin. Dusty and Twink followed her. Hardly had the door closed when they heard the first large drops of rain rattle against the cabin top. Lightning flashed and a loud boom sounded and then an eerie moan that suddenly rose to a shrill cry overhead made Twink's hair stand on end.

Piggy crouched down on the bed and whispered, "It's the Witch of the Lake."

"What are you talking about?" snarled Twink.

"I dreamed about it last night. It's the storm hag, the banshee. She's a wind witch who flies on the lake gales. She can smash the strongest ship to bits. Some call her the Witch of November, but that's her, all

30

right. She's here now."

A powerful gust of wind whistled through the *Ariel*'s rigging, and they all felt the boat tip suddenly. Thunder cracked again, right overhead as the rain began pounding against the deck and cabin top. The boat's gentle motion of a few minutes before was now much jerkier as it rolled and lurched. The wind continued to shriek overhead. That witch is whipping up the lake now, thought Twink. The *Ariel* tipped and fell down onto her side with a crash, and the cabin door flew open. Twink peered out.

She saw Skipper Sue, water streaming off her yellow rain jacket, bracing one foot against the engine box to stay on her seat as she gripped the steering stick. Steel gray waves with white crests swept by and Twink could see Skipper Sue's face was grim. Twink couldn't believe how quickly the calm blue lake had changed, turning dark gray and very lumpy in only ten minutes. This was different from the other day. If Skipper Sue was scared, then they really were in trouble.

Twink clambered out of the cabin and onto the rain slick engine box and wailed, "I don't want to drown."

Skipper Sue frowned, "You don't belong out here. It's not safe."

"You're telling me?" shouted Twink.

But Skipper Sue ignored her as she pushed and pulled, steering to keep the boat straight. She was too busy to bother with a cat. The rain had stopped, but the wind, now quite cold, was blowing as hard as ever, and the waves were definitely getting bigger. Twink could see ragged low gray clouds scudding by overhead, while the waves were already lifting their white crests of broken water higher than the side of the boat. The wind rumpled her fur, and she climbed down from the engine box and wedged herself in a corner of the wet cockpit. Then, as Twink began counting how many lives she had left, something flashed past the boat. She looked up and saw Harry effortlessly riding the storm winds, cutting through the air like a knife blade of ivory.

He wheeled sharply and swooped down again across the *Ariel*'s bow as he shouted at them, "The Wind Witch won't catch you today. Ride it. Ride the wind. Steer your course, and let your little ship run."

Skipper Sue saw the bird. She wiped her glasses clear of the rain with one hand to watch Harry, and then leaned forward to peer at the compass. She said, "It's too rough to go to Canada. We're going to head down the lake to Oswego, Twink. We've got lots of room to run. We'll be OK."

Twink could see that even though the waves were now higher than the whole boat, the *Ariel* was staying on top of them. She rose to each big wrinkled gray ridge of water, then dropped into the hollow behind it. She swooped up and down over the lumpy lake just like Harry was doing as he played with the wind overhead. Not a bit of water was coming into the cockpit. Their yacht was climbing over every wave.

Then an extra large lump of lake moved swiftly towards them looming high overhead. This lump was as big as a small hill. Twink crouched down and pressed against the engine box, certain that this time *Ariel* would be caught. The curl of white at the top of the wave would topple forward and crash down upon them and fill the cockpit. It would flood the boat and sink them, and she'd be swept away and swallowed up as Dusty almost had been. She saw light glinting off the wave crest as she dug her claws into the wood underfoot. It looked like the glint of sharp white teeth to her. But once again *Ariel* avoided the lake's greedy grasp. She lurched sideways sharply as Skipper Sue turned her towards the big wave and then she effortlessly leaped up and over the wall of water, nimble as a cat.

Harry had been right about their boat. She was taking care of them. Nice job, *Ariel*, Twink thought as she watched the backside of the receding monster wave rushing on down the lake, snarling and hissing in useless rage as it went. After that one, Twink relaxed a little. *Ariel* was old and fat, but boy, she could still move. She was quick enough to dodge the wave crests and stay on top of them. As she ran down the lake before the wind, she climbed over every wave. She never stumbled or grew weary. Not once did she fail.

Two hours later the *Ariel* entered Oswego harbor. The little city sat at the mouth of a river, its harbor cradled and protected by the long arms of two stone breakwaters. Several large concrete silos, some big round gas storage tanks, and a large metal building stood on shore, and a single gray ship lay beside the silos on the west side of the otherwise empty windswept harbor. Once safely inside the breakwaters, Skipper Sue took the sails down and turned on the engine to steer around the end of a point of land where a huge grain elevator stood like a tall watch tower. Behind it lay a protected basin filled with small boats. After securing *Ariel* at one of the docks here for the night, Skipper Sue went ashore to pay the dock fee. Dusty stretched and settled back down onto the bunk.

"That was quite a ride. I hope we don't have to do anything like that again."

"Yeah, I'm glad that's over. We came through it OK though. Old *Ariel* did a great job," said Twink.

But Piggy sat with a far off look in her round green eyes. At length she said, "I've got a feeling that this is not the last we've seen of the Wind Witch".

Twink tried to brush the thought aside, and Dusty changed the subject asking if anyone had noticed the really big dog on the next dock. But Twink wondered if Piggy was right. The witch knew about *Ariel* now. She'd be watching when they tried to cross the lake again.

4. Twinkle Toes and Dusty Have a Gam With an Old Salt

All night long the wind yowled and wailed through *Ariel's* rigging like an angry tomcat. The next morning Skipper Sue got out of bed, filled the food dishes, and made breakfast for herself. As she sipped her coffee, she told the cats, "We're staying here today. It's too rough to cross."

Twink could clearly hear the thunder of big waves crashing against Oswego's seawall. Some of the spray from the waves spilled right over the top of the ten foot high cement barrier. She was extremely relieved not to be sailing to Canada on this day. After breakfast, Skipper Sue picked up her notebook and told the crew to stay put as she was going up to the big city library on the hill to do something she called research. When the sound of her footsteps had faded, Twink glowered at Dusty and Piggy, both stretched out on the bunk half asleep.

"We're not going to find any stories lying around here."

Piggy said, "I'm not going out there. You saw that huge dog on the boat next to us when we came in."

Twink climbed up on the counter next to the little camp stove and peered out the round port hole window. The dog was nowhere to be seen. The window was closed, but the latch wasn't screwed tight. Twink poked and worked and worried at it until the latch slipped open. She put her head out and looked around cautiously. No dog in sight.

"Come on Mom. Let's see if we can find a story."

She slipped out the window and keeping low, hurried past the boat with the dog. Then she ran down the dock to shore. Here she hid under a parked car until Dusty joined her. They crouched looking out at the row of boats before them wondering what to do next. As they surveyed the quiet harbor, they heard the ka-chugity-chunk of an approaching boat motor. It sounded like *Ariel's* two cylinder engine only deeper voiced and with a slower more deliberate thump.

"There it is," said Dusty."Let's go watch it dock."

She and Twink walked out to the end of the pier for a closer look at the strange yacht. It was a sail boat. Like *Ariel*, it was built of wood and had a white painted deck house with several round port holes in the side. But unlike *Ariel,* its hull was low and lean, and it was much bigger and had two wooden masts and a long pole sticking out in front of its bow.

"What the heck is that?" said Twink.

"I think it's old. Maybe antique," said Dusty.

"Older than *Ariel*? No way. I thought we had the oldest slowest boat on the lake."

The strange yacht slipped past them. Its graceful black hull gleamed in the morning light as it moved along leaving scarcely a ripple astern. Twink saw a fat yellow cat sitting on top of the cabin beside the after mast. The yacht turned into a slip, and as its crew tied it up, Dusty said, "Let's go check it out."

Twink followed her, thinking maybe there's some kind of a story here. After all, it was an odd looking boat.

The yacht's people were nowhere in sight when the cats reached the dock, so Twink and Dusty strolled down to the pier's end and sat side by side to study their find. The big cat was on deck, and he looked over and hailed them with a cheerful meow.

"Avast. Are you fellow seafarers?"

"That's our boat over there, the little one with the wooden mast."

"Oh! You're sailing on a woodie, too."

"What kind of boat is this?" asked Twink.

"It's called a schooner. A schooner has two masts with the biggest one, the main mast, at the back of the boat."

"I never saw one of these before."

"Well, they're not so common now, but once there were hundreds of schooners on the lake. My great great times ten granddad sailed on a schooner out of Oswego. They carried grain over from Canada. His job was to catch rats so they wouldn't damage the cargo. Would you like to come aboard and look around?"

Twink hesitated, but her mother said, "Why thanks very much." and hopped down onto the deck.

"Welcome aboard the schooner *Sara B*. My name is Chauncey. I'm named after the commodore of the American battle fleet on Lake Ontario during the 1812 War." he added proudly. Chauncey was quite plump with a round face and a splendid set of whiskers that were even longer than Miss Piggy's. His straw colored fur was short and thick and striped with darker reddish- brown tabby markings.

"My it's so roomy," said Dusty. "And it doesn't smell of motor exhaust, like our boat."

"That's because it has a diesel. My crew uses veggie oil for fuel so it doesn't stink."

"I thought I smelled food," said Dusty who never missed a clue when it came to eating. "Come on, Twink. It's safe. These decks are nice and wide."

Twink plopped down beside her mother and looked around. Chauncey continued. "My boat is a little old fashioned, but she's very comfortable. Come on, I'll show you around."

As he led them forward, he said, "You know sometimes old stuff works pretty well. *Sara B* was built about sixty years ago in Nova Scotia. But several shipyards built schooners right here in Oswego when Granddaddy Reuban sailed."

"Why did they build schooners here?" asked Twink.

"Because of the trade. This port was the biggest and busiest on all the Great Lakes once. A dozen or more mills used the river's current to turn millstones that ground wheat into flour, and seventeen malt houses made malt for beer. Over there where the power plant is now, were and lumberyards and saw mills. All of those industries sent cargoes down the canal."

"What canal?"

"Why, the Erie. Surely you've heard of the Erie Canal? Oswego was

38

connected to the Erie by its own canal a few years after it opened. Boy, things started happening then. People came pouring in buying up everything in sight. City lot prices doubled in a few weeks. Oswego is a whole lot quieter today. The only time you hear about us now is when a big snow storm blows off the lake and dumps on us. We got twelve feet in five days last winter. But back in 1832 this place was bigger than either Chicago or Buffalo."

"How come it didn't stay big?" asked Twink.

"The ships on Lake Ontario had to get around Niagara Falls to go west on Lake Erie. Canada built the Welland Canal around the falls, but they made it so small a decent sized vessel couldn't get through. So a lot of the shippers sent their cargoes down the Erie Canal from Albany to Buffalo on Lake Erie above the falls. They had to pay a toll to use the canal, though. It cost them so much per mile, so they were real interested in running their ships and cargoes on the lake directly from Oswego through the Welland to Lake Erie and from there on to Chicago."

"They built their ships as big as possible to squeeze through the canal locks. Once in awhile a new boat even got stuck if they measured wrong. Then there was trouble. One time a man's new steamer got to the lock, and it was an inch too wide to get through. The guy who built it had put every dollar he had into his new ship. They say he got off the boat, went into the woods nearby, and shot himself with a pistol he had with him."

"So Oswego lost out to Buffalo because of that?" asked Twink.

"Yes, but not before one of the greatest inventions in maritime history was first used to make money here. It was the-"

"I know," Twink broke in. "The screw propeller. So that's why Captain Throop was so interested in it."

Chauncey looked a bit surprised. "How'd you know that?"

39

"A muskrat named Mattie told me."

"Well, for a few years ships with propellers kept Oswego in the running, but then they dropped the tolls on the canal and Buffalo won out."

The three cats strolled up to the wide foredeck, a pleasant warm sunny spot. Twink eyed the sturdy round spruce mast. It looked a lot like a tree.

"I bet you could climb that," she said.

"I have but I don't usually go aloft," said Chauncey. I'm getting a bit too fat for that sort of thing."

He flopped down on the warm wooden deck."Stay and have a gam."

"What's a gam?" asked Twink.

"That's sailor talk for having a friendly conversation," answered Chauncey.

The cats settled comfortably, and Dusty asked "Where did you sail from?"

"We came in from Sackets Harbor a couple hours ago. It was a great romp. We had eight foot waves pushing us along," said Chauncey.

"I never heard of that place. What's it like?" asked Twink thinking about the story search.

"It's an old military town. Some say it's the most historic harbor on the American side of the lake. During the War of 1812 thousands of soldiers and sailors and workmen came from the coast to build ships there. The shipyards in Sackets and Kingston launched some of the biggest wooden ships that ever sailed on fresh water. They built a ship of the line in Sackets that was the most powerful American battleship of her time. It would have taken more than a thousand men to sail her and man her guns, but the war ended before she was launched. She sat for seventy years, rotting away. Reuban my ancestor, saw her there."

"Hmph," said Twink, "sounds like a waste of money to me."

"Well, they didn't know for sure that the war was really over when they started building her, you see. News didn't travel as fast back then before cell phones and the Internet. The *New Orleans* was so big she could never have left the lake. She was like a ship in a bottle. Her keel was 187 feet long, made, they say, from three of the greatest white oak trees that grew in all of New York State. Her planking was six inches thick so the cannon balls would bounce right off it."

Chauncey paused and gazed up at the top of the foremast beside them. "Think of pine trees a hundred feet high and six foot thick at the bottom. That's what they used to make masts for those ships. This mast is a toothpick compared to those spars."

Dusty said, "We're going to Kingston because Skipper Sue is writing a book about the lake. She's researching the War of 1812 for it. I was reading some of her notes last night. She wrote that the hull of the *New Orleans* was built in just 90 days with all the planks and timbers made by hand. No power tools back then."

"Did she have anything in there about the time when 200 men all worked together to carry a huge rope hawser more than thirty miles? It weighed over four tons-"

Chauncey broke off as the three of them heard a distant voice calling "Here kitty kitty kitty."

"Uh oh, that's Skipper Sue," said Dusty. "I guess we'd better get back to the *Ariel*."

"Well, if you get another shore leave come back. I'll tell you about when Granddaddy Reuban sailed here and what happened when he got caught in a blizzard on the lake."

"Thanks, we'll try to do that," said Dusty.

"Yeah, agreed Twink. "I'm looking for stories for Skipper Sue's book."

The two cats then jumped onto the dock and trotted down it and hurried back to the *Ariel*. Skipper Sue looked relieved to see them.

"I wondered where you guys went. It's dangerous out there. I don't want you wandering around alone."

Once again she shut them below, this time making certain the windows were all latched tight. After eating lunch, she left, telling them they were much safer on the boat. The cats settled in for a nap. Except Twink. She did not intend to stay here when she had a chance to perhaps collect a good story. She'd never met an old salt like fat Chancey, the schooner cat. He was pretty interesting and he was full of stories, too. She knew she could get at least one out of him for Skipper Sue's book.

"What'll we do now?" she said to her Mom.

"Oh, another nap might be in order."

"Maybe for you, but I'm not spending the whole day on the boat listening to Piggy snore. We can't go home until we get that stupid book filled up," said Twink.

Dusty yawned, "Well, go on ashore then and find a story."

Twink prowled around the cabin wondering how to get out. She felt a tiny stir of air under the stairs that led down from the cockpit. She crawled beneath the steps and into the dark space beside the motor. It was oily and smelly, but here she saw a small opening in the deck overhead that ventilated the engine. Sunlight was streaming in through a big rip in the ventilator hose connected to the opening. I bet I could just squeeze through there, she thought. Twink clawed her way up the torn vent hose and tested the opening with her whiskers. Plenty of room. A few seconds later she was on deck in the sunshine.

She quickly put her fur in order and then set off down the dock for Chauncey's schooner.

She was about half way to shore when she heard two things- a shrill cry of warning overhead and the scrabble of large clawed feet on the dock planks behind her.

"Dog! Run for it!" shouted the voice above.

Twink darted down the dock and streaked across the parking lot towards a parked car. She heard the dog gaining on her. His panting breath sounded like a locomotive bearing down on her. He was closing.

"I'll break your neck," he snarled under his breath. He was only a few yards behind her. He would, too. She had seen him earlier. He was about the size of a horse with mean little eyes and a massive bull neck and shoulders. Her claws were no match for a set of huge jaws filled with gleaming white teeth. One hard shake of his head after he grabbed her and she'd be a goner. He'd snap her spine in a second.

She ran with all her strength, leaping ten feet at a time. The dog continued to gain. She imagined she felt his breath. Her lungs were burning. Just as she was about to stop to make a desperate last stand and try to claw his eyes out, a shape flashed down from overhead. She heard the dog sliding and scrabbling and snarling. Twink gave her last ounce of strength to reach the parked car. And made it. The dog, distracted briefly by Harry's sudden plunge across his bow, now resumed chase. He thundered up to her refuge, shoved his head in after her and began barking. Twink edged towards the middle of the car, her heart racing. The dog roared and raged, spit and slobber flying all over. He tried to jam himself under the car, but his chest and shoulders were too massive. Then Twink heard "Sampson! Get back over here! Sampson come!"

The dog pulled his head out with a curse and trotted away. Twink crouched under the car, shaken and still winded until her heart slowed to 300 beats a minute. Then she crept to the light and looked out. He really was gone. Twink emerged to see Harry sitting on a nearby piling.

"Coast is clear," he called.

"Thanks Harry. He almost got me."

Harry's eyes twinkled with amusement, but he gave a sympathetic cluck. "The waterfront's full of toughs. You gotta keep a weather eye out around here."

"I guess you got that right," said Twink.

"You're in safe harbor now. I'm going up to McDonalds for some dumpster fries. I'll catch you later."

Harry spread his wings and flew off heading up the river. Twinkle Toes watched him go. Darn lucky he had been around just then, she thought. Then she looked over at the two masts of Chauncey's ship a few yards away. The dog was gone. She was this close, so why not continue? Cautiously she started out across the open pavement for the schooner.

Chauncey was on deck. "I heard the dog. Come aboard."

Twink dropped down off the dock onto the yacht, and settled in the sun grateful for the safety of Chauncey's boat. "Dogs sure are a pain. That was as close as I want to cut it. I think I used up a life back there."

"Good thing you had a lookout on watch up aloft," said Chauncey.

"Yeah, I owe Harry one for that all right. I don't know why dogs even exist." Twink did a bit of rearrangement and tidy up work on her coat. After she had put her fur back in order, she said, "You were going to tell me more about your ancestor and Oswego. What was your ancestor's boat like?"

"Granddaddy Reuban's schooner was a two master about 90 feet on deck. She could carry around 250 tons of cargo-that's about what five or six tractor trailer trucks can haul today. She was named the *Gazelle*."

"What kinds of cargo did sailboats on the lake carry?"

"Before the Civil War they carried just about everything that needed shipping. Great Lakes schooners carried salt, hay, flour, dried fish, barrels of apples and potatoes, lumber, railroad iron, coal, and stone. See that stone building over there? Schooners brought those blocks of limestone here from Canadian quarries. They carried thousands of immigrant families to Chicago and the western plains. And they carried lots and lots of grain."

"It was hard work. And dangerous. Hundreds of ships lie on the bottom of the Great Lakes today. Granddaddy almost got wrecked once here on the lake. I had another ancestor on a schooner that was caught in a bad storm on Lake Erie. He was rolled right over. The boat was carrying lumber, and they stacked too much up on deck. It made the boat top heavy, you see."

Chauncey got up and walked over to the foremast and stood up and stretched reaching up as high as he could and worked his claws up and down a few times to sharpen them up. "A good sailor always keeps his claws sharp so he can keep his footing on the deck," said Chauncey.

Then he continued, "Those old time sailors were tough. They didn't just sail during the summer like we do on our yachts. They had to make money, and they couldn't do that staying in port. They fitted out in late

45

winter and sailed as soon as the ice was out of the harbor. And the best paying cargoes were in the fall when it was most risky to travel the lake and when the new grain had just been harvested and needed to be carried to market."

"It gets stormy in the fall," said Twink.

"It does indeed. And in November the storms move faster. They pick up energy from the warmer water of the lakes, too. They can become as strong as a hurricane in just a few hours. The lake sailors call those storms weather bombs."

"I heard when the iron ore freighter the *Edmund Fitzgerald* went down on Lake Superior it was blowing fifty miles an hour and there were thirty foot waves," said Twink.

"Why, I've seen videos of seventeen foot waves right here on Lake Ontario. And once in awhile a rogue wave comes along that's twice as big as the rest of the waves in a storm. It could have been a rogue that sank the *Fitz*," said Chauncey. "And there's also the cold-- one time Granddaddy Reuban went out in November and got caught in a blizzard. It was the worst storm to hit the lake in forty years. The canal boats froze in before they could finish their runs, and there were twenty foot drifts of snow on land. It blew so hard it moved a couple of railroad cars parked on a siding in Oswego. It blew the water down Lake Erie so it raised up twelve feet in Buffalo and dried the harbor right out in Toledo. Yes sir, that was the worst snow storm Granddaddy Reuban ever lived through, and he wouldn't have survived if he hadn't done his job."

"What was his job?"

Chauncey closed his eyes. He wrapped his tail around his feet and assumed that wise look all cats have as they sit and think. A breath of chill air, like an ancient memory, stirred Twink's back fur. "It was late in the season, times were bad, and money was scarce," said Chauncey.

46

5. Reuban Outwits the Great Cat of Winter

Reuban could barely keep his eyes open. He had been staring at the rat hole behind the warm galley stove for nearly an hour hoping the sneaky thief would forget he was there and poke his sharp little nose out. He got up and stretched and looked at Mollie the cook who was hard at work scrubbing out a pot that the crew had just emptied of a rich beef stew. Surely there was one crumb of meat left in there. He mewed a polite inquiry.

Mollie paused in her work and looked down at him saying, "Oh, Reuban, I wish we weren't going on this run. It's late now to be trying the lake." She set the pot down and stared off across the cabin before continuing, "But we have to make one more trip or we'll lose our boat to the bank."

That wouldn't be so good, he thought. November was no time to be cast away on a city street without a comfortable ship's cabin, a full food dish, and a warm bed. A nearby voice up on deck called out "Weather's breaking. We'd better get this old wind wagon underway."

With no hopes for a snack, Reuban turned his back on the food dish, strolled across the cabin, and leaped up the short stairway to the after deck outside. He settled down into a crouch next to the wheel box and watched Mollie's husband, Captain Ben, and the crew hustling about getting their schooner ready to sail. They had a long run ahead of them, down nearly the whole length of the lake to get their load of wheat from Toronto to Oswego. Normally, their vessel would have been laid up by now, and Reuban would have been snug ashore with his captain and cook in their cottage in Oswego. But there had been a huge harvest of wheat that fall, and the farmers were anxious to get it to market, so every ship that could was making extra runs and carrying cargo late this season. The farmers needed pay for their crops just as much as Captain Ben and Mollie needed the money from this last trip of the season to keep their schooner.

The cat shivered as a breath of bitter wind ruffled his thick fur and he wrapped his tail tightly around his front feet to keep his toes warm. Already a skin of ice, clear as a pane of glass formed the night before, covered the harbor waters, and the *Gazelle's* deck was slick with frost. The Wind Witch's great white cat of winter crouched just over the northern horizon on this late November day. Time had about run out for the shipping season of 1880.

The small black and red tug, followed by a plume of dark coal smoke, came alongside to tow their two master out into the open lake. The crew passed over the heavy hawser, and soon the tinkle and crunch of thin harbor ice gave way to the steady rush of water flowing past the ship. Reuban looked up at the sky. Although the November sun gleamed dim and pale through a layer of thin cloud on the horizon, he knew bad weather was coming. The cat of winter was stalking them and nearly ready to pounce.

Once clear of the wharfs, the tug cast them off leaving them with a cheerful hoot of her whistle. She was going back to the safe harbor. But a hundred miles of steel gray winter lake lay before the *Gazelle,* now under full sail dipping and rising to the gentle swells that were shoving her along towards Oswego.

By late afternoon, the sun had dimmed. Then it disappeared behind a smear of charcoal colored cloud. The wind grew stronger and raised its voice in the rigging, moaning and growling. Occasional stronger gusts sounded the winter cat's angry yowl overhead. Back in the harbor before towing out, the crew had lashed a barrel of rock salt to the base of each mast, and Captain Ben told them "keep it flying." The boys were throwing scoops of salt around now as the growing waves were beginning to board the ship, slapping and thumping against her sides and icing her decks. The coils of line that controlled the sails were hung high in the rigging, but they, too, were being covered by ice. The cat of winter was toying with the *Gazelle*, as Reuban would slap a small mouse about with his front paws.

Mollie stood wrapped in her heaviest wool cape beside Captain Ben by the wheel. She said, "It's freshening. We should get some sail off her before the gear ices up."

The captain nodded agreement and cupped his hands to his mouth to shout orders to the four young men that made up the crew. Then he went forward to assist the boys, while Mollie took the wheel to steer. Reuban watched the spray that was now beginning to freeze into a solid coat on the tall masts and the rigging and worried. Ice was heavy. If enough of it built up on the ship's masts, it could roll her right over. And if it coated the ropes and pulleys and froze them solid, the crew wouldn't be able to lower sail. It would be impossible then to control the ship in the rising wind.

"Reuban, you'd better get below. There's weather coming," said Mollie.

He looked aft. A cloud darker than the fur on a rat's back filled the sky to the northwest behind them. Wisps of pale smoke-like snow slanted down to the lake from it. As he watched, he heard a sudden boom of thunder oddly muffled by the snow. Reuban jumped up onto the big wooden box that held the ship's towing hawser and other ropes. The top wasn't too icy yet, so he could hold on. He'd stay on deck and stand watch with his crew.

The cloud raced down the lake and overtook the *Gazelle* before the crew had finished furling the mainsail. When the squall's strong wind slammed against the ship and seized them in its grip, Mollie at the wheel had all she could do to keep the ship under control and sailing before it. The wind grabbed the mainsail and tore it from the crews' hands. The stiff heavy canvas rose up and flogged and snapped in the wind, but Ben and two of the crew fell upon it and held it down before it could rip into shreds. The cat of winter had stopped playing with them. Now the Witch had taken over, and she was all business.

Snow swirled so thick around them that the boys up forward were lost from sight. They were working to get the last jib in, pulling on ropes and staggering about on the icy deck to tie down the thrashing heavy canvas. The wind driven snow burned and stung like fury against bare flesh. Reuban couldn't feel his nose or his ears any more, and he felt sorry for the humans who had no fur on their faces to keep them warm.

"We'll heave to and wait it out," gasped Ben when at last he came aft still breathless from fighting the sail. In the thick driving snow that surrounded them they were blind as new born kits. Even Reuban couldn't see anything beyond the ship's rail. But Reuban could clearly hear the icy spray striking against the reefed foresail and the deck. There was nothing else to do. After adjusting the single staysail forward and a bit of the mainsail aft so the ship could ride the waves more easily, Ben lashed down the wheel with some light twine, and everyone went below to escape the snow and bitter wind leaving the ship to look after herself.

No one slept much during the night as the *Gazelle* drifted slowly down the lake, jogging along under reduced sail. The wind eased around midnight, and the waves dropped so the ice stopped building up on the ship. The horrible din in the rigging quieted, and at the first dim gray light of dawn in the east, the crew pounded the stiff frozen canvas free and raised sail again. It was now intensely cold, and clouds of mist rose from the water and swirled around them forming a freezing bone chilling fog that coated the schooner's gear with white rime ice.

As they got underway, Reuban wondered and worried. Where were they? He heard Captain Ben speaking to Mollie about the danger of missing Oswego. The deadly wave-washed shore of Mexico Bay at the end of the lake lay beyond it. If their schooner blew down into that bay, she would have little room to battle her way out against the wind and waves. It was shallow down there, too. When the waves felt the bottom there, they grew higher and steeper. Such seas strike and smash with vicious fury against a ship driving it down onto the shore. No sailing vessel once trapped there in a winter storm had ever escaped from Mexico Bay. Dozens of good ships and crews had died on its ice-bound shores at the end of the lake. Reuban did not want to be added to the toll.

"I think we should steer south. I want to be sure we don't miss Oswego so we need to get closer to shore," said Captain Ben as he peered into the gray mist that surrounded them. Once again Reuban took up his lookout post beside the captain. Every other member of the crew did the same, listening and straining to see through the fog. Though they must sail close to land to hear the fog signal at the harbor, if they worked in too far, underwater rocks and shoals waited ready to rip into their hull and tear the life out of their ship.

It began to snow again. Now big soft feathery flakes came down as thick as white fog. With less wind, the lake was calmer, but big swells still pushed them along. And again they were blinded. This was even worse than the freezing fog. Beyond the *Gazelle's* outward pointing bowsprit, a wall of swirling snow wrapped around them like a cold white blanket. It blocked sound, too, so the lookouts couldn't hear Oswego harbor's warning fog horn or the noise of the city somewhere ahead of them.

Guided only by her compass, the schooner sailed on. Somewhere ahead lay unseen a shore. Had they already sailed past Oswego?

51

Reuban's keen ears heard it first. A deep growl, filled with menace and threat. Despite the icy footing Reuban leaped up onto the deck box glaring into the white void before him. Now muffled heavy crashes interrupted the steady rumble. Reuban growled back. He raised his own voice in a warning wail challenging the winter cat's roar.

"What is it Reuban?" asked Captain Ben who was standing beside the man at the wheel.

Reuban yowled, "Danger. Danger ahead!"

Captain Ben shouted to the lookout forward "Get the lead-line out. Take a sounding. Hurry."

Moments later the crewman called back, "Four fathoms."

"Standby to wear ship-there's no time to bring her about!"

The crew hurried to their positions to shift the sails and heavy booms as Captain Ben at the wheel spun it quickly to turn the ship away from the land. Still, the waves pushed them onward towards the invisible land, and to Reuban it seemed as if the *Gazelle* would never turn. Now even the humans could hear the surf pounding the shore. They must shift the sails quickly, yet if they acted too fast, the wind might catch a sail and rip it as it slammed over. Without her sails, the *Gazelle* would be helpless. The hungry surf and the rocky shore waited. The lake was all too ready to wash over her, pound her to pieces, and devour her.

"Now Tommy-jibe ho! Nate, take up on that tackle!"shouted Captain Ben. With a rattle and a thud the heavy mainsail suddenly slammed across the deck as the wind caught it. The ship swung around and began working away from land, pushing steadily against the waves that tried to press her down against the shore and crush her against the rocks.

Watching the schooner fight her way through the water, splitting and shouldering aside the waves with her strong bow, Captain Ben nodded approval and said, "Good job, Reuban. We'll sail out to ten fathoms and then run along shore and keep the lead going. That'll keep us close enough in to hear Oswego."

If we didn't already miss it thought Reuban to himself. An hour later the snow stopped. As the curtain of white lifted, the crew saw the dark land along with the buildings and coal smoke of Oswego's factories. The crew also heard a tug's steam whistle sounding to guide them in, and they saw Oswego's stone lighthouse tower with its flashing beacon. Guided by her captain's sure hand on the helm, the *Gazelle* slipped safely into the harbor where a little tug waited to take her hawser and tow her to the elevator where she could unload her cargo of wheat.

Chauncey concluded his story; "That was the last trip they made that year. A week later the harbor was frozen solid. But now they had money to pay the bank and keep their boat." Chauncey paused to look out over the quiet sun-lit harbor. Then he added, "A lot has changed since the old schooner days. Now we have engines, and radar, and satellite navigators to help us get into harbors. We don't sail in November either like they did. But nature still calls the shots out there. Even in the summer boats get into trouble and people die. You must never let your guard down while sailing on the lake. And never trust the water."

Twink thought of yesterday's squall and of how Dusty had nearly drowned in Sodus Bay. She nodded. For sure Chauncey had that right. The lake could be treacherous.

Chauncey continued, "A mariner can cope with some pretty heavy stuff if he's prepared and skilled. And if his crew all works together and watches out for each other. You need to learn and then practice your skills all the time, and keep a good watch, too, while you're sailing. It's not always easy, but you have to do it if you want to sail the lake and come back."

Twink looked around the marina with its rows of boats sitting at rest in the strong afternoon sun. It all seemed so safe and orderly in the harbor. Yet even here dangers lurked. Dogs lunged, cars rushed by, and always the water waited. Tomorrow they would cross the lake. Anything could happen out there. She wouldn't let her guard down. The Wind Witch of the lake wasn't going to catch Twink unaware.

6. Twink Stands a Watch

The Wind Witch was nowhere in sight the next morning as *Ariel* chugged out of Oswego Harbor. In fact, the lake was as flat as the floor of Twink's living room back home. As they passed the steel tower of the lighthouse and entered the open lake, Skipper Sue said with a sigh, "Guess we're going to be a motor boat today."

Since it was calm, she let the cats up on deck to escape the noise and fumes of the engine. Even Piggy came out and huddled in a cockpit corner next to Skipper Sue's feet. Twink wondered how many hours they would have to listen to the racket of *Ariel's* two cylinder motor clattering away under foot. She jumped up on the seat next to *Ariel's* captain and said, "I'm bored."

Skipper Sue looked down at her. "We have to use the engine, Twink, if we want to get across to Canada. We've already lost two days, and I want to get to that lecture. Anyway, you'll like Kingston. It's the oldest city on the lake. The French built a fort there called Cataraqui, back in the 1600's. It was the most important fort they had on the Great Lakes. Cataraqui was the gateway to all of the rest of Canada and the great northwestern wilderness."

CAT-araqui, well duh. Of course, it would have been important thought Twink. The sound of Skipper Sue's voice and the steady chuggety chug of the motor were making her sleepy. She closed her eyes for a brief catnap wondering how many hours it would take for poky old *Ariel* and her little ten horsepower engine to cross the lake.

She woke up around lunch time and went up on the fore deck to join her mother. Dusty was looking ahead to where a dirty gray bank of mist lay upon the water. "I think we're in for some fog."

"Uh oh, how will Skipper Sue find Kingston?" wondered Twink.

"She doesn't have one of those satellite navigator things Chauncey talked about."

"She's got the compass. That will tell her the way," said Dusty.

Twink shook her head. "I wouldn't bet on it. Remember last year when we ended up in Port Bay instead of Fair Haven? She's a rotten navigator."

Piggy joined them, her green eyes round and wide as she stared at the dark mass of cloud ahead that was rolling towards them. "I don't like this. I feel trouble coming."

"Oh, don't be such a scaredy cat," growled Twink. Then *Ariel* plunged into the mist, and in a moment it became much darker as the air and water around them became a void of gray. They chugged on. Tiny beads of water formed all over each cat's fur coat, and the air grew clammy. Twink shivered with the abrupt chill that enveloped them. It was surprisingly cold for a summer day. Water began dripping off the sails, and the decks grew moist.

"I'm going below," said Piggy, and she slunk aft. Dusty followed her.

Twink went back with them to the cockpit but decided to stay on deck. She didn't like being wet, and the penetrating cold was uncomfortable, but she remembered what Chauncey had said about keeping a good watch. Much as she hated to admit it, she agreed with Piggy. She, too, felt there was trouble ahead out there in the fog. And Skipper Sue had goofed up her navigation before. She'd been reading a book instead of watching the compass that day when they had ended up in Port Bay. I'd better stay up here and keep an eye on her thought Twink. Like all cats, Twinkle Toes had a very good sense of direction. Right now, it definitely felt to her like they were on a wrong heading.

Unfortunately, she was quite correct. *Ariel* was off course, but Twinkle Toes couldn't tell Skipper Sue what course to steer as she didn't know herself. This time, though, it wasn't the Wind Witch that was preventing their little ship from reaching Kingston. Ahead of *Ariel* just under the water lay a strange formation of rocks called Charity Shoal, a shoal like no other on the lake. Its rocks formed an almost perfect circle around a deep hole. And within that hole a mysterious magnetic force was at work.

Thousands of years ago a giant comet had fallen from the sky and struck in Canada. Just before it hit, a piece broke off. That smaller part crashed into Lake Ontario in a vast blaze of fire and steam. In a fraction of a second, the impact released as much energy as a hundred nuclear bombs. The monstrous blow also changed the very rocks of the lake bottom and magnetized them. Now the rocks below silently reached out to *Ariel's* compass to pull its indicator away from the earth's north magnetic pole. Unaware of her error, Skipper Sue was no longer steering *Ariel* towards Kingston even though she was watching her compass closely.

Twink stayed on deck sitting beside Skipper Sue while the cold fingers of fog wrapped themselves around her. Although she knew the engine was pushing them along steadily, nothing seemed to change around her. Time dragged slower than a garden slug crossing a six lane highway. Five minutes felt like an hour as she stared at the gray water and gray air while the cold seeped deeper into her bones. Finally she was so stiff and shivery that she decided to take a short break. She went down into the noisy but somewhat warmer and drier cabin. Back on Skipper Sue's bunk, she busied herself with drying off her fur. As she did so, she wondered what else a good crew person should do to help her ship in a fog.

"I wish we were home," said Twink as she worked on her wet feet and thought of the warm soft dirt and summer sun in her garden. "Who is this famous writer, this Meow-what guy, in Canada Skipper Sue wants to see anyway?"

"I think he wrote a book about his dog," said Dusty.

Twink stopped drying herself and glared at Dusty. "Ah, c'mon. How could a book about a dog make anyone famous? That's ridiculous."

Dusty was about to reply when the steady chuggety chug of *Ariel's* engine stopped. The motor coughed, skipped a couple of times and then with an apologetic wheeze fell silent.

All three cats stared at the now quiet engine compartment. This is not good, thought Twink. No motor and no wind. No way we'll get to Canada or anywhere else now. She went immediately back up on deck.

Skipper Sue had the top of the engine box off. She was peering down at the top of the silent motor. She wiggled a spark plug wire half heartedly and said to Twink, "I bet we're out of gas." Then she looked up at the small radar reflector hanging in the rigging. "And I have no idea where the shipping lane is. I sure hope we're across it."

Skipper Sue opened the cockpit locker and took out an old grimy yardstick. She unscrewed the gas cap on the side deck and pushed the yardstick down until it hit the gas tank bottom with a distinct "tonk." She pulled it up and Twink could see that only the bottom half inch of the yardstick was wet.

The silent fog surrounded them like a nasty clammy blanket of soggy cotton. Water dripped off the boom and landed on Twink's head. We'll be out here all night, she thought. With the huge ships. One of them could run us over and never even know it. Twink stared into the fog listening for the rumble of an approaching ship. Their boat rocked gently on the glassy water. Without the steady putter of the engine, the quiet pressed in, and Twink felt squeezed by it. More water plopped down on her. Twink decided if she was going to be run over by a ship she might as well get comfortable. She went back down into the now peaceful cabin.

Piggy was sitting up on the bunk wide awake. She had heard the exchange about no more gas and the shipping lane and didn't much like the idea of waiting for a 700 foot freighter to show up. It was late afternoon, not too long until supper time. Dusty looked at the stove and said, "Well, if we're going to die I wish we could do it with full stomachs."

Piggy who also was very fond of food also looked at the stove and licked her chops. Then her expression changed as, still looking at the stove, she half closed her eyes and appeared to be thinking. She said, "Skipper Sue puts 'flame juice' in there to make the stove hot when she cooks hamburger. Maybe she could put that same stuff in the engine to make it hot again."

Twink had been glowering at the floor thinking her own thoughts-- like how incredibly stupid Skipper Sue was. Only a complete idiot would set out across the lake with an empty gas tank. She, too, now looked at the stove and then stared at the front of the box upon which the stove sat that served to cover up the front of the engine and its heavy spinning flywheel. When *Ariel's* engine ran, it gave off heat, as the lingering warmth of the cabin around them proved. Maybe fire juice would work. Twink glanced over at Piggy-the stupid lump might have come up with an idea for once. They certainly needed to do something.

The image of a ship the size of a shopping mall blundering around in the fog flashed through her mind. Even now one might be rumbling along, its steel bow pointed straight at them. If it hit their little egg shell of a boat, they wouldn't have a chance. They would be smashed into a mass of floating wood splinters in seconds. Somebody had better do something and it probably wouldn't be Dusty. She wasn't much for action other then when it was time to eat or get ashore, and Piggy was totally useless. So it was up to her to help her ship. And the sooner she started, the better.

"Hey, you just might have an idea there," Twink said to Piggy.

Twink to the rescue. I'll get us out of this mess. I'll tell that dim bulb up in the cockpit what to do, Twink said to herself as she hopped down from the bunk and once again ran up the three steps to the cockpit. Here she sat down on the floor and glared up at Skipper Sue as she said as clearly and loudly as she could, "Flame juice. Put flame juice in the motor."

Skipper Sue had been sitting hunched over in the chill with her arms folded tight against her stomach staring off into the fog. When she heard Twink she looked down. "Are you hungry Twink? I guess it is getting late."

"No stupid, not food. Flame juice!"

Skipper Sue patted Twink on the head and said, "Maybe I should heat some soup up. I've got some beef soup you guys would like. Hot food would taste pretty good right now. Who knows how long we'll have to sit here waiting for wind. I wonder if the stove needs any kerosene?"

Twink glared at Skipper Sue. Really. Humans were so unbelievably dense. Give me a break already! She jumped up on the engine box and shouted, "Flame juice dummy. To feed the motor!"

Skipper Sue said, "Twink don't be such a pest." Then a funny look appeared on her face as she sat there with her mouth half open looking at Twink on the engine box. "Kerosene! The engine might run on it. We had an old fashioned tractor back home that ran on kerosene after it was warmed up. This motor is pretty near that old. Maybe it will run on kerosene, too."

Skipper Sue got to her feet, lifted the cockpit locker cover and pulled out the one gallon jug of kerosene for the galley stove. She unscrewed the fuel tank cap and dumped it in. Then she said "C'mon motor!" as she turned the key. The engine started immediately, and Twink beamed in approval. Never before had she been so happy to have the noisy smelly old thing puttering away underfoot. Its racket was music to her ears, and the aroma of oil, hot iron and exhaust fumes smelled better than a clump of cat mint. "Let's get out of here before a ship comes along," she said to Skipper Sue who must have been listening this time because she shoved the shifter lever forward and started the boat going ahead again.

With the revival of *Ariel's* engine, there came a change of luck. Less than a half hour later, the fog began to thin. As the air cleared, a low dark line appeared before them on the horizon. Land! We're coming to Canada! Twink could actually smell the new country a few miles away. Canada had a sweet cedar fragrance mixed with dead seaweed and wet rocks and a touch of fish. Skipper Sue saw it, too, and changed course. As *Ariel* chugged steadily closer, a small white wooden lighthouse appeared perched on the end of a long low lying point.

"There must be a harbor in there," said Skipper Sue. "I don't know where we are, but we're going in. Maybe someone will sell us some gas."

All the cats were on deck as *Ariel* carefully felt her way into the harbor through an entrance scarcely wider than she was. On either side ledges of concrete colored rock awaited the unwary or inattentive pilot. It wouldn't take much of a bump to crack one of our planks, thought Twink and then we'd sink for sure. But this time Skipper Sue steered carefully and held a true course, gliding over the clear green shallows past the watchful lighthouse into a protected cove. Once inside, she steered over to a wooden dock and stopped *Ariel* in front of a sizeable rust stained work boat that was tied up there. She climbed up onto the dock with the dock lines, tied up the *Ariel* and then came back aboard and shut the engine off. The cats looked around at Canada.

Without the noise of the motor, Canada was very quiet. No lawn mowers, no motorboats, not even any cars driving past on the gravel road by the harbor disturbed the peaceful evening. A large glittering green dragonfly settled on Ariel's cabin top as the quiet chatter of a dozen swallows overhead sounded. The still water reflected the shore and where a motionless heron stood near the entrance waiting for a fish to swim by, a second upside down heron image mirrored by the surface waited with him.

"Man, this is a real gunk hole," said Skipper Sue. "I wonder where the heck we are."

A thicket of gnarled wind twisted trees stood on the north shore, and down at the cove's end several big willows formed a dense screen of foliage. A half dozen cabins and cottages with small neatly mowed lawns, wooden racks draped with fish nets, and several old boats beached on shore, were clustered together on the south side of the cove. One house had a flag pole in its yard. A beautiful red and white flag waved in the gentle wind. "We made it," said Piggy. "There's the maple leaf of Canada."

Near one house a man in plastic coveralls and high rubber boots was unloading a small aluminum boat pulled up on shore. They heard the clang of metal as he heaved a garbage can out.

"Smells like fish," said Dusty. All the cats remembered that it was well past dinner time now.

"Hey, look at that," said Twink.

A few yards from the dock a boy in a battered little aluminum boat had just caught a small perch. As he pulled it in, a sizable stocky bird streaked with brown burst out of the willows with a loud squawk and flapped across the water to land on the back seat of the row boat. The boy laughed and said, "Sorry I'm keeping this one." He reached down into his bait box and tossed the bird a minnow. The young night heron gulped it down and settled himself on the seat to wait for more.

"Wow, I've never seen anyone share their bait with a bird back home," said Twink.

Piggy noticed a sign by the dock "It says wildlife sanctuary over there."

"They must really mean it," said Dusty. "Remember a couple of years ago when we were still living in Watertown, hearing about how those fishermen went to Galloo Island and clubbed a bunch of baby cormorants and stomped on their eggs and nests?"

Piggy remarked, "Well, maybe there's room for both birds and people in this place."

Twink, gazing at the shore line trees reflected in the still water, saw a young deer appear, bend down for a drink, and then fade back into the thicket.

Beside her, Dusty said, "It's nice here. I wonder if the rest of Canada is like this."

Their observations were interrupted by the arrival of a rusted blue pickup truck at the end of the dock. A gray haired man dressed in dungarees and a red and black checked shirt got out and walked down the dock toward them. He greeted Skipper Sue with a cheerful "Welcome to Canada. I'm Will Beman. I'm the harbor master here at Fisherman's Cove when I'm not fishing. How long is your boat?"

"Twenty three feet," said Skipper Sue.

"Then it'll cost you $2.30 to stay on the dock for the night. Anchoring is free of course. And you can pay me tomorrow-- if I remember to come back," he added with a laugh.

Skipper Sue reached inside for the band aid box where she kept her Canadian money and counted out the dock fee. "That's a very reasonable price," she said.

"It's ten cents a foot, and your boat is pretty small. Did you come across from New York today?"

"Yes, and I'm all out of gas. Can I buy any fuel here?"

"Well I've got a full jerry jug in my boat. I can sell you five gallons .Is that enough?"

"I hope so. How far are we from Kingston? We got a little lost in the fog. "

Mr. Beman laughed. "I wondered how you found us. This place is pretty out of the way nowadays. We don't get many yachts here anymore. But it's only 35 klicks to Kingston."

"What's a klick?" asked Skipper Sue.

"I forgot. You're a Yank. Thirty five kilometers that's a little over twenty miles."

Skipper Sue looked relieved. "Five gallons would be plenty then."

"I'll bring it over after I get my gear put away and my boat cleaned up."

After Beman drove off, Skipper Sue set about cooking her dinner. She put food out for the cats, and after dinner decided to go off around the cove to look at Mr. Beman's fishing boat and his nets and cottage telling the cats that she wanted to find out more about the fishing business. However, she forgot to latch the porthole. Twink pushed it open and slipped out on deck. Soon Dusty followed. Finally, after several minutes, Piggy got up her nerve and squeezed out of the window to join them.

The sky had cleared, and the three cats sat on the cabin top watching the orange and gold of sunset gradually fade into a softer dull red. They heard the sharp yap of hunting foxes in the distance as a chorus of crickets began an evening concert on shore joined by a trio of frogs in the harbor.

Twink longed to go exploring. The quiet harbor, tall grass, and grove of trees called to her. Surely she could find a story here in Canada.

"I'm going to take a walk," she announced.

64

"Are you nuts?" said Piggy. "This is a foreign land. You have no idea what's out there. You heard those foxes. There might be bears out there."

"Well, I'd rather meet a bear than another dog. Anyway, there are plenty of trees to climb."

"Bears climb trees, too. No sir, I'm staying right here."

"I'm going. I might find a story. The sooner we get enough stories the sooner we can go home."

Dusty gave Twink a quick lick on the top of her head. "Be careful."

Twink hopped up onto the dock and slunk down it, hurrying for the trees where she quickly blended with the shadows.

7. A Blue Water Voyager's Tale

The first bats of the night were beginning to zigzag over the harbor as Twinkle Toes stole through the tall grass and slipped into the deepening gloom under the trees. She knew Skipper Sue didn't want her ashore alone, but she would just take a quick tour around the harbor.

Twilight was Twink's favorite time to prowl. Her excellent night vision along with her keen hearing and a splendid set of whiskers made it easy for her to get around even during the darkest night. On this mild evening a waxing moon high overhead dappled the ground beneath the trees with spots of pale light, and the dew underfoot told Twink it would be a good sailing day tomorrow as she padded along. Suddenly she heard a soft rustle behind her. She whirled around.

A head poked out from behind a clump of grass and a lidless dark eye stared at her. Then some more of the creature flowed forward and stopped while Twink crouched.

"Hello, what have we here?" said the creature. "I don't recognize you. Are you going to the garden too?"

Twink retreated a step or two fluffed up her tail and hissed, "Who are you?"

"I'm Ellen, and you?"

"My name is Twinkletoes," replied Twink in a guarded growl.

"Well, Twinkle-Toes there's plenty of food to go around. Have no fear. Wonderful strawberries now and tender lettuce and fresh peas, too, so come along."

"Peas? Strawberries? Snakes don't eat vegetables."

"I beg your pardon dearie. I'm not a snake. I'm an eel, and it's really mostly slugs snails and worms that I'm after, not vegetables."

Twink looked more closely at Ellen. She was about three feet long and come to think of it perhaps a bit more plump than most snakes Twink had met. Nor were any scales apparent. And sure enough a long fin, now flattened, ran down the middle of her muddy brown back and two smaller fins stuck out from either side of her body just behind her head. Twink noticed the skin on her back and yellowish sides and white belly appeared to be moist and slimy as she lay in the dewy grass.

"We really ought to move along, Twinkle Toes. More eels are coming behind me, and we shouldn't hold them up."

Ellen began wiggling forward. Twink stepped aside and then began following her. Ellen called back cheerfully,"There should be a goodly supply of slugs around, too, with it so damp."

"I don't eat slugs," sniffed Twink. "I'm a cat."

"Mice," said Ellen. "You'll be a mouse hunter then, right? I've eaten a mouse or two in my time-not that I could ever catch one ashore. I'm not clever like you. But now and then one falls into the harbor from the dock. They are tasty. I like meat when I can get it, it's a nice change from fish."

Ellen paused to snap up a small earthworm that had unwisely started across the path. "Eels aren't picky eaters. We'll take just about anything we can catch."

"Do you live in the harbor?"

"Yes, I spend the day in a nice little cave between two boulders that the two leggers put in the water to protect the boat ramp. We eels work the night shift, though, so you might not ever notice us."

"Do you come out of the water very often?"

"Oh,no. Just when there's a really good reason. Like strawberry slugs. Ah, there's the garden ahead. Thank goodness. As you can see overland travel does not suit me, though this wet grass is tolerable."

"How long can you live out of the water?"

"Oh, quite awhile if it's damp and cool. Certainly a day or two, if there's no sun to dry me out."

At the garden Twink was startled at the strange sight before her. The neatly mulched strawberries and tidy rows of peas, string beans, lettuce, and spinach lay washed by the silvery moonlight. And at least a dozen eels of various sizes were busily foraging about, the moon gleaming off their wet bodies. Ellen wriggled out of the grass and onto the damp straw.

"I'm so glad this organic gardener uses mulch. I absolutely detest crawling over bare dirt. Do you know that my second cousin says in Germany the two leggers go out at night and run a furrow between the garden and the stream bank so eels are trapped ashore?"

"Why?" said Twink.

"Two leggers eat eels. They smoke us, pickle us, and bake us. Here on the lake they fish for us all the time. I never eat a worm I find under water because that's what two leggers use for bait here. They set out a long line with several hundred short lines tied on to it, each with a hook tied to it. Each hook has a worm. Or at least, they used to. Come to think of it, it's been awhile since I've seen a trot line."

Ellen paused to snap up a plump slug. Then she continued, "There was a foolish old eel that lived under the dock who was so stupid she ate a worm underwater. She said they tossed her in a garbage can with a hundred other eels, and then they all were dumped into a sort of floating pen of netting-it was dreadfully crowded, nothing to eat, and there was horrid blinding scalding sunlight all the time. She was shoved and pushed and banged around until she said she was one great big bruise. Then she found a hole in the netting and escaped, but she heard the two leggers packed those other eels up in boxes of damp moss and sent them off to Europe in some kind of boat that flew through the air. She's been scared to leave the harbor since. She must be at least forty now."

"How long do eels live?"

"Well, I'm thirty, but my grandmother got washed into a pond during a big flood and lived to be over eighty before another flood washed her out of it."

Twink said, "I notice you always speak of she eels."

"That's because all the eels in the lake are females. We're much braver and more adventurous than the males. We're stronger, too, so we come further than they do."

Twink was puzzled. She licked her paw and did a quick wash while she tried to figure this out. Where did the eels come from? And why did they bother she wondered. Ellen meanwhile wriggled off to pick more slugs from strawberries.

Between slugs she told Twink that no eel had ever been born in the lake. They had all made a long long journey to get there. "After I finish my supper, I'll tell you the legend of our people. It's a very old story and it should be told properly. "And," she added with a sigh,"I may be the last eel around to tell it to you if things don't change soon."

Twink's curiosity was now fully aroused. This definitely sounded like a story. "I'll go hunt for some dinner myself," she said. Then I'll come back in an hour or so."

"Splendid. Please do. I would love to recite for you."

An hour later Twink was back. Ellen was slowing down in the slug hunt, as she was getting quite stuffed. She settled in under some spinach leaves and began;

"This is a story like no other, the epic of the eel nation. One day soon I, like my sisters, will leave this place. Perhaps in a year or two. I know not the day but it will be soon for the thread of knowledge of the last journey runs through all of our race and all of us must take that final journey.

We are an ancient people. We are a thousand times older than this lake. We survived the last great extinction when the air caught fire and the world grew dark and the sea grew cold. Our people lived, but many others did not. They say no land creature larger than a cat survived."

The memory begins when the sea was much smaller than today. The world continent had broken and as the two pieces moved apart, the sea grew wider. It was warm then. Though we dislike sunlight, we love warmth.

We are born in a dark place far away from here, deep in the ocean a mile or more below the indigo blue sea surface. Our bodies begin as strange thin living ribbons narrow and long and clear as a dragonfly wing. Tiny and helpless, the young float upward to be caught by surface currents. Some are swept north by the Mother Current that the two leggers call the Gulf Stream. Others go westward beyond Florida and ascend the great river that drains half the continent. As I floated north, the Stream meandered and eddied. Some of us drifted ashore to seek small freshwater streams and big brown rivers in the south lands of Georgia and the Carolinas. Many of us sought the warm shallow waters of the Chesapeake Bay. A few of us even went on across the sea.

I ascended the St. Lawrence. The moon pulled me shoreward. I rode the tide west always moving at night. A year passed. I grew. I became bigger and stronger. My form shifted again and became as you see me now. At first I remained clear like glass, then I darkened and began to actively swim harder. Another year passed.

I came to water without tides. Now I and my sisters had to swim against the outflow of all the Great Lakes. It was difficult. Many fell behind. Many died. But we had to go on to The Lake a thousand miles away. As I struggled against the current, the water began to smell very strange. At times it was so bitter I tried to avoid it by sinking to the bottom and waiting. Once I entered a place of searing burning pain. I saw fish who were dying. I saw eels who were crippled, their bodies deformed. But most of us went on. We could not turn back. Many more of us died.

It was late spring when I reached The Wall. This was new. My mother never saw it. It didn't exist when she was young. Ours was the first generation to face the Wall. Perhaps we will be the last.

We searched for days to find a way around the great barrier. Gulls and herons and hungry big fish preyed upon us as we swam back and forth in the turbulent water. Finally a small group of us found a way around. It was the most difficult part of the entire journey, for we had to climb many feet. Sometimes we even left the water to crawl and climb. We moved in darkness and hid during the day. Crowds of gulls gathered to snatch up any straggler caught by daylight. We pushed on. At last I came to this place and here I have lived for thirty years.

Each year fewer young eels come to this harbor. Perhaps the way around The Wall has closed. Perhaps the stinking burning water has caused them to lose their way. It's been ten years since I've seen a young eel move in to Fishermen's Cove. Something is keeping them back.

I will go soon. I will change again into a new and strange body. I will put on my silver and bronze coat. My eyes will grow large so I can find my way in the dark ocean and my fins will lengthen as I ready for my journey. Even now I begin to store food in my body as oil, for I must travel thousands of miles without pause or food.

One fall night when the moon is dark, I will depart to seek the sea. I and my sisters will descend. Traps and barriers and fences will lie across the river. There will be The Wall and the bitter water. Humans who seek our flesh will capture many of us. If I survive and if I am strong, I will ride the tide to the sea.

Our numbers dwindle. I fear for our future. Our throng thins to a few. But the sea calls us home. In the far place of warm sweet salt water we will meet the males again for the first time since leaving the sea. Our future life carried within our bodies will mix with that of the males and we will die to be reborn."

As Ellen's story ended, an owl called. Deep and menacing, his hunting cry rolled forth on the still air and echoed off the trees. Ellen and Twink looked at each other and Twink suddenly felt very small and humble as she looked at this far traveler who had already faced so many dangers. Soon she would face more obstacles and hazards beyond anything Twink could imagine.

"The old boy's hungry," said Ellen. "Might not be a bad idea if both of us were moving along."

Twink looked down at her white feet. They practically glowed now in the moonlight and she now felt very conspicuous. And vulnerable.

"I think you're right. I should be getting back to the boat."

"Take care on your voyages. And perhaps we'll meet again, here or in some far place."

"Yes, I hope we do. Fair winds and calm seas to you, too, Ellen on your last voyage." said Twink.

Without a backward glance, she set off for the harbor taking care to slink along close to the rows of peas and spinach where she hoped the owl couldn't see her. Twink concentrated on moving as quietly and quickly as possible through the garden and then into the grove of trees. The rustle and whisper of movement among the dry leaves underfoot as she placed each paw softly down upon the ground told her others were also venturing about on this summer night. She saw moonlight laying a silver sheen on the grass beyond the trees as she neared the forest edge. Once across that grass and the gravel road beyond, she would have it made. She could clearly see *Ariel's* mast sticking up in the distance.

Just a few more minutes and a couple hundred feet and she would be safe.

The owl called again. Close. Its deep gruff voice boomed out into the night almost overhead. Twink flattened herself against the ground and froze. An owl could kill a cat. Those powerful talons could pierce the body of a full grown rabbit or a skunk and squeeze the life out of it. He'd tear her to shreds if he caught her. Twink's spine prickled with fear. His eyesight was as good as hers and his hearing as keen. Could he see her?

A black shape floated soundlessly out from the trees on broad wings. It drifted toward the harbor gliding slowly over the grass and the road. He'll be back. I'd better make a run for it, thought Twink. She gathered her haunches for the first leap. Then she burst out of the trees and raced across the grass, her white feet flashing in the moonlight. Another twenty feet, then the road, then the dock.

Suddenly a flood of brilliance blinded her as a car's headlights appeared from behind a curve in the road. Twink faltered, dazzled and confused. She was certain that the owl was coming back for her. As she dug in and crouched, she thought I'm not going to make it. At any moment he would strike. Panic flooded through her and washed every thought from her mind. She froze staring at the car's relentless rush. The right wheel was heading directly for her. It seemed as if everything was happening in slow motion. The car swerved. It straddled her. A couple of pebbles from the road stung her sides, then it was over. Just a cloud of dust and fading sound remained, as the car drove off. Its tail lights dimmed in haze as Twink huddled in the road. Then a voice sounded within her head. Run! Run for your life. The owl is coming! She got to her feet and bolted the last few yards to the harbor.

Twink rushed across the open parking area and pounded down the dock. She leaped onto the *Ariel* and pushed though the open window and plopped onto the bunk where Skipper Sue was reading with the other two cats snuggled up beside her. What a relief to be back aboard. That was a little too close. Yes, it was cramped and crowded, but for now, anyway, the *Ariel* was her home. And at least when tied to a dock, the *Ariel* felt a whole lot safer than being ashore right now.

After Skipper Sue finished reading and turned out the light, Twink told Dusty and Piggy about her near death experience and the eels. She concluded, "This story business is getting pretty strenuous. I think I might have gone through another life for that one. But it was worth it. I had no idea this stuff was happening and that the lake is changing so much. I wonder, does anybody else know about this? If all the eels vanish, whose next? Why did they build The Wall anyway, and would they have done it if they knew that it would kill so many of Ellen's people?"

Dusty spoke, "I don't know Twink. But you're right. These changes are important. We need to get this into Skipper Sue's book."

Piggy had crouched on the bunk listening intently to Twink's story. Now she spoke up. "I wonder what else is going on out there that we should know about?"

Twink shook her head. She gave a front paw a quick lick, something she often did when confused or uncertain and needed time to think. Ellen's people, an ancient and successful race, were disappearing. Someone had to find out what was going on and then tell people about it. The right people,the ones who could do something about it. Twink's stomach felt a little queasy almost like the first day on the boat. This project was not going to be easy. Especially for one small black and white cat. Did she really want to get involved with this? Was this something she should do?

"Hard to say what's going on, Piggy. But I bet Harry knows. Next time he's around, I must talk to him. Whatever's going on, it's bad."

8. Twink Suffers A Knockdown

The next morning dawned clear with a gentle west wind. Skipper Sue was in high spirits as she readied *Ariel* for a day of travel with a fair wind. She was anxious to get to Kingston and the museum.

"I sure hope I'll get to talk with Farley Mowat. I think I've read almost every one of his books. I think he'll be able to help me. The lecture isn't until tomorrow. We can still make it, no problem," she told the cats after they had shoved off. The lake flashed silver and cobalt blue before *Ariel,* and with the wind filling her sails, the plump little yacht bustled along at a good clip.

Why does Skipper Sue like sailing so much? wondered Twinkle Toes as she sat in the cockpit with the morning sun warm on her shoulders. She goes sailing every chance she gets. Twink had to admit that right at this moment aboard *Ariel* with a gentle breeze, it was quiet. She did appreciate that. Just the whisper and swish of the water alongside and the occasional rustle of the sails and creak of the lines overhead. The boat shuffled along with an easy swing that reminded Twink of sitting in a rocking chair. It was relaxing and restful and blessedly quiet without the motor. The Wind Witch was off somewhere hopefully far away this morning.

Perhaps one reason Skipper Sue likes to sail, is that it's something she can do by herself. All she needs is a bit of wind, a good boat, and time. She could go anywhere there was water. You could sail around the world if you had enough time. With her own little ship, Skipper Sue could go when and where she pleased. A cat could get to like the independence and freedom of sailing, Twink thought. At least when the lake was calm.

She watched the pastures and bean fields and cottages of the low lying countryside move past as they sailed east down the channel between Amherst Island and the mainland towards Kingston. Even though the wind was scarcely strong enough to ruffle her fur, *Ariel's* sails were catching enough of it to push along their two tons of food, water, tools, supplies, books, litter box, and boat as fast as a cat could trot. Pretty easy way to travel, thought Twink. And cheap, too, with free wind.

Before noon the hulking gray stone fortress of the old Kingston penitentiary was abeam, and by lunchtime *Ariel* was tucked away at a dock in the public marina on the doorstep of Kingston a few yards from the big City Hall building with its land mark copper dome and clock tower.

Skipper Sue went off to the farmers market behind City Hall for groceries, and all three cats used Twink's ventilator hose escape route to get out of the cabin. As they sat in the afternoon sun, a familiar voice called from overhead, "Ahoy *Ariel*!" Then Harry dropped down onto the bow and folded his wings.

"I thought I'd find you here. How was your crossing?"

"We got lost," said Twink. "We ended up in a place called Fisherman's Cove."

"Ah yes, I know it well. A sweet little harbor and great grub, too, with all the fish guts from the netters there."

Twinkle Toes then told Harry about meeting Ellen and her story, concluding, "So what is going on Harry? What are these changes out there in the lake and where is this bitter water Ellen talked about coming from?"

"Hard to say for sure. But I can tell you this. My people and other bird tribes on the rest of the Great Lakes also had trouble with this stuff you're talking about. It started back in the 1960s. Aye, those were bad times. Back then, a lot of us couldn't even hatch our eggs. Sometimes

77

an egg broke just from being sat on, because its shell was so weak. My wife, gone now these twenty long years, and I lost a dozen." Harry sighed and looked off across the harbor. "I'll always remember when one egg finally did hatch. Of course, the baby died right away--never even got all the way out of the egg. For years our chicks hatched wrong. A lot of the poor little buggers died right off. One was missing its eyes. Another had club feet and several had crooked bills. Some of them were twisted right up. They couldn't eat. None of 'em lived more than a few days. It was heavy going for us birds then."

"But about twenty years ago it got better. The humans had been poisoning the Great Lakes with stuff they call chemicals. For forty years they had let the crap run right out of factory pipes and dumps into rivers and creeks and even into the lake itself. But when they saw what it was doing to us, they stopped it. It's a right lot better now since the lake got cleaner. Our chicks are healthier. But lately there's new things happening that aren't so good. It might be that bitter water you was talking of."

Piggy spoke up, "Ellen said the baby eels aren't coming anymore. Is the bad water still in the St. Lawrence River?"

"Can't say what's happening to the eels. Last few summers there's hardly been any small ones around. I used to eat 'em by the dozen down at the power dam each spring. Aye, there's something different going on all right. For one thing, there's some new fish in the lake. The humans call them round gobies, though I've never seen 'em around before."

"What's a round gooby? A fish shaped like a ball?" asked Twink.

"Go-bees," Harry told her. "They're little nippers, about six inches long. They live under rocks near shore. They started getting sick a couple of years ago. And the birds that ate them got sick, too. Last summer hundreds of gulls and terns raising families on Little Galloo

Island died. Then, of course, with no one to feed them, all their babies starved. Nobody knows why the parents died. But I'm not eating any gobies for sure, and if you're smart you won't either."

"Do you think all the birds are going to disappear like the eels?" asked Twink

Harry drew himself up to his full height. His eyes flashed as he said firmly,"Gulls will survive. We're tough. We can eat anything, and we can fly away to other places. There's restaurant parking lots and dumps in Toronto or Rochester. But the terns and loons and other birds that only eat fish- they got rough seas ahead. And the fur folk like the mink and the big fish in the lake got no choice either. They have to stay here and eat fish. It'll be heavy weather going and headwinds for them I'm thinking."

Harry once again turned his head to look out at the distant lake. "I can shove off anytime and fly a hundred miles in a few hours. But this is my home port. I don't want to move to the coast and salt water. It's jammed full of huge houses and apartment buildings and roads and cars down there. There's no room for anybody on the beach except humans. You can make a good living, but it's a rat race fighting ten other gulls for every scrap at the mall parking lots. No sir, too hectic for me. I'll take the lake. I'm staying right here by the sweet water where I was born."

All three cats nodded. Home is also dear to a cat's heart. Right now, even on board *Ariel* safe in harbor on this pleasant sunny day in Kingston, the word sounded sweet to the ears of the three cats. Each closed her eyes and remembered her favorite flower bed, garden spot, or sun bathing place at their small house in the country. Twink then looked around at the harbor filled with big shiny white yachts. On shore behind the boats the windows of several tall apartment buildings gleamed in the morning sun, while the city traffic's noise sounded like the roar of the lake on a windy day. Their quiet little homestead on the other side of the lake seemed very far away indeed.

Harry was still standing up, and he, too, was looking out at the shore. Twink thought he looked unusually sad, and she felt a mix of sympathy and admiration for the hardy old seabird. He'd been around, all right. He'd seen the big wide world out beyond the lake, and plenty of trouble, too. But there he stood, head held high, ready to go on and take what came. He was no quitter for all the tough times he had lived through.

"I wish we could go home right now," said Piggy.

"Amen," chorused Dusty and Twink together.

Twink did a quick wash up behind her ears. Harry had confirmed her growing conviction that whatever was going on out there in the lake should be in Skipper Sue's book. First Ellen, and now Harry's tribe. It definitely sounded big and getting bigger. "I wish we had some answers here," she said.

"If you want to know what is happening anywhere around the lake, you go to Main Duck Island and talk to Sid and Richard." said Harry. Those two get all the gossip. And what they don't know, you can find out from Pearl. Pearl is over seventy years old. And her Mother and Mother's Mother lived on Main Duck, so Pearl knows more than any other animal on the lake."

"Where can we find Pearl?"

"Like I says, you hoist sail and shape a course for Main Duck. When you get there, look up Sid. She's the dock master there. Don't be put off by her looks. A lot of people say her tribe is sneaky and treacherous but it's all bilge water. Sid's as honest and true hearted as they come. She'll help you out any way she can. She's a reptile, like Pearl, so she knows her. She'll get you to Pearl."

"Here comes Skipper Sue," said Dusty. "Better get below."

With a quick good bye to Harry the three cats lined up to crawl through the deck vent and back down into the engine area. From there they made their way to the cabin. They were sprawled on Skipper Sue's bunk the very picture of contentment and innocence when she opened the cabin door to look in on them.

The next morning after breakfast, Skipper Sue went up to the marina's public showers leaving the cats locked in the cabin. Twink finished her own morning wash up, settled back on the bunk, and said, "I don't know how we're ever going to get to Main Duck. And I'm sick of this place anyway. I wish we could go home. How many stories have we got Piggy?"

"Only about thirty pages. We need lots more if we're going to make a book."

Twink hissed a very rude cat cuss word adding, "I never thought it would take this long".

"Maybe I could help get some," offered Piggy.

"You? You won't even get off the boat. You're hopeless."

Piggy's back fur went up and her already fluffy tail became considerably bushier."I can get a story as good as any of yours!"

"Spare me. If we wait for your stories we'll be here until the next ice age."

"Idiot!" Piggy spat.

"Hair ball," snarled Twink and she wound up and and let fly and whacked Piggy on the head.

Dusty spoke up, "Stop it you two. Fighting isn't going to get us home any faster."

But Piggy's blood was hot now. With a last furious curse flung over her shoulder at Twink, she sprang off the bunk and disappeared under the cockpit. Moments later Dusty and Twink heard her clawing up the vent hose and grunting as she squeezed through the deck opening. Her feet pattered overhead and then silence fell.

"Now you've done it, Miss Crabby. She'll go ashore and get lost," said Dusty.

Twink snarled, "That fat fur ball. She won't even get off the dock let alone go ashore. She'll be back in five minutes."

But she wasn't. When Skipper Sue came aboard and opened the cabin door only two cats sat on the bunk looking back at her.

"Where's Piggy?" Skipper Sue asked. She looked around the cabin, and peered under the bunk and inside the tiny closet where she kept her rain gear. She looked up forward on her bookshelf and used her flashlight to see into the anchor locker, and she searched under the cockpit back by the engine. There she saw the torn vent hose with sunlight showing through the exposed deck opening. "Uh oh. She got out. She must be on shore somewhere."

Skipper Sue looked very worried as she jumped off *Ariel* onto the dock leaving the door open. She jogged away towards shore calling "Here Piggy. Kitty kitty kitty."

Dusty glared at Twink. "Nice work."

Twink glared right back. "All right, I'll go find the stupid hair ball."

Twink leaped up the stairs into the cockpit, bounded onto the dock and galloped down its length to the shore. Here she jumped down onto the slimy rocks along the water's edge and crouched under the dock.

"Come out you stupid lump!" she yelled into the gloom. All she heard was a nasty shrill giggle from a wharf rat somewhere nearby. She shouted again. Silence. Twink climbed over several slippery rocks and tip toed along the mucky edge of the water in search of some sign of the departed Piggy. No footprints, no signs, not even a single long brown hair showed itself. Two hours later she crept aboard the boat where Dusty waited alone.

"Skipper Sue's still ashore looking for her. We've got to find her,

Twink. She's the only one who can work the computer."

"She can't be far away," said Twink. "Soon as I get a bite of breakfast, I'll look some more."

"It's nearly noon. Skipper Sue's going to miss her lecture with the famous author."

Twink was gobbling down her food and said something rude with her mouth full so Dusty didn't quite catch it.

Dusty got up with a sigh. "I guess I'd better help hunt, too." She slipped up the stairs and went quietly off down the dock. Her mother's departure left Twink feeling guilty as well as annoyed with Piggy. She bolted a last bit of food and then followed without even taking time to clean her whiskers.

Twink found Dusty under the dock. They agreed to split up with Dusty searching the waterfront up by the ferry dock, while Twink would go look down by the yacht club. "Be careful Twink. This is a big city. You don't know what kind of cat eaters are out there. There's a rat half as big as Piggy under the next dock," Dusty cautioned.

"Don't worry about me. I'll be fine," said Twink.

She hiked off along the very edge of the harbor basin, picking her way around the dead fish, piles of seaweed, and bits of plastic trash carefully keeping her clean white feet out of the oily water and the slime. By staying right next to the water, Twink was able to avoid using the street with its countless cars and people all in a tearing roaring cat trampling rush to go somewhere. Down by the Marine Museum was a little area of tall grass and weeds at the water's edge. That looked like a possible hiding spot, so Twink headed for it, working cautiously along the narrow strip of shore between a rusty steel seawall and the harbor.

It was indeed a hideout, but not for a frightened Miss Piggy.

Soft footed and slow, Twink crept towards the weedy clump. She stopped a few feet away and called out in a low voice, "Piggy? Are you there?"

A loud hiss exploded forth. Twink froze as a long white neck soared up out of the grass high into the sky. The neck belonged to the biggest bird Twink had ever seen. The thing was huge, darn near as big as Skipper Sue. It opened its beak and hissed again. Twink arched her back and stood on tip toe. She fluffed up her fur making herself as scary looking as possible as she slowly backed away on stiff legs. Better get out of here right now she thought. Then a flicker of movement off to the side caught her eye. Another one. Headed right for her.

Oh, Great Bast, thought Twink as she whirled around to face the second swan. It was as big as a battleship and it was swimming straight at her. A bow wave rolled off its breast, and its neck was stretched low towards her. Its black eyes glittered with rage as it left a large wake astern. He must be doing ten knots thought Twink. She had seen swans before. One had attacked her and Skipper Sue last summer. They had been out in the dinghy when one had charged them. Skipper Sue had said a swan could break a human's arm with its wing, and that swans had dragged small children into the water and drowned them.

With the swan's mate on her nest ahead, the seawall to the right and the male swan and harbor on the other side she had only one way to go- down the narrow beach back the way she had come. She began to run, scrambling over the slick rocks and piles of rotting seaweed. Her feet sank into the ooze sometimes up to her ankles, and she was soon gasping for breath as she struggled through the soft muck.

The male swan spread his wings and began flapping, lifting off enough to run across the water. Twink could hear his feet smacking against the water and the beating of his mighty wings. He was fast catching up with her. A gigantic bird was about to grab her. One hit with his wing to knock her off balance, then he would pull her into the

84

harbor and hold her under. Twink slipped on a slime covered rock and nearly fell. She recovered as she felt the wind stirred by the great wings flailing the air a few feet astern. The steel harbor seawall loomed five feet high on her left. There was just one possible thing remaining for her to do. She leaped.

It was the jump of her life, five feet straight up. She got her paws over the edge and scrabbled her hind feet furiously against the rusted steel wall as she tried to dig her front claws into the cement on the top of the bulkheading. She felt her claws grating and slipping across the concrete. No. She would not quit! She gave a heave and a last desperate wiggle. Then she was over. On solid land. No time to stop now. One flap of his wings and the swan would be up here, too. Twink streaked across the empty lot running with all her strength heading for a row of parked cars in front of an old brick building.

The swan also vaulted up onto the seawall with a single wing beat. But when he saw Twink fifty feet away hurtling towards the cars, he made no further chase. Twink ducked under the first car she came to and skidded to a stop beneath it on an oily patch of pavement. Looking out she saw the swan slowly marching down the wall. Then he raised his huge wings and dropped off the edge and out of sight back into the harbor.

Twink had had enough. If Piggy had run into those things she was a goner. Likely she was dead anyway wherever she was. If a swan hadn't gotten her, a car or a dog probably had. After her heartbeat got back to something like normal, Twink crept out from under the car and headed back to *Ariel.*

As she skulked along the shore, mindful of swans, rats, dogs, and other hazards unknown, she felt a growing weight of guilt and dread settling on her shoulders. Piggy the lump was, after all, a part of *Ariel's* crew. Now she was gone, And it was her fault. Without Piggy there would be no more story seeking for the book. She could forget finding out about the vanishing eels. And Skipper Sue had missed her lecture. Holy Whiskers, she was really in trouble now.

When Twink saw the dock with *Ariel* waiting beside it, her spirits lifted. She was actually glad to see the stupid boat. She dropped down into the cockpit. No one here. She looked into the still open door. There, chowing down at the food dish was Piggy. Dusty was washing up on the floor beside her.

"Where did she come from?" asked a wide eyed Twink.

"She was hiding under the dock. She got up on top of the big float thing that holds the dock up so nobody saw her."

Piggy looked up from the dish. "I'm sorry, Twink. You were right. I didn't find any stories. It's harder than I thought to get a story."

Twink jumped down into the cabin, walked over and licked the top of Piggy's head. "I'm glad you're back, Piggy. You're a fat fur ball, but we need you."

9. Twink Hauls Her Wind And Lays A New Course

It was well past lunch time when Skipper Sue returned from her own search ashore. Upon seeing her lost crew-cat, her eyes widened and she exclaimed "Piggy!" She swept the cat off her bunk and cuddled her. "I thought you were gone. Where on earth were you? I thought I'd never see you again. I'm so glad you're back, Piggy."

Piggy closed her eyes in bliss, safe and snug in Skipper Sue's arms as her purr rumbled forth, and despite herself, Twink found she was purring, too. Skipper Sue sat down on the bunk still holding Piggy and stroked each cat in turn. "We gotta stick together you guys. It's a tough world out there." Then she looked at the clock on the small shelf by the cabin door and sighed, "Well, I missed the lecture. Guess I'll never get a chance to talk to Farley Mowat now about my book." She set Piggy down on the bunk and stared at her book shelf. Then she pulled a book out and leafed through it. "He's such a good story teller. Here's his book *The Boat Who Wouldn't Float* about sailing his wooden schooner in Newfoundland. This is one of my favorites. And he was quite a sailor, too."

Skipper Sue read a paragraph or two to herself. "He sure knows how to make you see things with words."

She closed the book with another sigh. "I'll just have to try to do it without him. She shelved the book, reached for her canvas bag with her notes and got up saying, "Guys, I'm off to the library. Don't any of you dare get off this boat 'til I get back."

Skipper Sue went out into the cockpit, stuffed a rag in the ventilator opening and then closed the door and left. But she forgot to screw the porthole window latch down tight. With Piggy's help, Twink managed eventually to persuade the loosely threaded latch open enough so as to release the window. Once outside, she flopped down onto the warm deck and stretched out in the sun. Soon Dusty joined her. They were both dozing off when a cheerful "Ahoy *Ariel!*" sounded overhead. The cats looked up at the long white wings of a gull against the blue summer sky. Then Harry dropped down beside them.

"I heard you crossed tacks with the Swan Family, Twink," he said with a glint of amusement in his yellow eyes.

"He tried to kill me," said Twink.

Harry threw his head back and laughed a loud gull laugh and said "Welcome to progress and 21st century waterfront development. Those fancy high society Swans are taking over everywhere on the lakes. They moved up here from Long Island and the Hudson Valley about ten years ago. They're pushing out all the working folks like the Mallard and Geese families with their great big show place nests. The loons can't stand 'em. They won't even let the herons fish out in front of their places. Before long there won't be room for any of us ordinary folk on the lake to make an honest living."

Dusty could see that Harry who, for the most part usually seemed to be a pretty cool character, was starting to get his feathers ruffled over the Swan takeover of the waterfront, so she changed the subject. "Skipper Sue missed her program. So now her book is in trouble."

"What program was that?"

"It was a talk by a Canadian author named Mowat. She said he was a really good writer."

"Too bad she missed him. He is pretty famous. He's sold more books about nature and the north lands than probably any other Canadian writer. He is a great friend of animals. His books have helped change laws and made some people take action to protect wolves and birds and sea animals. He makes people care by writing about problems and injustice. My cousin down on the coast went out with a ship that tried to stop the seal hunt off Labrador. They went partly because of Mowat's writing. The whole affair was run by a man named Paul Watson who knew about Mowat and had read some of his books. Watson has three or four ships out there on the ocean right now chasing Japanese whalers and outlaw fishermen. He calls them 'Neptune's Navy'."

Twink spoke up, "Well, we got a problem right here on the lake. We need to find out why the eels are dying and what's making the new goby fish sick. Then Skipper Sue can put that in her book. We've got to get to this Main Duck place and see that Pearl and Sid you talked about."

Piggy, recovering in the cabin from her terrifying ordeal ashore of hiding under the dock for three hours, had heard Harry arrive. As he talked, she poked her head out the window, looked around and then came cautiously out on deck and joined them. Now she spoke up, "Yes, Harry, Skipper Sue goes to libraries to find out stuff. How can we get *Ariel* to Main Duck if there's no people and libraries there?"

Harry stood on one foot and scratched the back of his head with the other. Then he suggested, "Your old shipmate Chauncey is a couple docks over with his schooner. I heard them talking about going to Main Duck. Maybe he's got an idea."

Dusty spoke up. "Hey, Twink, what was that Mowat book Skipper Sue was just looking at. Didn't she say it was about a wooden schooner?"

Piggy's ears pricked up. "Yea, Twink. Skipper Sue likes old boats. If you 'ran away' over to Chauncey's boat while she was watching, she'd follow you. Then maybe Chauncey's crew would get her interested in going to Main Duck. Harry could go over and get Chauncey up to speed about how we need to go there, so he'd say something to his people."

"Worth a try," said Harry. "Can't see you got much to lose." He flew off to brief Chauncey.

"I like it," said Twink. "It's got potential."

Chauncey's a smart old salt, she thought to herself. It would be fun to see him again, anyway.

Skipper Sue returned from the library near supper time as the sun began to disappear behind the City Hall dome and the shadows of the tall apartment buildings across the street were creeping out over Confederation Basin Marina. When she opened the cabin door, Twink darted out and jumped onto the dock.

"Get back here, Twink! Right now!" said Skipper Sue.

Twink looked over her shoulder her yellow eyes round and innocent and then trotted off.

Skipper Sue said a rude word and climbed up on the dock and ran after the cat. Twink scooted down to the dock where Chauncey's big black boat was tied up. Skipper Sue lumbered along behind her, and as Twink galloped out on the dock and jumped down onto the schooner she thought, this is almost too easy. Humans are so simple minded.

Chauncey greeted her with a wide smile and a cheery, "Ahoy!"

Twink settled in beside him with a purr saying, "Hey, Chauncey, good to see you again. Wait 'til you hear what happened to me this morning."

Skipper Sue clumped down the dock in hot pursuit and pulled up beside the *Sara B*'s cockpit where a man and woman were sitting each with an empty dinner plate and a cup of coffee.

"Excuse me, I think my cat just jumped on your boat."

"Is it a little black and white kitty? We just saw one go by. I think she's up forward visiting with our cat," said the woman.

"That's her," said Skipper Sue who could see Twink sitting on the foredeck with a fat yellow cat.

"Well, come on aboard."

Skipper Sue stepped cautiously over onto the side deck and looked around. "This is an amazing boat," she said.

"Welcome aboard the *Sara B*. I'm Sally Bates and this is my husband George.

Skipper Sue flashed Twink a dirty look, before she turned and smiled at the couple. She gawked up at the tall wooden masts and studied the hand-made fittings and the spliced rope work and rigging of the old yacht. "I've never seen a boat like this."

Mr. Bates said, "There aren't very many of them left. Say, would you like a cup of coffee? We've just finished dinner but we've got a bit of dessert if you'd like some."

Skipper Sue sat down and Mr. Bates passed her a mug followed by a plate of fresh baked cookies. Skipper Sue selected a plump cookie and asked, "Where did your boat come from?"

Mr Bates said "She was built in the Canadian Maritimes. Boats like this were used to catch cod and herring before World War II. They were called Tancook schooners after the name of an island in Nova Scotia where many of them were built."

"I have a wooden boat, too, but it's nothing like this one. How old is she?"

"She's about sixty. We've had her for five years. She's a very comfortable cruiser."

"I bet. Do you sail around the lake much?"

"We generally get a good three or four weeks in. We're both teachers, so we get a long summer break. We're headed for Main Duck Island tomorrow. Then it's back home to Little Sodus Bay."

"Where's Main Duck?"

"It's a half day's sail south of here. It's the most remote island on the lake and it's beautiful-- wild and windswept and empty. No one except boaters goes there. Fortunately, it's a public Canadian park so developers can't build houses on it. There aren't many spots left like it on Lake Ontario. We go there every year."

"Sounds interesting," said Skipper Sue.

"Oh, it's that all right. But it's dangerous too, lots of rocks and ledges around it. It's bad holding for anchoring. You don't want to be there anchored outside in a north wind or you'll drag right onto the rocks. And it's tricky getting inside the boat harbor, too. A couple summers ago a big motor boat hit a rock going in there and sank. They say there's buried treasure on the island. And old graves too. And snakes? I've seen six footers there! You watch where you walk. But it's a special place. We stopped there in September once when all the goldenrod was in bloom. The island was covered with a carpet of yellow. There were thousands and thousands of monarch butterflies resting and filling up with nectar from the flowers while they waited for a north wind to help them fly across the lake. They were all headed to Mexico for the winter. The island was thick with them, " said Mr. Bates.

Twink, listening in on the talk from the foredeck where she was sitting with Chauncey, was delighted to see Skipper Sue looking even more interested. It's working, she thought. Chauncey looked smug and purred.

"I'm not crazy about snakes, but the place does sound kind of cool."

Mr. Bates said, "Why not sail with us? We could show you how to get into the harbor. You have to be real careful, but it's worth it to visit the place. And it's supposed to be good weather and westerly winds tomorrow, perfect for getting there."

"Why not?" said Skipper Sue. "I guess there isn't a lot of reason to stay here any longer. And I should be starting to head home, too," said Skipper Sue.

"Excellent, then. We'll leave bright and early. Is 7 am OK?"

Skipper Sue nodded.

Mr. Bates settled back leaning against his boat's cabin side and went on "Main Duck is like no other island on the lake. It's Canadian, but fifty years ago it was owned by one of the most powerful people in the world, an American lawyer and diplomat named John Foster Dulles who became Secretary of State under President Eisenhower. In the 1980s the Queen of England visited there when cruising Lake Ontario with her yacht. There are dozens of wrecks around it, and no one really knows who was buried on Graveyard Point or how they all died. Some say they were French."

Mrs. Bates passed the coffee pot around for refills.

Skipper Sue sipped her coffee and asked, "Do you think there could really be treasure on the island?"

Mr. Bates said, "There might be. Nobody knows for sure. There's a story that during the French and Indian War about 250 years ago the crew of a small French warship drove their vessel ashore on Main Duck after it struck Charity Shoal. It was late November, or so the story goes, and the ship was sinking fast beneath the crew's feet, when through flurries of snow they sighted the low dark island a few miles away. Working the pumps and passing buckets up hand to hand from below, the crew tried to slow the rise of the water in their ship's hold as they steered for land.

The Captain ordered some of the men to chop away the rails of the ship with axes and cut the lashings on the guns to push them overboard to lighten her. They set every sail they had to drive the sinking ship towards the island. They ran her ashore and she hit the rocks hard. Then a wave picked her up, flung her one last time and she came down with a crash. The ship rolled over and broke her back, and the yards and spars and heavy blocks fell from overhead and more men died. Icy waves beat at the hulk and washed more men overboard and they, too, drowned in the freezing water. Some, mercifully, were drawn under quickly by their heavy clothing.

About a dozen soaked soldiers and sailors crawled or staggered ashore on numbed feet as the snow whipped around them. As night fell, they huddled in a grove of trees with no food or fire. More men died that bitter night. The survivors gathered what they could from the wreckage on the shore the next day. They buried their dead on the little point on the island's east end, and some say, they also buried a pay chest of gold and silver coins that they had been carrying to the soldiers stationed at Fort Niagara. They hid it so their British enemies wouldn't find it.

With little food and shelter, they continued to die one by one. At last a single man was left. He had scraped out shallow graves and buried the last of his companions. Many years later his skeleton was found on the south side of the island far from the graves. He had died of hunger and cold alone on the winter island, watching the distant horizon for a rescuing sail."

After a pause Skipper Sue asked, "And no one ever found the treasure?"

Mr. Bates shook his head. "Not so much as a coin. A few buttons, a couple of rusted swords and bayonets, and some other things have been found. The fishermen have pulled ancient military weapons up from the lake bottom in their nets and once they brought up a brass cannon. But no treasure. Lots of people don't think there ever was one," he added.

After another cup of coffee and more talk, the two yacht skippers agreed to depart at 7 am sharp. Skipper Sue then thanked the Bates and headed back to the *Ariel* carrying a contented Twinkle Toes in her arms.

As she walked along she said to Twink, "If I found some of that gold, I could retire, and we could sail all summer and I'd write books about it all winter."

Oh great, not more sailing, thought Twink and she gave Skipper Sue's stomach a small dig of disapproval with her hind claws. Then she wondered if there really was treasure on Main Duck and where you would search for it.

The Canadian flag atop the military college's main hall rippled in the warm summer wind as *Ariel* followed the *Sara B* out of Lake Ontario's oldest harbor the next morning. After Skipper Sue had gotten *Ariel's* main and jib up and the engine shut down, she let the cats out telling them, "If it gets rough, you guys have to go below."

By now the crew knew the routine. They stayed by Skipper Sue in the safety of *Ariel's* cockpit whenever they were underway on the open lake. All three sat on the seats and watched their companion boat slipping along under full sail. They could clearly see Chauncey perched on the cabin top beside the main mast. Harry flashed by a streak of white and gray against the blue water. He skimmed across the *Sara B's* bow and swooped up over her masts.

"She's as graceful as a gull," he cried out in admiration of the schooner.

Ariel's cat crew watched the easy glide of the schooner's low lean hull. She moves like a fish, making scarcely a ripple, thought Twink.

"Chauncey's boat is beautiful. Look how she handles those waves. She makes it look easy," said Dusty.

"I've never seen a sailboat like that," said Twink. "She seems almost alive, the way she goes through the water."

Twink thought of Chauncey's comments the night before as she had sat on the foredeck with him while Skipper Sue ate cookies. He had said sadly then, that there seemed to be little room in the world today for old fashioned but beautiful boats.

"All people care about now is how fast it goes or how big the bathroom is and how many beds it has. *Sara B* was built like a work boat--her job was to look after herself so the crew could catch fish and then she got them home safely. She isn't fancy but she's sea kindly. Owning a pretty boat isn't as important as it once was. Even boat names aren't pretty like they used to be. Now owners call them *Snapper,* or *LunaSea* or *Aloanatlast.* They used to name yachts after mythical beings and magical creatures like *Atalanta, Lotus,* or *Titania."*

To which Twink had added, "Or *Ariel,* the wind spirit in Shakespeare's story."

Twink looked up at their own mainsail now filled with power and curved white against the blue sky. She listened to the music of *Ariel's* bow wave. It reminded her of the cheerful gurgle and swish of the little creek behind her garden back home. She looked over at her mother and said, "Grand sailing today." Dusty, settled on Skipper Sue's lap, agreed.

"We're moving right along, ought to be there by lunch time."

The smooth rise and swing of their own boat as *Ariel* romped over the waves lifted Twink's spirits. Even Piggy's stomach stayed settled today. But as they watched Chauncey's boat moving along with steady sure-footed ease through the chop, Piggy, seated by Twink on the cockpit sea,t said, "I don't like it. Two times now we've been out with good weather. That Witch is still around. She's saving something up for us. I know she is."

Kingston's skyline fell away astern, and before long the *Sara B* sailed off effortlessly leaving little *Ariel* far behind. They watched the schooner's sails dwindle into a distant bit of white and then they were alone on the wide lake again. Just steer south once you're clear of Snake Island and keep well off The Brothers, Mr. Bates had told Skipper Sue. Today she paid close attention to her chart and compass, and shortly before lunch time the thin dark line of Main Duck island appeared over *Ariel's* bow right where it was supposed to appear.

It came up rapidly over the horizon for fat little *Ariel* was romping along, shoving the water aside with great enthusiasm thanks to the brisk west wind in her sails. To the cats it seemed almost magical to see the island expand and fill out before them, details growing sharper and larger and more distinct before their gaze. At first, Main Duck was just a few tiny tree tops like a string of dark dots, soon it became a low solid line, then the white tower of the light house appeared on its west end. After that, the pale gray stone beach at the water's edge on the island's north side showed and they knew they were almost there. When *Ariel* slipped close under its lea into the calm water behind the island, the cats smelled the sweet fragrance of summer meadows, wild strawberries, and resinous cedar. But where was Chauncey's boat? None of the tree lined coves along the curved crescent of the island's north shore showed a black schooner at anchor.

Skipper Sue was wondering also as she dropped sail. Then Twink saw two varnished masts tipped with white showing over the low trees. "There's *Sara B*-- she's inside the island," Twink meowed at Skipper Sue. At that moment *Ariel's* radio came to life. Mr. Bates was calling them.

With *Sara B*'s crew giving directions, Skipper Sue cautiously steered through a very narrow channel hardly wider than *Ariel* into the boat harbor. Twink had never seen such clear water. Every joint and crack in the flat gray ledges showed beneath them in the watery light. It seemed as if *Ariel's* keel was surely about to hit the rocks, yet her depth sounder showed ten feet of water under the boat. It's like we're floating in air, thought Twink. You can't see the water at all.

An abandoned cottage, its windows covered with gray squares of plywood stared blindly at them as the *Ariel* slowly tiptoed into the harbor. She passed some stone ruins close enough almost to touch and went by a miniature island barely big enough for one willow tree to grow on to starboard, and then the dock appeared. Skipper Sue sighed with relief after they were safely inside. The dock was saggy and crooked but solid enough for little *Ariel*. (Chauncey's boat had anchored out so there was plenty of room.) Dusty and Piggy jumped up on the seat beside her to watch as Skipper Sue steered over to the dock, got off and tied the boat up. After she shut the engine down, She climbed back onto the dock and scanned the harbor before her.

"I wonder if there really is treasure here. That would be something wouldn't it guys? All I'd need is a little handful of gold coins and I could retire," Skipper Sue said to the cats.

The three cats joined her on the dock and looked around. It was very quiet except for the soft rustle of the wind in the tall grass on shore and the murmur of small surf on the island's south shore.

"Awesome," said Piggy.

"Very cool," agreed Twink.

And Dusty simply sighed with pleasure. Before them lay an island with buried treasure and no other humans on it. What could be better?

10. Twink Picks Up A Pilot In Main Duck

Skipper Sue finished tying *Ariel* up and was still gazing out at the peaceful sheltered harbor with its fringe of tall cattails rippling in the wind when Mr. Bates rowed up to the dock with his dinghy.

"Come on out and have dinner with us," he invited. We've got plenty of food. We're having steak and potatoes and fresh corn on the cob from the farmer's market."

"Sounds a lot better than Tuna Helper," said Skipper Sue. She quickly set food out for the cats down below and left the cabin door open telling them, "Don't go too far." Then she went off with Mr. Bates in his dinghy to the *Sara B.*

Twink ate a couple of bites and then hurried up on deck. Here she sat and surveyed her surroundings. She listened to the surf's murmur from the south shore of the island and the cheerful bubbling song of several black and white bobolinks flying over the tall grass east of the harbor. The open flat land around her was so low she could see across the entire island to a line of trees marking its far edge. She watched a muskrat swim across the harbor and saw a large gray fish glide past in the clear water beside the dock.

Dusty and Piggy came padding up into the cockpit having cleaned up their food dishes. They sat down for an after dinner wash up.

"I wonder where this Sid person is?" said Twink.

"How will we know her when we find her?"asked Dusty.

"Harry said she was the dockmaster. She must be around here somewhere."

She jumped off *Ariel* and landed lightly on the dock. Dusty followed with Piggy bringing up the rear and looking around constantly.

Piggy said, "Didn't Harry say something about her looks- like maybe she was kind of scary?"

Twink tiptoed slowly down the dock, her whiskers and ears on alert for any sign of the dock master. For all her bold talk, she, too, was uneasy. She crept out onto the area of short grass at the end of the dock and looked around. No sign of Sid.

"Uh oh, what's that," Piggy growled behind her. Twink barely heard the rustle by the water. Then she saw a darkness in the grass next to Piggy. Piggy's tail bushed up and she retreated back up onto the dock. Then the biggest blackest snake Twink had ever seen flowed out of the grass, stopped a foot or so away and lifted its head.

"Good afternoon. I'm SSSid. Welcome to Main Duck Island. Were you looking for me?"

Twinkle Toes felt like following Piggy back up onto the dock. She'd seen snakes before but nothing like this. Sid was as big around as Skipper Sue's arm. Her scaled body shone against the grass like black marble and her eyes gleamed with quiet intelligence. She flicked a bright red tongue quickly towards them. Was she deciding to strike? She looked quite capable of eating a cat. But Twink stood her ground. They had to find Pearl. How else was the stupid book going to get written?

"Um, a friend told us you'd be here. He said you could help us out."

"Well, I will certainly assist you if I can."

Twink kept staring at Sid whose long body gleamed like polished ebony. There was something hypnotic about the animal sitting so still before her. Sid was beautiful yet strange. Twink wanted to say something but the words seemed to back up and clog her throat. Her mind went blank as she looked at Sid. All she could think of was how queer this legless creature was. No wonder people didn't like snakes. They were different. And downright odd.

The snake smiled, "Cat got your tongue?"

Dusty, sitting a bit further away, said, "We're trying to find out about the changes in the lake. Harry the gull said you could help."

Sid's smile vanished. She hissed out a sigh and her head sagged. Then she drew herself up into a coil and settled into a comfortable position resting her chin on part of her body so her head was at a level with Twink's own.

I wonder how she does that, thought Twink. She's so limber. She's even more flexible than a cat. Twink felt a bit braver.

"We need some answers about the birds and eels and what's killing them."

"Oh yesss, the dying. Richard and I have talked about this often. There were people here just a few days ago-ssscientists. They came ashore from their boat and picked up some of the dead fish and carried them off."

"Why?" asked Twink.

"They're ssstudying them. Or ssso Richard sssays. Perhaps you should talk to Richard. He's very intelligent." Sid looked a bit brighter. "He's a wonderful sssinger, too."

"Could you introduce us?"

"That's easy. Follow me."

Sid slithered down to the water's edge and traveled a few yards along the water. The three cats followed at a respectful distance. She stopped beside a clump of pickerel weed where a half submerged log lay along the shore.

"Richard. There are sssome folks here to sssee you."

Two golden eyes emerged from the shallows beside the log, followed by a wide green head. Then a large and very plump bullfrog raised his broad shoulders clear of the water.

He boomed forth a greeting. "Hello there. You're looking for me?"

"These visitors want to know about the dying."

Richard pulled himself up on shore so he was mostly out of the water. He roared "It's a disaster. A tragedy. A catastrophe. It makes me hopping mad! And it was completely avoidable. The way humans have acted on the lake has been criminal. I tell you we need a frog to run for president and for prime minster, too. If we had some amphibians in office maybe we'd get more balanced policies. See, we live both on land and in water so we understand both sides. There's just 'way too much emphasis on short term terrestrial profits today with nobody paying any attention to the little guys afloat or ashore. Take roads-a few towns put toad tunnels in where a road cuts between swamps and forests. But most of us just have to take our chances on getting across. Do you have any idea how many toads (and frogs!) get flattened by cars on a rainy night? Millions and millions! And all these bulldozers filling in our spring ponds and puddles and ripping out all the shrubs and trees-why does everybody want a huge parking lot or a shopping mall or stupid five acre short grass lawn and a paved drive around their house!And then then there's bug sprays and poisons and weed killers."

"He sure does talk a lot," whispered Dusty.

Twink waited until Richard took a breath and then jumped in, "But what about the dead fish and birds?"

"It's the Seaway. It's all stupid Eisenhower's fault. And GATT and NAFTA and McNamara and the Trilateral Commission and-"

"Hold it a second!" said Twink. "Please. I don't understand."

Richard took a deep breath and puffed himself up and then let it out slowly. He continued in a quieter tone

"Ok. Here's the deal. The Seaway connects the Great Lakes to the Atlantic and to all the rest of the big wide world. Ships take saw logs, grain, and stuff out of here and bring fertilizer, ore, salt, and aluminum and other stuff in. Ships have tanks in their bottoms that they fill up with water when they're empty. Without ballast they would roll right over in a storm. When they come here from somewhere else empty and pick up cargo, they dump the ballast water. If they started out from another freshwater place like the Baltic or the Caspian Sea (which aren't really very salty seas) they carry all kinds of critters in the ballast tanks. When the ships dump it to take on cargo, the critters get dumped, too. And some of those guys are really pushy. Now we got all these strangers in our lake like *Bythotrephes,* and *Dreissenia* and *Eurytemora* and *Cercopagis* and.."

Seeing that Twink was getting a glazed look, Richard stopped and then began anew.

"The really big one was the zebra mussel. Those guys stirred up huge trouble in the lakes."

"What's a zebra mussel?" asked Twink

"It's a little shellfish, a clam kind of thing, that filters tiny and I mean really really tiny plants and animals out of the water. They got in here about twenty years ago. They showed up first near Detroit. Now they're everywhere! They found 'em way out west in Lake Mead last year.

They ate everything up so all the open water folks don't have enough food. They have totally screwed things up. And now we got another problem, Chinese carp."

Sid saw that the cats looked more confused than ever. She spoke up, "Richard, maybe they should walk down to the beach and sssee for themselves how things are."

Richard by now had worked himself completely out of the water and onto the beach. He seemed to be just getting into his stride. He blinked and then fixed his gaze on a plump brown beetle walking along the shore. He snapped it up and then said "Good idea. Come on back later, and I'll tell you more."

With that he turned around and with a powerful leap bounded back into the harbor, landing with a loud plop and disappearing.

Sid glided along the well trod foot path a short distance towards the beach with the cats. As they went, she said "Perhaps this evening after sssupper you could come back. The moon is nearly full tonight. It would be a lovely night for a concert. Richard might sssing one of his ssongs for us. He has a wonderful voice. Now the beach is straight down that way-it's about a two minute ssslither."

Sid slipped off into the grass, and the cats headed for the beach.

Piggy spoke up, "Isn't it kind of weird to see a snake and a frog hanging out together?

Dusty said, "I think Richard and Sid might be an item, or at least Sid thinks they are. That's probably why she doesn't eat him."

The south shore of Main Duck lay only a few hundred feet away, so the cats were soon pushing through the bushes and shrubs at the top of the beach. They emerged into the late afternoon sun and paused to look at the lake before them. White crested rollers of green water surged across the wide ledges of rock. Dozens of huge rounded boulders lay scattered among the surf. Their dark wet forms looked like stranded sea monsters to Twink. The roar of the waves pounding the shore made her uneasy as she picked her way carefully out onto the pebble beach. Much of the shore was covered with a thick layer of white shells that crunched underfoot. Before her feet lay a small dried dead fish.

Twink said, "These must be the goby fish Harry talked about."

"Look, here's another one," said Dusty.

"Don't touch it! Remember what Harry said," hissed Piggy.

The three cats stalked slowly over the rocks passing hundreds of sun blackened withered corpses scattered around like bits of trash, their eye sockets empty, white bones poking through their torn skin.

Then Piggy further down the beach said, "Uh oh."

Twink turned to see a large mushy smelly fish lying near the water. A mass of pale maggots wiggled and twitched in its gill cavities and eye sockets as the larvae reclaimed its body, speedily devouring it. Soon the decaying fish would be transformed into new air-borne insect life. A few feet away a large partially eaten bird with black feathers lay grotesquely sprawled, flies buzzing loudly around it.

"What is *this*?"exclaimed Piggy. She pawed at a cluster of flies on the ground beside the bird. The flies hopped around and buzzed in circles. "These are freaky. Look, they've all only got one wing."

"I don't like this at all," said Twink, her fur lifting slightly along her back.

"The bitter water. It's here, too." said Dusty in a low growl.

A big hairy fly buzzed around Twink's head. She swatted at it. "I've seen enough. Let's get out of here."

The three cats retreated back to the footpath and headed for *Ariel*. Each was silent with her own thoughts until Piggy stopped before a large bush lush with smooth green leaves.

"That's strange,"she said.

"What is?" asked Twink.

"This is a lilac bush. People plant these by their houses for the pretty flowers. I wonder how it got here?"

"Maybe the seeds floated here on the wind?"

"Lilac seeds don't float on air," said Piggy. "Besides there's another bush there, and one there. They look like they were laid out along the path, like people planted them in a row."

Dusty had gone over to sniff around in the brush and grass beside the bush. She called, "Here's some stones, and a piece of rusty steel."

Piggy joined her. "There were houses here once. See? That's a peony bush over there, just like Skipper Sue's. And this is a foundation. People used to live here."

"I wonder what happened to them. Why did they leave?" said Dusty.

"Maybe they died. Let's go back to the *Ariel*" said Twink.

Back aboard the boat the mood was somber. Twink decided a good bath was in order. She felt the lingering stink of the beach still upon her. As she set to work washing, she wondered about the dead fish and what Richard had said and about the old house ruins. The frog had talked about pushy strangers changing the lake with their new ways. But that didn't explain the deformed flies or why all the goby fish were dying. How were the strangers killing everyone? How could a fish kill a bird? And what had become of the human islanders? Had they, too, gotten sick and died a long time ago? As she finished up her bath paying special attention to her white front and feet, she thought we should go back and listen to Richard some more. He's a wind bag, but maybe he's got some answers.

Skipper Sue was still aboard the *Sara B* visiting with the Bates. She had left the cabin door open for the crew to come and go as they wished, so Twink headed up on deck again. Twilight was Twink's favorite time for prowling about. Soon Dusty and Piggy joined her in

107

looking out over the calm harbor. The nearly full pale gold moon gleamed against earth's soft gray night shadow low in the east over the water. In the gathering darkness overhead, the first stars were emerging. Twink loved this time of shadows and dim light, a time when often the wind grew still and smells arose into the night air. It was the changing of the watch. The sun's favored creatures headed for their beds, while those who were most active at night came awake.

"Let's go back and talk with Richard," said Twink.

Dusty looked around the quiet harbor." I wonder who else hunts at dusk around here. I suppose it's safe enough to go just that far."

Piggy looked doubtful, but when Twink hopped onto the dock followed by Dusty, she decided to tag along. Single file the three cats moved silently along the harbor's edge heading for Richard's log. Around them insects chirped and whirred in the grass and an occasional frog called out from the shallows.

They found Sid and Richard both relaxing on their waterfront patio-log beside the clump of pickerel weed. After an exchange of greetings, Twink said "Richard, I didn't quite understand a couple of things when you were talking about the Seaway--"

"Take cover!" Sid hissed. In a flicker of movement she dropped off the log and disappeared into the grass saying, "This way-under that bush. Quick!"

The cats leaped after Sid. Behind them they heard a loud plop as Richard dove into the shallows behind the log. All three cats crowded under the dense tangle of the bush with Sid and crouched together looking sideways towards the cause of Sid's alarm. A huge long legged gray bird dropped out of the sky with wide spread wings and landed in the water a few feet from the log. It folded its wings and stood motionless staring into the shallows. It was a good four feet tall and had a long neck and a sharp spear-like beak at least six inches in length.

Sid whispered, "I've seen him kill a full sized snake. He aims for the head."

The great blue heron scanned the shallows. He was only a yard or so from where they had last seen Richard. One stab of that deadly dagger and there would be no more songs or stories from Richard. Ever again. As soundless as any cat, the heron lifted one leg clear of the water and slowly advanced a single step. He lowered his head to within a foot of the water. Clearly he saw something down there. Was it Richard?

"He stabbed a frog here last week and swallowed him whole. He's deadly," whispered Sid.

Like the heron, the cats had excellent night vision, and the moonlit scene before them was perfectly clear to their eyes. Twink saw a ripple on the still water's surface. Someone was swimming directly towards the motionless heron. Someone who was about to die.

The bird drew his head back, much as Sid would do. Then he struck. It was too fast for even a cat's eye to follow. The heron withdrew and struck again and again, stabbing the prey at his feet with repeated powerful lightning quick blows. They saw him raise his head holding a half grown muskrat in his beak. Bleeding and mortally wounded, it twitched weakly. Then the heron swallowed it. Twink watched the bulge of the muskrat slide down the bird's long neck. The heron shifted from one foot to the other and ruffled its feathers as if settling its meal. Then with a loud "grawk" it spread its wings and lifted off into the night.

Sid slid out into the open saying, "He doesn't usually hunt here this early. We'll be safe now, though. This is his spot, and no other heron would ever dare fish here."

Richard clambered back up onto the log. "He got my cousin Klem last week." Richard shrugged. "Guess it wasn't my time. Yet." Richard settled himself and said, "Sid tells me you wanted to hear one of my songs. I think I'll sing you a bluesy little tune I've been working on. I'd like to record this someday. Maybe I'll put it on You Tube."

The three cats sat down in a line in the grass at the water's edge. Sid drew herself up into a comfortable coil and gazed at Richard with a look of pure rapture as he began to sing. Deep powerful and resonant, his voice rose into the night. Frogs in the little wetlands all over the island and even as far as the lighthouse a half mile away heard Richard. Undaunted by his near brush with death, he sang with assurance and with growing passion. Out in the harbor aboard the *Sara B* Skipper Sue said to the Bates, "Listen to that bull frog. Now that's some voice!"

The song began with a praise of sweet warm summer winds that swept over Main Duck's green grassy meadows and marshes, beloved island home of Richard and Sid and numerous other good folk, a land that lay all alone in all the lake. Richard sang of the life that filled the meadows, the people of fur, of feathers, and of the insect nations. As his voice boomed forth across the harbor, countless midges rose up out of the grass and gathered in a half dozen large swarms over the willows beside the dock and began their own life dances, whirling and spinning in dense clouds that looked like puffs of smoke stationed above each tree in the moonlight.

Richard sang of far traveling birds like the bobolinks whose liquid lilting shouts of joy had rung out over the plains of Paraguay three months before their return to the island. He sang of the tiny sanderling and graceful curlew who had stopped over at the island to rest before they journeyed north to the unspeakably vast lands of the tundra. And he sang sadly of those who no longer came to Main Duck. The hundreds of mighty brown sturgeon who had once lazed over the sunlit shallows of the island's ledges, and of strong silver trout and sleek salmon who had flashed through the green depths off the island's northern shore now going, nearly gone, all gone.

The countless eel nation, once so abundant that every ledge and rock was home to an eel, now they, too, dwindle. And what of the ducks, whose flocks darkened the sky and gave the island its name? Their joyous clamor as they returned to their island, gliding down with wings set so smooth and sure, to land in its lee on a fall afternoon. He sang of geese and of native swans from the far north whose mighty wings had once flashed white against the sky. He mourned their passing, their dying, so much dying here in the lake. Then he concluded;

"Let others celebrate the cities of man, let them sing of traffic on roads,

I will remember the humble while I can, the dancing golden mayflies, the sweet trilling toads.

Beneath the clear water the turtle so sure,

she waits and watches and tries to endure.

You, out there listen up, pay heed. I'm telling you true and I'm nearly done.

The poisons you use into our water now run.

Strangers among us push us aside.

And now many, too many, of us have died.

You can take our water, oh, you can drink the lake dry,

but we're all connected, man and snake, and dragonfly.

And Man, you won't live long, after we're all gone."

After Richard's last notes had boomed forth and faded in the silence that followed, the cats heard another voice raised in a distant response. It cried out, a long sorrowful howl, heart breaking in its minor key, rising in pitch, pure and clear, then breaking off and dying away. An unshed tear gleamed in Sid's eye as she whispered, "That's Loon. His wife failed to return with him this sssspring. He is alone now."

The cats sat still and silent, staring at the moon-washed harbor where a few glints of silver danced on the water. Loon's cry had pierced Twink's soul. She would never forget this place and time.

Piggy's eyes were round and black. Dusty sat as still as a little gray stone cat. All were frozen by the haunting coda to Richard's lament.

Finally Dusty got up. "I suppose we should be heading back to the boat."

She and Piggy slipped off into the grass, small soft-footed shadows in the night.

But Twink lingered. She said to Sid and Richard, "I don't know. This whole business is enough to make anyone howl. It's just so sad and so wrong. But what can any of us do?"

Sid lifted her head up and looked Twink in the eye."Don't give up on us, Twink. Others must hear."

As Twink looked back at her and saw her quiet strength, her own courage grew stronger and stiffened her resolve. Yes, she thought. She

112

had to put this in Skipper Sue's book. This story needed to be told. The life of the lake deserves no less. Yet much remained unclear.

"But how can I possibly do it? There's so much I don't understand."

"Go sssee Pearl. Go listen. I'll show you the way."

Twink nodded. "Ok. We'll do it."

"It's a long walk out to the far end of the island. We should leave early."

"We'll go as soon as we can get off the boat tomorrow," said Twink.

11. Twink Presses On

Twinkle Toes awoke in darkness. No moonlight streamed in through the *Ariel's* port holes now, and she heard the boat's halyards slapping and banging loudly against the wooden mast overhead. The wind had come up. That's what had broken her sleep. Twink felt the boat shifting and fidgeting around the dock lines creaking as the wind keened and strummed in her rigging. She also heard the lake. Big waves were breaking against the island's outer shore. They boomed and crashed in the night making a thunderous roar. Mixed in with the bellowing of the waves, Twink thought she could hear faint high pitched cries and distant shouts, almost as if shipwrecked sailors were calling for help. After a long time, she fell asleep again, though hers was an uneasy restless and dream filled sleep.

The next morning was calm again. Dawn brightened the clear eastern sky and the roaring surf of the night had quieted to a barely heard grumble. But the feeling of unease persisted. After Skipper Sue had served breakfast, Twink went up on deck. She saw Mr. Bates rowing towards them in his yacht's dinghy. This time he had Chauncey along. Bates hailed Skipper Sue cheerfully as he came alongside the dock.

"I thought I'd give old Chauncey a little run ashore before we go. We're heading back to Oswego this afternoon."

Chauncey hopped up onto the dock and seeing Twink called out, "Ahoy."

"Hey Chauncey, I see you got shore leave." Twink greeted him with a purr.

"So did you find the treasure?" he asked.

"No, only dead fish and ruins. I wonder what happened to the humans that lived here?

114

"I've heard about that vanished village from my skipper. He said that used to be where the fishermen lived. Thirty or forty families lived here. They caught perch and whitefish and lake herring--thousands of pounds of them. They lived here all summer, had parties and bonfires and cookouts on the beach, and dances and dinners together. They built a school for their children and a few families even stayed through the winter. But most went back to the mainland when the weather turned cold. They could catch enough fish back then to live all winter on their earnings."

"Why did they leave?"

"The fish all disappeared. So they moved away, since there was nothing for people to do here without any more fish in the lake. Maybe they went to work for the government or helped make movies in Toronto. I don't know where people are getting fish from these days. Maybe from fish farms?" Chauncey sighed and looked out over the harbor. "This water is full of chemicals anyway so a lot of the fish are polluted. We're not supposed to eat the big ones from Lake Ontario more than once a month."

"Did the fish die from the chemicals?" asked Twink.

"I don't think so. Mostly I guess the people just caught them until they were all gone." Chauncey looked over towards his yacht sitting on her reflection at anchor in the harbor. "It was so much simpler back when *Sara B* was built. In those times people used rowboats and sailboats like her to catch fish. It took a lot longer to fill up a boat. They used long trot lines with hooks and small gill nets that they could haul up by hand so they mostly caught just the kind of fish they wanted. Once they started using motors it all changed. Boats got bigger and faster, and they could tow big trawl nets that they raised with power winches. They dragged the trawls along the bottom and swept up everything. What the people didn't want, they threw back, but nearly all the fish and other animals they threw back died. Sometimes the trawls tore up the bottom and that made it harder for the animals that were still down there to find decent places to live, too."

"Well, that was pretty dumb," said Twink.

Chauncey sighed again. "Sometimes I think humans just want too much too fast. You never see a human sitting in front of a mouse hole for an hour. They're so impatient. And they figure why leave any fish for tomorrow or the next day? Another fishing boat will come along and catch them first so I'd better grab them all now."

"But when all the fish are gone, nobody can catch any."

Chauncey nodded, "I know. But nobody thinks ahead. They just want it all right now for themselves. And I wonder, compared to back then, are they really any happier now? Those fishermen from Main Duck worked hard in the summer, but then a lot of them could take the whole winter off to be with their families and relax. People have more stuff and more money but less time now."

The two cats heard footsteps approaching. They moved aside as Skipper Sue and Mr. Bates walked by talking as they went.

"I'm going to stay one more day. I want to look around some more. It would be really cool to find that treasure," said Skipper Sue.

Bates laughed, "Good luck. Keep an eye on the weather. There's a storm out west that might move in so we're leaving for Oswego right after lunch."

"I got my radio. I'll listen to the forecast."

Mr. Bates spoke to Chauncey "Come on old fellow. Let's get a little walk in."

Chauncey said to Twink, "Guess I got to go. Maybe we'll see you again back on the south shore."

"I hope so. See you later, Chauncey and take care."

Skipper Sue tidied up the boat, checked the dock lines, pumped out the bilge water, and then climbed onto the dock with her camera. "I"m going ashore. You guys, don't go too far."

The three cats watched her stride down the path. Then as her figure dwindled in the distance, Sid flowed out from under the dock. "Are you ready to go sssee Pearl? It's a long walk so we should get ssstarted."

Piggy looked like she was thinking up excuses to bail. Twink gave her a hard look and said. "We're ready."

"Follow me then. We're going to the light house."

Finally, thought Twink. Maybe we'll get some answers from this Pearl person. The dead fish and birds on the beach, the disappearing eels, and the deformed flies and Harry's chicks, Twink has a sneaky suspicion these were all somehow connected. Would Pearl have an explanation?

The three cats walked in single file behind Sid as she headed for the beach, the easiest and safest route she explained. Main Duck had recently acquired a fox. But he would have little chance to sneak up on them if they stayed on the shore where the upper edge of the beach was lined with big trees. You'll never be more than a few yards from a tree to climb she assured them.

"What about you?" asked Dusty.

"I can ssswim. I'll ssseek shelter under a rock in the water or dive down deep," Sid replied.

Sunlight poured down upon the beach where a broad swath of dazzling white shells at the water's edge contrasted sharply with the jade colored shallows. Last night's waves had died away to a gentle surf and the morning heat lay like a heavy blanket along with the smell of rotting fish as the cats emerged cautiously from the bushes. Dozens of fish carcasses were strewn about on the shore before them. Scattered among the gray pebbles under foot were more small dried dark bodies. The beach was very still except for the buzz of flies and the swish of the wavelets.

"Those dried up little ones are gobies," said Sid. "The big ones are mostly carp, poor things. I used to believe carp were indestructible, but even they are in trouble now. The gobies washed up a couple weeks ago--thousands of them. And all those shells are from zebra mussels. Pearl says they first showed up here about ten years ago."

Twink picked her way over the sharp edged shells underfoot. Sid flowed out onto the beach gleaming like a ribbon of ebony against the bleached shells as she headed for the shallows. She slipped into the warm water. "Ah, this is much nicer. Come on in."

"No thanks," said Twink. What's killing all the fish?"

"You'll have to ask Pearl. This has happened before, but never as bad as this year."

"What about this?" asked Piggy. Twink and Dusty looked over to see Piggy poking cautiously at the body of a large black and white bird. It had been dead for sometime.

"Before the white shells began washing up, Pearl says there were very few dead birds. Perhaps theres a connection between the shells and the dying. The mussels did change the lake. It became a lot clearer, and Richard says we have different plants and more algae in the water now."

They walked for some time. It was hot and smelly' and Twink began to grow bored.

She asked Sid, "Have you ever heard anything about buried treasure on the island?"

"Yes. Pearl sssays that ssstory has been around for a long time. She sssaid a hundred years ago a man found a big boulder with writing carved on it."

"Did he find the gold?"

"He found trouble. Bad trouble. Very sssad."

118

"What happened?"

"Here's how I remember Pearl telling it:"

"Once there was a fisherman who spent his summers on Main Duck. In that time the fisher folk stayed in a settlement of shanties and cabins here during the warm season. They rose at dawn and worked all day, rowing and sailing many miles, pulling their nets, setting and hauling seines from the beach, and laying and bringing up their trot lines from deep water. They pulled shining silver fish from the water and salted and dried them. Then they took their catch ashore to the mainland and exchanged them for silver coins.

"But one fisherman was lazy. He didn't want to row hours a day and haul fish up out of the lake. He didn't want to help the others pull the long heavy seine nets onto the beach. He had seen the Frenchmens' graves and the boulder with the carving on it, and he decided to find the chest of gold. He dug in front of the boulder in the thin soil and soon hit rock. He dug behind it and hit more rock. He dug a circle all around it and found nothing. He was certain the gold lay right beneath his feet. I'll find it tomorrow he thought. While the other boats went off to set their nets, his skiff stayed ashore and he dug and dug in the hard thin dirt. His hands grew blistered, and his back ached more than it ever had when fishing. But he knew the gold was there.

"When the other fishermen asked him to help clean the fish and salt and dry the catch on racks in the sun, he turned his back on them and went off alone with his pick ax and shovel. He peered into cracks and holes under the great slabs of limestone that form our island. He pried and pounded and broke the very rock. At night he dreamed of gold coins glittering in the darkness of a cave. The next day he searched and pried and pounded anew, crawling through the thickets of brush and thorns and tearing at the rocks with his bare hands until he bled upon the earth.

"One day a vision told him seek the gold in the graves. He went to where the shipwrecked men were buried, and he dug up their bones. There was no gold. Grave after grave he ripped open with his shovel and pry bar and pick ax. The dead laughed. Then they cursed him for his greed.

"And so he went mad. He walked to his skiff pulled up on the stone shore. He shoved it off and rowed away. He was never seen again."

Twink said, "That fisherman was about as smart as all those people feeding slot machines with quarters hoping to hit the jackpot."

Sid nodded. "There is treasure here, to be sure, but not gold coins. It's the treasure Richard sssings about--meadows filled with wild flowers, flocks of free flying wild birds, and shining ssschools of sssilver minnows. Digging and ripping and destroying the land for treasure-- it can only end badly," said Sid with a sigh.

The snake swam on through the water, while the cats trudged after her on shore. By now Twink's feet ached. She knew from the occasional stumble and "ouch" as someone stubbed a toe behind her, that Dusty and Piggy were also footsore and tired. The late morning sun poured down on the beach, making the stones uncomfortably hot underfoot. Twink glanced at the shade under the bushes and trees at the top of the beach and wished they could sit down and rest for a few minutes. Piggy with her shaggy thick fur was drooping the most. Twink could hear her panting like a little dog behind her.

A jumble of driftwood piled up around a big log blocked their way. Sid swam effortlessly ahead, leaving Twink to trudge around it. When Twink rounded the pile, she found Sid up on dry land coiled and waiting. "Look," she said.

Twink saw a small aluminum hulled motorboat pulled up on the shore in front of them a few yards away. There were no humans anywhere, but Twink caught a smell suggesting they hadn't been gone long. Dusty, too, sniffed the air as they waited for Piggy. "Smells like beer."

"Smells like trouble," said Piggy.

"Somebody's having a beach party," said Twink.

"I don't like it," said Dusty eyeing some empty styrofoam takeout food trays and trash and a discarded shirt scattered about on the beach by the boat. "I think we should steer clear of this party."

Sid agreed, "Sssometimes people come here from the mainland when the lake is calm. They break into the caretaker's cottage and look for things to sssteal. Ssstay alert."

They moved on past the boat. A few minutes later they climbed over an outcrop of limestone and saw before them a wide shallow pan of barren rock and rubble. The island's shoreline curved inward sharply forming a deep crescent. "If we cut across that we'd save a lot of walking," said Twink."

Sid was reluctant to leave the water. "No cover. Danger."

Dusty agreed, "It's wide open out there. If a hawk or a fox comes along, we're history."

"No fox is out hunting in this heat," argued Twink. "And we haven't seen a hawk anywhere on the island."

Piggy was too tired to argue. She sprawled in the shade of a boulder and panted.

Sid still looked unconvinced. "We can rest in the shade, then go on."

"I hope those people from the boat aren't around," said Dusty.

"It's not even a hundred yards, let's go," said Twink. She struck out boldly headed straight across the dry basin.

They were perhaps two thirds of the way across the basin when they heard the voices. Then a burst of loud laughter followed by the smash of breaking glass and more laughter. The sound of twigs and dry branches crackling underfoot grew closer.

"They're coming this way," hissed Sid. "Take cover".

The cats split up and crouched behind rocks. Sid crammed herself into a hollow under a flat rock that was barely big enough to hide her. The voices and noise approached.

Twink saw them first as they emerged from the brush. Two young men, both shirtless in the summer heat, one rather flabby, the other taller and thinner. The short fat one was carrying a bottle. They began stumbling over the cobbles and rocks occasionally cursing at the bad footing. They were headed for their boat, directly behind the animals. The bottle carrier stopped, put his bottle to his lips and tipped it up to drain it. Then he flung it hard at a distant gull standing by the water and laughed as it broke spattering shards of glass everywhere.

Twink's heart pounded as she flattened herself against the ground. This was trouble. Only a kitten would assume otherwise. These kind of kids set black cats on fire for Halloween.

The teens were perhaps twenty feet off when they paused to rest. "If there's treasure here, I'll eat it. Nothing but snakes," said Fatty. "Did you see that one by the lighthouse? I know it was a moccasin."

"We could go around to the harbor with the boat."

"Nah, I wanna get outa here before the wind picks up You know how it always gets rough here after lunch."

"Ok, ok. Then let's move. I'm sweating like a pig."

They started forward. A rock turned under Fatty's foot and he lurched and stubbed his toe. Several very loud and rude words followed. As he bent down to rub his foot, he caught sight of Sid's tail.

"Snake!" he yelled and pointed.

"Whoa, look at that sucker. He's huge!"

Fatty picked up a fist sized rock and lobbed it at Sid's tail.

His companion strode over to a stout piece of drift wood lying nearby and seized it. He moved to the flat rock and pried it up, exposing Sid.

"Gawd! Kill it!"yelled Fatty. He picked up another stone and threw it. Sid fled, dodging the stone by inches.

"Go around! Cut it off!" shouted Fatty.

The other teen scrambled over the rocks with his stick in both hands. He slammed it down at Sid and missed. She twisted and doubled back and came up against a big boulder about six feet from Twink's rock. Trapped.

Sid's tormentors approached slowly. Fatty picked up a basketball sized rock. "I'll try to hit its head," he told the club holder. Twink watched, choked with helpless horror and fury. What could a ten pound cat do against two nearly grown male humans? But she couldn't stop her tail from lashing. The teens paused to gauge their distance. They'll break her back. They'll smash her to a pulp, thought Twink.

Fatty lifted the small boulder. The movement of Twink's tail caught the eye of his companion. He turned to see if another black snake was sneaking up on them saying, "What's that?"

As his gaze fell upon her, Twink rose to her feet from behind her rock and looked back, her hair on end, eyes blazing and screamed with all her strength, "Now Sid!"

The snake launched herself from the boulder backstop and darted forward. A solid column of muscle, she literally leaped through the air and flew between the club bearer's legs. Thinking he was being attacked, the boy roared in fright, twisted away, stumbled, and crashed down onto the rocks. Fatty flung his stone at Sid. The snake was moving like a black streak of lightning now. The rock missed her by at least a yard. She dove under another large flat rock.

Twink also bolted, racing for the jumble of driftwood just beyond the boat. Dusty and Piggy sprang up and ran for cover, both heading for the line of bushes and trees at the land's edge. Shaken severely by

Twink's wildcat wail and Sid's 'attack', the teens had had enough. Stringbean staggered to his feet and limped to the boat cursing at every step. Fatty followed closely. He chanted as he scrambled over the stones, "Omigod omigod. Did you SEE that?"

By the time Twink reached the driftwood's shelter, the teens were already at their boat shoving and pushing to get it afloat. As they yelled back and forth at each other about what had just happened, Twink was transformed into a black panther and Sid became an eight foot cobra, the monster of Main Duck. Twink collapsed in the shelter of a driftwood tangle. Weak with relief she crouched and watched as the teens shoved their boat into the water and scrambled in. The outboard coughed to life, and the boat accelerated onto plane. Its roar became a distant drone, and the hull dwindled to a dot on the horizon.

Only when the sound of the outboard had completely faded, did Twink crawl out from the tangle of dry wood. Still feeling a little shaky, she hurried across the open rocks stumbling and slipping over the rough footing. When she reached the shade of the bushes at the top of the beach, she stopped and called, "Mom? Piggy?"

Silence. She was alone on the island. Surrounded by a dense tangle of underbrush, she crouched and wondered about that fox. Perhaps he was even now watching her. Her anxiety was intensifying into panic when a rustle sounded. Sid flowed out from behind a log.

"A near thing. You sssaved my life friend Twink."

Twink shook her head, "It was totally an accident. I couldn't keep my tail quiet. When he looked at me I didn't even think. I just screamed at him."

"You are more courageous than you give yourself credit for being," said Sid.

A stir behind a nearby clump of weeds caught their attention. Dry leaves crackled. Then Dusty pushed her way through the weed stalks.

Twink bounded over to her mother and licked her face and head. Dusty nuzzled her back. Both cats purred with joy at finding each other. After a few moments Dusty said, "Now where's Piggy?"

The three animals split up and began to search. Dusty and Twink calling Piggy. Where are you? Piggy-- come out! Their yowls echoed among the trees, but no Piggy answered. Then Twink heard a faint cry that was more of a whimper than a reply.

"This way," said Sid.

Another weak mew sounded, this one from overhead. "There she is," Sid pointed with her head.

Piggy was clinging to a limb near the top of a large oak. "Piggy come down!" shouted Twink.

"No. Too dangerous."

Twink sat down and glared at the dark furry lump overhead. Dusty joined her and started coaxing. Finally Piggy crawled along the branch to the tree and slowly backed down the trunk. But she stayed close to the comfort of her tree. "I want to go back to the boat."

Twink growled, "No way. We're almost there. We're not quitting now. Come on!" She raised a paw to slap Piggy who cowered against the tree and hissed back.

Dusty pushed between them. She kissed Piggy gently on the top of her head."Piggy we have to go on and see Pearl. We need her help for Skipper Sue's book"

"It's too scary," whimpered Piggy.

"We'll stay right by the trees."

Piggy shook her head and pressed back against her tree again.

Twink got up. She looked over at Sid and winked. "Come on Sid. Let's get going."

Sid started off and Twink with head and tail high, followed calling out, "We're leaving, Piggy."

Dusty trotted up alongside. "She won't stay there alone," said Twink.

Dusty glanced back at the thicket behind them. "I don't know. She's awfully stubborn."

They had traveled perhaps fifty feet when they heard something running through the grass and brush. Then Piggy bust out of a clump of shrubbery calling, "Wait. Wait for me."

Twink glanced sideways at her mother and whispered, "Told you so."

A few hundred yards further on they came to an overlook. A miniature harbor opened before them. It appeared to be a man-made basin with its concrete walls and narrow entrance. Behind the shallow harbor stood a massive white tower that soared high into the sky. More dead carp lay along the shore of the shallow basin.

"That's the light house, one of the biggest most powerful lights on all Lake Ontario. It has warned the ships away from Main Duck's rocks for nearly a hundred years. The keeper used to keep a little boat in this basin that he used to go ashore for groceries," Sid told them.

Twink remembered Fisherman's Cove. There the small friendly wooden lighthouse at the entrance had been a welcome sight, a cheerful guide telling *Ariel's* crew here you'll be safe. You can rest. But be careful as you approach this snug harbor.

This great tower was another guardian and beacon. It stood stern and tall against the storms and waves of the lake on the very edge of the island, warning mariners of danger. But what danger was it that lay out there beneath the lake's surface that was now killing so many of the lake's fish and birds?

"Wait here," Sid told the cats. I'll return with Pearl."

12. Twink Braces Up and Hauls Her Wind

Sid swam off into the green weedy shallows of the lighthouse pond. Soon she returned accompanied by a huge snapping turtle. Both animals hauled out on the rocks beside the cats.

"This is Pearl. She can tell you about the bitter water and the dying."

Pearl was obviously ancient. Her skin was wrinkled and gray and a coat of dark green moss grew on the back of her shell. She looked the three cats over with a slow deliberation, and in her eyes the wisdom of her years sparkled brightly. When she spoke her voice was low and strong. Twink felt small and very ignorant before the giant snapper.

"Welcome to Main Duck. I'm afraid our island is not at its best these days. I'm sorry that you had to see its shores so filled with death."

Twink spoke up. "That's why we're here. We want to find out why so many fish and birds in the lake are in trouble."

Pearl said, "You must look back far into the past to understand what is happening today, for humans have changed things so much. The humans who lived here a thousand years ago, the people now called the First Nations or the Native Americans, who knew this whole great land as Turtle Island, made small changes. They were few in number and lived lightly upon the land. But then a new tribe of humans appeared. Their ways were different. There were many more of them, and they made big changes to the land and the lake.

They cut down the forests and dammed the rivers and streams to provide energy for their mills. They built houses and towns and cities and dumped their wastes in the water. As the land changed so did the rivers and the lake. The water grew foul and the streams dried up. The new people caught most of the fish and then raised different fish and put them into the lake. The humans even changed the waterways themselves by digging new channels and canals and by building the great dam across the St. Lawrence River to produce electricity for their factories and homes. That's the 'wall' that has killed so many of the eel nation. Many of the lake's peoples could not survive the changes. When they died, the newcomers moved in.

"How did the new animals get here?" asked Twink.

"The strangers came here through the canals the humans had made, and they came on ships from across the sea. Some of them were placed in the lake by humans on purpose or accidently. The zebra mussels, alewives, gobies, red shrimp, spiny water fleas, mud snails, and others, over a hundred different newcomers have now moved in. There was lots of room for them in the lake with so many of our own people gone."

"But what about the dead fish? Some of the new fish are getting sick. What's happening to them?" asked Twink.

"Unfortunately diseases came with the the newcomers. A sickness

128

that the invaders had lived with for hundreds of generations was new and deadly to our people. Some of the lake's own fishes were already weakened by the foul water from the factories. New combinations of living creatures and man made chemicals are now re-arranging the web of life here in the lakes. So more of us die. That's what you see happening now."

Piggy spoke up, "We go to the vet and get a shot every year so we won't get sick. Is there anything that could stop the diseases in the lake?"

"Some things can be done. The humans are trying to be more careful about the ballast water carried by ships, and they have changed how they move fish and fish eggs around at their hatcheries and bait farms. But mostly it will be time that cures the diseases. This sort of thing has happened in other places and times. Possibly some of our lakes' fishes will eventually be able to live with the diseases. Unfortunately, some will not and they will disappear forever."

Twink got up and paced back and forth along the water's edge, her yellow eyes bright with anger and her tail lashing. "This is wrong. And wicked. There must be something we can do besides just wait for it to get better. We can't just give up!"

Pearl watched and waited until Twink stopped pacing and sat down again. Then Pearl said, "The humans who have changed the lake so much, must themselves change. Humans have always been very good at learning. They learned to farm, they learned to write and count, and they learned to make metals and form tools and weapons. As they learned, they changed the world they lived in. Now they must learn to make something else. They must learn to make a community."

"What's a community?" asked Twink, the independent minded cat.

"A community is a group of beings that work together, like you working as a crew on your boat. The humans are part of a vast

129

community of nature. Unfortunately, they have forgotten this. They have tried to make things to suit themselves without thinking about the rest of us. But they can't live only behind fences and seawalls and inside their homes. They need soil, pure water, and good air. They need plants and animals and the tiny unseen ones humans call bacteria and fungi who cleanse and renew our world."

"Many humans do know they are part of the community of nature. They are working to preserve it and to shift peoples' behavior so others will re-discover the community. Together we can make things change. But humans must first choose to change. They have done it in nations and cities of the past. It can be done again."

Pearl paused and turned to look slowly over the beach and at the wide lake that lay beyond. Then she said, "Know this. Life will continue. Its strength will not be denied. My people were here when the dinosaurs walked. We survived while the greatest of them died off. I cannot tell you if there will be room in the lake of the future for frogs or snakes or eels or for us snappers. But we have endured for 200 million years.

"Perhaps the humans now so busy building their houses upon our shores will fall victim to disease. It seems possible that this will occur again, as it has in the past. I don't know what the lake of the future will hold, but there will be life of some sort within it."

In the silence that followed Pearl's speech, the cats sat mulling over what they had heard, each busy with her own thoughts. Twinks' were mostly dark. Stupid stupid people. How could they be so dumb? She thought. Sid must have noticed Twink's black scowl as she glared down into the calm water of the little pond, for she said to the cat,

"Twink, don't give up on us. Even if a few of us manage to sssurvive, we can come back. We've done it before. We can live with the newcomers. My people and hundreds of others lived on after the great comet struck here ten thousand years ago. We 'll make it, if we just have a little help."

Pearl remarked, "I think our friends have had about as much information as they want for now. That sky out there is warning that it's time for these mariners to be starting back to their boat. I think their captain might be waiting for them."

The three cats followed Pearl's gaze out over the lake and saw a pale white film of high cloud climbing up from the western horizon. A ghostly halo of light like a pale rainbow surrounded the sun, and to Twink the still air felt heavy and the lake now had an oily look to it.

Twink said, "I think you're right Pearl."

Sid bid her friend farewell. "We'll be off then. I'll sssee you sssoon Pearl."

The three cats got up to follow her. Twink brought up the rear and paused to say, "Thank you Pearl. We'll try to do something to help. And we'll get this into Skipper Sue's book."

"Go well and sail safely. Fair winds."

Pearl turned and lumbered slowly back into the water and swam off.

As the cats hiked back along the beach with Sid, Twink asked, "Sid, what can we do to help?"

"If you ssspeak for us in your book that might do sssome good. You could try to get your human to eat differently. Have her feed on more local food grown without chemicals. Ask her to buy and use less new ssstuff and repair more old things. I'll sssend Harry along with a list of things that will help the lake and the land, too, when we get back. It's a list that Richard and I made up a while ago."

"I don't know. It all seems so hopeless," said Twink as she stepped around yet another goby corpse.

Sid paused and looked back at Twink and spoke with a calm certainty. "It isn't. As Pearl sssaid, sssome humans are trying to mend

131

the web of life. People have changed their ways before. They can do it again. There are great and famous ones, ssscientists and musicians and leaders in government. There are thousands of lesser known humans, too, working for us, nuns, teachers, movie ssstars, engineers and business people. Ssso even if you're a sssolitary cat writing your book alone, you are one of many. You must have faith, Twink. You'll only truly fail if you give up."

When the snake and the cats reached the path that led from shore back to the dock, they said their good byes.

"Have a sssafe sssail home."

"We hope to. We'll look for Harry with the list over there," said Twink. "And thanks Sid, for taking us around."

Piggy and Dusty murmured their thanks as well. Sid nodded. She raised her head up out of the grass and smiled down on them and Twink saw the kindness in her eyes. Then she slipped silently off into the grass.

As the cats headed back to the boat, Twink thought that she would have to change her views about snakes. Sid had done everything possible to help them out. She was a very decent sort of serpent, not loud and opinionated and judgmental like Richard. And when she did say something it seemed worth listening to. It was a shame so many folks said such bad things about Sid's tribe.

When Skipper Sue saw the three cats trotting up the footpath towards the dock she called out "There you are! I've been looking all over for you. We have to head out, the radio says there's bad weather on the way. A three day blow is coming in late tonight. We gotta go right now and get over to Oswego or I might not make it to work Monday. Come on!"

13. Twink Seeks Safe Harbor

Ariel chugged out of the harbor and onto the nearly flat lake as the sun touched the horizon. Once clear of the island's outlying shoals, Skipper Sue swung her boat's bow to the south and steadied the *Ariel* on the correct compass course for Oswego. She boosted the engine throttle up to *Ariel's* five mile an hour cruising speed and stared ahead to where two tiny smoke stacks on the horizon marked Oswego's power plant beside its harbor.

"We should make it before the bad weather gets here, we'll be there in six hours if the motor keeps going," she told the cats who all were sitting in the cockpit with her.

The western sky was unusually colorful as the sun slipped under the water. The lake reflected a hundred hues of gold, orange, rose, and red in a rainbow of shifting intensifying color. Twink sitting on the cockpit locker opposite of Skipper Sue, looked back at the low island astern, black against the evening sky. As she watched Main Duck grow smaller and begin to sink beneath the horizon, she thought about the hidden treasure. That's it right there, she thought. Sid had it right. The island itself, soon to be unseen and unknown again to *Ariel's* crew, is the treasure. A hidden quiet place on the lake where nature's folk still live freely without fear (most of the time anyway) is rare and valuable indeed in this crowded noisy world.

Twink hoped with all her heart that Main Duck would remain safe for Sid and Pearl and Richard and the rest of its residents. No houses, no golf courses, no shopping malls, no lawns, no people. Just trees and brambles and sumac and poison ivy. Just grass and wild strawberries and daisies and milkweed, for the butterflies and midges and swallows and snakes. She wished there would be room for the wild ones to live there for many years to come.

The colors in the western sky dimmed and faded, and one by one summer's stars began to appear. Bright Altair, Deneb, and the planet Jupiter, looking like a drop of silver solder against the growing darkness gleamed overhead, while the waning moon floated up from the lake to the east. Skipper Sue checked her course and steered *Ariel* toward a big bright star low over the water in the south. After twenty minutes or so, she picked out another star to steer towards, as the swarm of stars and galaxies overhead slowly wheeled westward. Up by *Ariel's* spreader hung the hazy arch of the Milky Way and over her mast hung a single star gleaming against the dark sky.

"That's Vega. Ocean sailors use it to fix their position with their sextants," Skipper Sue told Twink. A tiny bead of light crawled south among the other fixed stars. "That's a satellite. Maybe it's one of the satellites that sends out positioning signals for GPS plotters. Too bad we don't have a receiver."

The lake was quiet, but it was also very big and dark and empty around them. They were nearly twenty miles from land as they puttered on into the blackness. It felt lonely being the only boat out here, and Twink crawled into Skipper Sue's lap. Skipper Sue put one arm around her kitty and steered with the other. *Skipper Sue is feeling it, too,* thought Twink.

She wondered where the old Wind Witch was. Would she notice little *Ariel* in the dark as they crawled across the wide surface of the lake? To the Wind Witch up there somewhere in the clouds, *Ariel* probably looked like an ant crawling across a polished gym floor.

Ariel's engine chugged away steadily underfoot as the Milky Way rose high overhead followed by the moon, and the night chill settled and grew. Twink became sleepy in the warmth of her captain's lap, while the engine purred away. She dozed off.

"Crap!" Skipper Sue said. Twink, startled awake, looked around. Then she looked up. The stars were disappearing. Already more than half the sky was covered by a cloak of cloud. Skipper Sue reached for the throttle and boosted it up a bit more. Then Twink felt a light breeze stirring her whiskers. It was from dead ahead. She did see us, thought Twink. Maybe that's her witch's cape up there covering the stars.

Twink peered around the boat's cabin. She saw a cluster of tiny distant lights ahead low on the horizon. There's Oswego, she thought. One bright light blinked in a steady pulse-- the main harbor light. Twink remembered the small steel light house at the entrance when they had departed Oswego four days ago. It seemed much longer since they had sailed to Canada. The breeze picked up and whimpered through the *Ariel's* rigging.

"Ten miles to go. Two more hours, if it doesn't blow too hard," said Skipper Sue.

The boat was beginning to bounce around as she pushed ahead, for the Wind Witch was roughing up the water out there in the darkness around them. *Ariel* smacked into a lump of lake and a splatter of spray came aft. Skipper Sue jammed the tiller in place and went below to snatch her rain jacket from the closet. Soon *Ariel* was throwing spray back at them almost constantly as she thumped and pounded and shoved her way south butting against the chop. Skipper Sue fretted.

"This is going to slow us down. And the longer it takes, the bigger the waves are going to get and then we'll go even slower," she told Twink as she gripped the tiller tightly. Out in the darkness the Wind Witch smiled. Now and then a breaking wave top flashed alongside. Twink thought it looked like the gleam of Her teeth. The wind picked up a bit more and a soft low moan sounded overhead in the rigging. "I've got you now," Twink thought she heard the Witch laugh.

It began to rain. Twink was soon soaked. She shivered and thought about going below into the dry cabin. Twink peered around the side of the cabin again. The blinking light was much higher and brighter. They were getting closer to Oswego. Boy, it was cold. And wet. Come on engine. Keep chugging. Twink began to shiver, partly from nervousness. *Ariel* punched into the biggest wave yet and sent a solid sheet of water aft right into Skipper Sue's face. Twink managed to crouch down behind the cabin and missed most of it.

It was really dark now. Like the inside of rat hole. All Twink could see with her keen cat eyes was blackness and a cluster of city lights and now and then some spray up forward from the bow, lit up by the red from *Ariel's* port side running light. "Another half hour and we'll be in the harbor," Skipper Sue said. Twink decided to stay on deck with her Skipper.

Ariel lurched and stumbled as another big wave slammed against her bow. The Witch was starting to get mean, throwing some hard punches at them now. Twink dug her claws in to keep from sliding off the cockpit seat. Had the engine faltered? She listened closely. The steady chuggity click continued, and *Ariel* came upright again and pushed aside another wave. It wasn't a very strong engine, but it was stubborn and steadfast. It wasn't about to quit. We'll do 'er the little boat seemed to be saying as she faced the waves squarely and shouldered them aside. I'm not afraid of witches and wind as long as I've got a good crew on my deck and a steady hand on my helm.

However, Skipper Sue was fidgeting around and scowling into the darkness. She stood up, then sat down. "We gotta be close. Where's the stupid entrance?" She tried to wipe the rain and spray off her glasses and reached into the locker for the folded paper chart. Of course, Skipper Sue, like all humans, was blind as a bat in the dark, so she had to use the flashlight she had stowed earlier by the engine box to see the chart.

Twink shut her eyes when Skipper Sue turned her light on to look at the chart. Twink knew that a sudden bright light makes it impossible for anyone, even a cat, to see anything in the darkness. She didn't want to be blinded. After a few seconds, Skipper Sue snapped the light off and peered into the rain and wind. "There. That's a blinking red and a blinking green. That's gotta be it. That's the channel." She stood up to see over the cabin and steered for the lights saying, "Red right returning." Overhead Twink thought she heard a shrill sharp sound almost like a mean little giggle as a gust of wind whistled past the rigging.

She can't possibly see anything, thought Twink and she sneaked a quick look for herself. About fifty lights appeared to be in front of them. City street lights, distant red tail lights of cars on a road, and yes, at least six blinking lights that must be on the buoys in the harbor. And, Twink saw, Skipper Sue was steering straight towards a ten foot high wall made of huge rocks.

Twink leaped up onto the cabin top and started yelling. "Hey! Look out! We're heading for the rocks!"

Skipper Sue was dim sighted, but she did see Twinkle Toes with her four white feet up on the cabin. And she heard her. She wiped a hand across her rain speckled eyeglasses and then gasped. She slammed the tiller over. *Ariel* swung sharply to the right. A wave rolled her towards the wall of rocks and she leaned over. Twink slid across the rain slick cabin top and dug her claws in with all her strength to hang on. "Oh Great Bast. We're finished now," she thought. The rocks loomed over them a boat length away.

Somehow *Ariel* scrambled over the wave that had tried to shove her into the wall. Then both Twink and Skipper Sue saw the end of the jetty with a fringe of white water foaming around it and a green light flashing on top of it. The entrance. A few seconds later *Ariel* slipped through it, quick as a cat. Inside, in the smooth calm of the harbor, Skipper Sue dropped the tiller and kicked the engine shifter into neutral with her foot. She picked Twink up and clutched her tightly against her chest. Twink felt Skipper Sue's hands shaking. She tried to purr, which is very difficult to do when you're soaking wet and being squeezed half to death.

"We made it. We're ok," she mewed.

"Man that was close. Way too close," said Skipper Sue. She put Twink down, picked up the end of the tiller and pushed the shifter back into gear. Then she steered the *Ariel* up the black rain speckled river to the cement sea wall near the canal entrance where there was a place to tie up. Safe. In harbor at last. Out of danger. The *Ariel* had slipped out of the Wind Witch's grasp again.

*   *   *

Gray clouds scudded low overhead, and big waves pounded against the breakwater the next day. Skipper Sue slept late and then went ashore to eat breakfast in a restaurant. Twink stretched out beside her mother on the bed. It was wonderful to be safe in a quiet harbor. It was fine with her if they stayed here all day. The cats went back to sleep.

"Ahoy *Ariel*. Anyone aboard?"

Twink woke and said, "That's Harry!" She stood on her hind legs and peered out through the porthole. Sure enough there he stood on deck outside, unruffled and keen eyed on this windswept morning. A few minutes work and she had the latch loose so she could crawl out on deck.

"You beat the weather, I see," he said cheerfully.

"Barely. The Witch almost got us. Skipper Sue tried to take a short cut through a stone wall. I yelled and she saw it just in time."

"You aren't the first boat to try that route. Just last month a big houseboat piled up there at night. Tore her bottom right out."

Dusty and Piggy had joined them. Dusty spoke up, "Harry, did you see Sid? Did she give you the list?"

"Yep. Got it right here in me head."

"Piggy, go turn Skipper Sue's computer on. We'll write it down now," said Twink.

Harry stuck his head in the window and over the next few minutes told Piggy what to type as she worked on Skipper Sue's computer down below on the bunk. When Harry and Piggy had finished the four animals went up to *Ariel's* foredeck where the boat's cabin blocked the chilly wind. Twink settled down and said with a sigh, "I wonder if it'll do any good, all this writing."

Harry said, "Well, we're on a lee shore alright, but like Pearl told you, there's some real good hands aboard working to keep us afloat. It's going to be rough going for a few years, but that's when the tough get going. You take in sail, batten down the hatches good, and man the pumps. You never leave the ship until she leaves you, and then you step up into the lifeboat."

The three cats sat quietly thinking of their cruise and what might lie ahead. Twink thought of Ellen getting ready for her last voyage and wondered if any young eels would return next spring.

As if reading her thoughts, her mother said "I guess it comes down to faith. That's all any of us has in the end."

"Yep, that's about it," said Harry. "You do what you can to get ready for the big blow, but in the end you just have to hang on."

Three days later Twink got up from Skipper Sue's chair, yawned stretched and jumped to the living room floor. It was so good to be back home. No more Wind Witch, big waves, wet fog, or nasty swans, and sure was nice to have some elbow room again. But there was still one thing left to do. Skipper Sue was sitting at her desk with the computer on. She was looking out the window at her flowers by the tool shed. Twink leaped up on Skipper Sue's lap and then jumped on to her desk and walked across her keyboard, taking care to step on the key Piggy had told her to hit.

"Ah, Twink, get off of there," said Skipper Sue, sounding cross.

Twinkle Toes strolled over to the window and sat on the sill. Behind her she heard Skipper Sue say "What's this stuff. 'The Piggy File?' I wonder how that got on here. Maybe I'll take a look."

Skipper Sue read;

Main Duck Island lies alone in the lake. Waves batter its stony shore and The Witch of November sends strong winds sweeping across its low lying barrens and grass lands to tear at its scanty groves of oak and hickory and cedar. No humans live here now, but the island is haunted with memories. There have been shipwrecks, here. Mad men have died here and hapless smugglers and lost crews from ships, too. Here the rich and powerful twisted the life paths of millions of ordinary men and women to serve their own ambitions...

Hmm, this sounds kind of interesting. Maybe I'd better read this. Skipper Sue settled back into her chair and Twink purred.

Oh yes, here's Sid's and Richard's list to help your neighborhood lake, stream, river, or bay that Harry gave Twink in Oswego. This list is a starting point. Readers young and old can generate their own lists and/ or start up a project of their own, too. Skipper Sue is planning to grow more vegetables in her garden next year. She says she'll slow the slugs down with dishes of stale beer!

Sid's and Richard's List

Watch what you dump down the drain. And be very careful about what goes into the toilet too. Don't flush away perfumed products or stuff with artificial fragrances and NEVER put any kind of medicine or pills into sewage or down the drain.

Keep lawn fertilizer use to a minimum. When plant food and fertilizers called phosphates from lawns and farm fields get into the streams and bays and lakes, they can cause too much algae to grow. Richard says, why do people put plant food on the lawn anyway? The grass grows faster and needs to be mowed more. Lawn mowers are VERY hard on the frogs and toads in your grass. And gas powered mowers are noisy!

Avoid using extra plastic and plastic packaging like throw away water bottles and plastic bags. The manufacture of some of them may be associated with chemicals that cause trouble for wildlife.

Use chemicals carefully. Chemicals have caused many problems to animals and fish in the lake. Be sure that any unwanted paint, or bug spray or motor oil or other chemicals are disposed of properly.

Never burn anything plastic in the burn barrel or fireplace. This produces some very nasty poisons. Try to re-use things. Skipper Sue fills old tires with dirt and grows strawberries in them.

Help things grow where the soil is bare. Bare soil is bad for streams, bays and the lake. When it rains and the soil washes into the water, it clogs up and smothers things and carries chemicals and fertilizers in with it. If there is any bare soil around your house, plant some grass or plants to hold it in place. A lot of erosion occurs from hill sides. Trails and roads from dirt bikes, hiking or other use can also make soil wash into the water. Home made mulch can help (please don't buy that colored stuff from Wal-mart), but growing plants and trees with roots and leaves are better.

Think about ways to save water. Pretty much all the water that comes into your house eventually leaves as sewage. If you use less water, you make less sewage. There are many gadgets to put on the faucet, or shower so that it uses less water. Fix leaks. Richard says save on laundry by not wearing clothes! (He's a frog. Don't listen to him.)
If you know a boat owner like Skipper Sue, tell him or her to go easy on the soap when cleaning the boat. Lots of time you can scrub your boat pretty clean without using any soap. And washing your car with lots of soap on a black-top drive way is just about as bad.

Use as little electricity as possible. Most electricity comes from a big power plant located by a lake or river. The power plant uses water and fuel to make that power. It produces waste and waste heat, too. The power plants use water from the lake to get rid of the waste heat, killing fish and small animals (plankton) in the process. Sometimes they put some chemicals like chlorine into the water, and this also is hard on small animals in the water. So try to save electricity whenever you can. Turn off the lights when you don't need them, don't open the refrigerator and stand in front of it, use less hot water, if you have an electric hot water heater, and try to use less power any way you can. Insulation can help. You'll save money, too, while helping the lakes. A number of websites on the Internet have ideas for saving power. http://www.ase.org/content/article/detail/965 has lots of good ideas

Roads are not good for water. Oil and grease and gas collect on them and then run off into the water. Pavement also keep rain from soaking into the ground. That hurts streams and wetlands. If you can drive less and *use roads less,* this helps the lakes and bays. Anything you can do to keep people from building MORE roads (and parking lots!) is a good idea, too.

Eat food that is produced outdoors in fields closer to your home, when you can. This will help the problem of making more roads and using more energy. A lot of human food travels on trucks and comes from far away. In the winter all those fresh vegetables and fruits may easily be trucked thousands of miles to a store near the Great Lakes or might be grown in a green house heated with fossil fuel. Do as Richard and Sid do, and eat fresh food that was recently grown nearby whenever

142

possible. Growing your own food in a garden is a good way to help reduce energy costs.

While you're out looking for food, try to find food grown on smaller farms. Large "factory" farms where two or three thousand cows produce milk or ten thousand chickens sit inside a big building and lay eggs, often make so much manure that it is hard to dispose of the waste without polluting local waters. Often, (though not always) food labeled "organic" is grown on smaller farms.

Many scientists think global warning will cause more droughts and that this will be bad for the Great Lakes. *Do whatever you can to create less CO2*. One important way to do this is to use less fossil fuels like gasoline or heating oil.

Last but not least, *get involved*. Work with others, write letters, go to meetings at your town and tell your elected officials that the Great Lakes are important.

ps. Sid wants to add something. She says if you have a garden and a yard and want to help out her cousins, leave some stuff around for them to hide under like a brush pile, old logs or some firewood. The young snakes will work in your garden and eat some of those pesky slugs.

Websites

Here are a few Internet websites with more ideas to help out the community of nature.

Children around the world are planting trees, adopting streams, writing songs and raising money for energy saving appliances, digging wells in Africa, for low electricity use light bulbs and other causes.
Some of their stories are here: http://www.unep.org/Tunza/children/

The Water Keeper Alliance has a number of Great Lakes groups under its umbrella. One of these is the Lake Ontario Water Keeper Group based in Toronto www.waterkeeper.ca
Lake Erie also has a water keeper group

An International group of lake watchers based in Buffalo is Great Lakes United, a broad coalition of U.S. and Canadian groups that promote, agitate, educate, and otherwise try to raise awareness of Great Lakes' issues.

A good source of information and link collections is the Great Lakes Information Network which has lists of organizations, labs, and activist groups on its site: http://www.great-lakes.net

Glossary

aback or *taken aback* a sudden wind shift may cause the sails to fill from the forward side causing them to push rather than pull the boat. Also the expression means to take by surprise

Bast An ancient Egyptian goddess of the sun associated with cats or regarded as a patron of cats also known later in history as Bastet

cockpit a small seating area at the back of the boat where the crew sits to steer. Usually has some seats and lockers and a place to put your feet. (And your cat or dog).

dockmaster the person (or animal) in charge of docking vessels and collecting any fees due.Sometimes the harbor master may also perform this function

fathom used to measure water depth and equal to six feet

gam a friendly conversation, often between the crews of two ships at sea

gunkhole much the same as backwater or eel rut, a little out of the way harbor often too shallow for big boats to visit

bow front end of the boat

hawser a large thick rope also called a cable in the old days- used to anchor or tow a ship

*heave t*o this is a way of 'parking' a boat so that it slowly drifts with the wind. Usually a *headsail* (a sail in the front such as a jib) is pulled to windward or "backed" and the rudder is set so that the boat would normally turn into the wind but is stopped from doing so by the jib.

jib small sail furthest forward on *Ariel* or *Sara B*

jibe to change course by turning the stern of the vessel through the wind

keel the main timber backbone of a wooden boat, or sometimes the fin projecting from the bottom of a sail boat to keep it from going sideways while sailing

lead line a light piece of line marked off in fathoms with a weight of lead on the bottom, used to take a sounding, that is to measure the depth of the water.

145

mainsail On *Ariel* or *Sara B* it would be the large single sail furthest aft

port The left side of a boat when you are facing forward. Or a harbor or anchorage e.g. the port of Oswego

shoal a shallow area sometimes hazardous to navigational

shorten sail to reduce the amount of sail carried

staysail the second small sail back from the front of a boat

starboard the right side of the boat when facing forward

stow sailor talk for putting something away in its proper place

tiller A sturdy stick connected to the rudder and used to steer the boat.

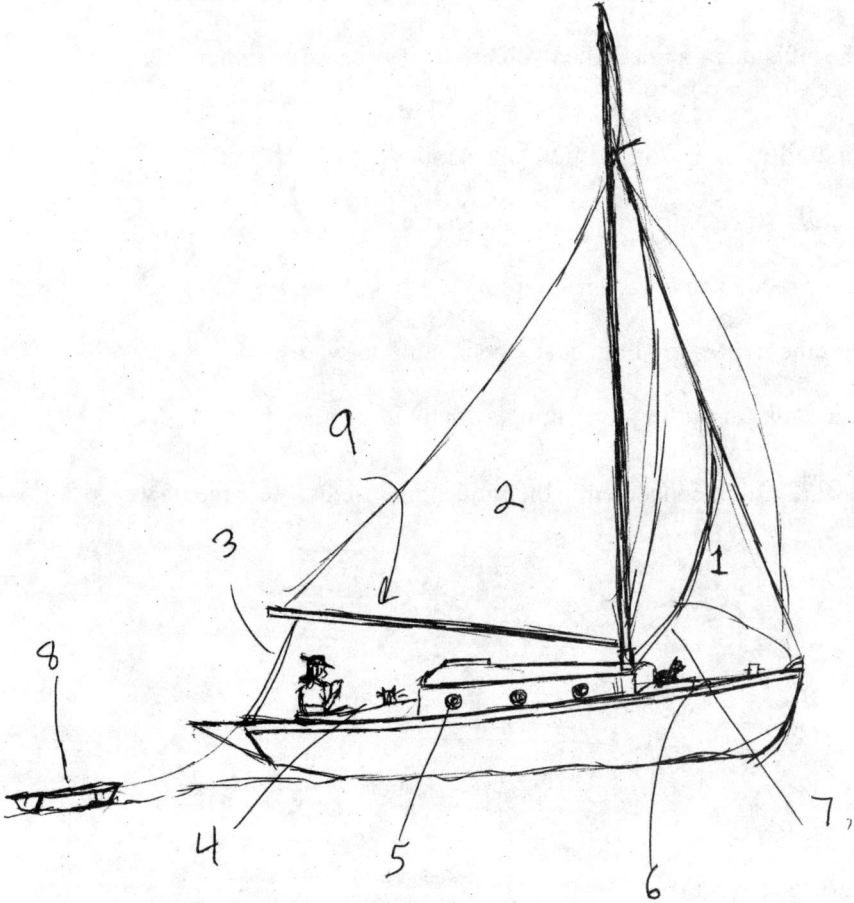

Boat Parts Sloop *Ariel*

1 jib 2 mainsail 3 mainsheet 4 cockpit 5 port hole escape route
6 foredeck 7 jib sheet 8 dinghy (also carried on deck) 9 boom

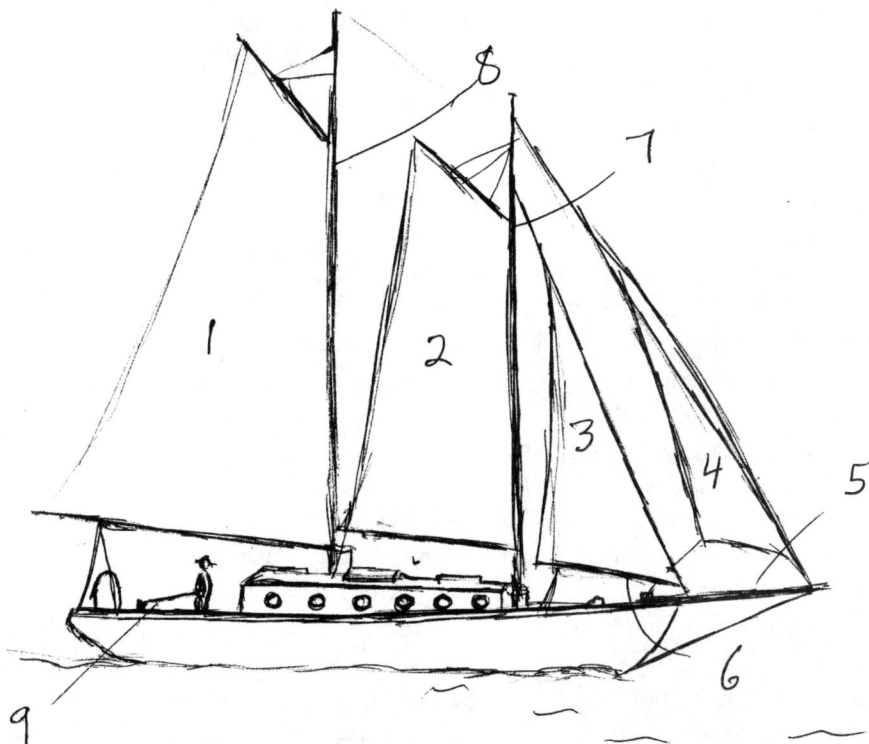

Boat Parts schooner *Sara B*

1 mainsail 2 foresail 3 staysail 4 jib 5 bowsprit 6 staysail boom
7 foremast 8 mainmast 9 tiller

Part Two: Skipper Sue's Notebook

The Great Lakes Today; Introduction and Overview........................150
Throop and the Underground Railroad Mattie's tale............................154
A few notes on slaves and Lake Ontario to go with Mattie's tale.......159
Climate Change and the Great Lakes 162
The Vandalia, A Lake Ontario First...168
Historic Sackets Harbor...170
Excerpt from Ariel's World printed in 1995...170
Great Lakes Weather 175
Did a comet kill the schooner Annandale?...179
Two Nations and the Great Lakes...182
Eel Update for Lake Ontario...184
Endocrine Disruptors in the Great Lakes...186
Recent Botulism Outbreaks..189
Viral Hemorrhagic Septicemia Virus (VHSV)....................................193
Waterfront Land and Swan Conflicts..195
Territorial Swans...197
Farley Mowat Canadian Conservationist and Author.........................199
Aliens Among Us...200
Carp And Carp Diseases..206
Spring Viremia of Carp...207
Disappearing Diporeia..208
Ship Ballast..211
Community Builders..212
A Note About the Cats and the Boats..215

The Great Lakes Today; Introduction and Overview

Welcome to Skipper Sue's note book. Here's where she put all the 'science stuff' while she was ashore at the library or talking to people in the labs around the lake. You can skip around or just grind your way through it from front to back. At the end you'll find a personal note about the boats and the cats that she sailed with.

Some well informed observers with scientific credentials believe the Great Lakes ecosystem is nearing a tipping point and subsequent collapse. Other lake watchers, like this writer, have their fingers crossed in the hope that we can still avoid such an outcome. However, it is clear that a combination of changing land use within the watershed, pollution, and the continuing immigration of unwanted "alien" species, is at work to de-stabilize the lakes. As more and more plant and animal species are eliminated and the ecosystem becomes more simplified, a crash becomes more likely.

As Pearl tells Twink, humans and other parts of the natural world make up a community. Communities thrive and prosper through connections. However, the subtle and intricate flows of energy along those connections are not obvious to the average mall shopper, land developer, town supervisor, highway worker, or business person operating within the Great Lakes watershed. In fact, even the mere concept of "watershed" is pretty hazy or downright nonexistent in the minds of many people, adults and children alike, all of whom live in one.

There is also the notion that one person's activities are inconsequential. What difference does it make if I clear these trees off and build a house here? How could one more paved driveway or one more trip into town with my car have any effect on the Great Lakes? Just as one single brief exposure to a few millirems of radiation will not kill you, one more individual seawall along a two hundred mile long coast will not suddenly destroy the beach. But environmental impacts, like radiation exposures, are cumulative. Tens, hundreds, and thousands of individual actions such as sea wall building in front of one's waterfront residence, do bring about widespread reductions in beach replenishment. A lot of people, this writer among them, believe our tiny individual actions have had a global impact and have collectively shifted the climate of the entire planet.

Another problem with trying to promote sound and sustainable environmental policy is the way today's actions can impact the future. In the environmental assessment business the notion of "secondary impacts" is supposed to be considered when a proposed project is being evaluated for its effects on the environment. A secondary impact is something that happens after the first action or project is allowed. Sometimes the secondary impacts are far more devastating to the environment than the original action that set them in motion. An example would be putting a town waterline in after a housing development is allowed. This, in turn, could spur more housing and road construction, sewers, and other development.

Scientists have identified several key sources of stress to the Great Lakes ecosystem. The ongoing input of nutrients from fertilizers and sewage remains excessive in the inshore portions of Lakes Erie and Ontario. The resulting nuisance growth and decay of algae contributes to high bacteria counts on swim beaches and to the outbreaks of botulism that have killed tens of thousands of fish eating birds. Excess nutrients can also reduce oxygen in deep water, killing off important bottom dwelling animals. The problem of too much nutrients, too much algae, and too many "weeds" is most acute in the protected bays and creeks where so many of the lake's fishes begin their lives. Over thirty years after the Clean Water Act's passage, excess nutrients continue to degrade water quality here.

Toxic chemicals are also recognized as a continuing problem in the Great Lakes. Sometimes the effects of these are subtle and not easily observed. Cancerous tumors and deformities like the large goiters seen in some Great Lakes salmon are far more alarming than subtle invisible effects such as reduced immune system function or scrambled hormones that reduce fertility. Some of the chemicals, like the various pharmaceuticals that are now being detected in municipal water supplies, enter via sewage. Some arrive as fallout from the atmosphere. And some reside in sediments that are disturbed by storms or dredging. Surface runoff from the roofs, roads, and parking lots of urban areas also can carry lead, cadmium, oils, and greases.

A subtle but very real source of stress and simplification throughout the lower Great Lakes is that of habitat destruction and change on land. Originally the Great Lakes watershed was heavily forested. Those forests were cleared for farming with marked impacts on stream flow, soil erosion, and groundwater supplies. Now the region's second growth forests are being logged and clear cut and in some places fragmented by houses and lawns.

The Northeast Midwest Institute, a think tank devoted to policy analysis in the Great Lakes region, reported in 2005 that "forest management and conservation should be a major component of Great Lakes ecosystem restoration." This same priority was acknowledged in the 1990 federal Great Lakes Fish and Wildlife Restoration Act's listing of priorities. However, forest quality continues to decline throughout the region.

To the casual eye it would seem that we have plenty of trees remaining along Lake Ontario's south shore. But patches of trees do not make a forest, at least not in the ecological sense. A forest is more than simply a collection of trees. Forests were once the dominant land cover, extending unbroken for many thousands of acres in this area. The various plants and animals and soil organisms within the extensive forest evolved together for many centuries. Then in the 19th century much of the watershed was cleared for agriculture with small areas of mature trees left for farm woodlots. By the 1900s some marginal farm fields were being abandoned and allowed to revert back into trees. Some of these second growth forests were a good approximation of the original land cover, though they did differ from the virgin stands of trees in the lack of several native species such as the white pine and American chestnut. Still, these second growth mixed forests gradually aged and assumed many of the characteristics of the original stands of trees. But in more recent times, that second growth forest has come under increasing stress and fragmentation.

As demand for hardwood for domestic use and export to Asia has risen, so, too, has local timber harvest. Much of that harvest, at least along the shore of Lake Ontario, is conducted on small privately owned wood lots and is rarely done with any sort of sustainable harvest objective in mind. Many of the land owners simply want to make a bit of money. Poor logging practices and grading techniques such as selecting all the high quality trees and leaving behind those of poorer quality are now causing declines in the health of our local forests. So has clear cutting and increased fragmentation (the breaking up of a large wooded area into a series of smaller stands separated by non forested land). A forest that is broken up by clear cuts or lots for houses cannot regenerate into a diverse healthy stand of mixed hardwoods if the parent sources of seed are lacking or if the soil is depleted of nutrients by erosion.

Wetlands that are important to ground water and the plants and animals of the nearshore Great Lakes' waters have also been drained and converted to farmlands. In Ohio it's estimated over 90% of the state's wetlands have been turned into farmland. Urban sprawl has also taken a heavy toll of both forest and wetland. The heavily populated area west of Toronto, on the end of Lake Ontario, is one of the fastest growing regions in Canada. Even in areas of the

Great Lakes where populations are stable or declining, undeveloped rural land continues to grow houses. Buffalo at the east end of Lake Erie showed almost no population growth between 1982 and 1996, yet urbanized land areas increased 52% within its metropolitan area.

As habitats are lost, individual species of plants and animals disappear and the overall ecosystem becomes less resilient and able to withstand further changes. The system becomes more vulnerable to new invading species such as the pretty purple loosestrife flowers that over run marshes, or the zebra mussel. It then is less stable and more likely to experience sudden large changes in populations of plants and animals.

The water within the Great Lakes is a vital life-giving resource used by the people of lake shore cities and towns. It's also used by manufacturing industries and by fossil and nuclear powered generating stations. Energy production is a big industry along the lakes. It's there because it needs the Great Lakes water. Power plants probably now remove more water by evaporation from Lake Michigan than the volume of flow through Chicago Sanitary Canal. Lake Ontario, the Great Atomic Lake, has 16 nuclear plants along with a number of conventional generating stations, all of which depend to some extent on the lake's waters.

Because of their open spaces, an increasingly scarce commodity in a world of low density residential development and sprawl, a number of people are looking to the Great Lakes as being good places to build offshore wind farms. Winds over open water tend to be stronger and steadier and thus better suited to power production than onshore winds. And all those conventional power plants along the lakes' shores provide good tie in points to the electrical grid for the wind farm operators.

Wind turbines have been criticized for killing migrant birds and bats. But the vast volumes of water used by conventional and nuclear plants for cooling that is then discharged at elevated temperatures back into the lake or boiled off as vapor from a cooling tower also take their toll on the Lakes' tiny fish and the planktonic plants and animals that are their food. Pros and cons aside, the Lakes, now home to oil, coal, nuclear, natural gas, and the big hydro plants on Niagara Falls and the St. Lawrence, will continue to be vital to North America's energy production. The International Joint Commission's original purpose way back in 1913 was in part to help settle hydropower related water use issues.

An old ex-military man I know says the next Civil War in the U.S. will be fought over water. I hope he's wrong, but he's not alone in his concerns.

153

Comprehensive and sensible planning for sustainable flexible water use policy is possible. But human history is littered with civilizations that failed and fell because they lacked such planning and policies. Sid's list is a good start for individual action to protect and preserve the lakes. But we also badly need collective co-ordinated comprehensive action by and leadership from the U.S. and Canadian governments. The people who live by and care for the Lakes must speak for them. We must let every level of government from local lake shore town up through county state and federal governments know the Lakes are important, and that they must be preserved and restored.

We've been living high on ecological credit for generations. At some point, just like those short sighted investors who bought into all that junk grade debt pushed by Wall Street traders and dealers as high yield safe investments, we're going to pay the piper. Mother Nature will collect on those debts. She always has, and she always will. The longer we wait to start paying it down, the more pain the human race will feel when the bill finally comes due.

Throop and the Underground Railroad Mattie's tale

Captain Horatio Nelson Throop came from a sea faring family. His father, Samuel, had sailed salt water aboard a whaler and had named his first son for the greatest British sea warrior of the day, Admiral Horatio Nelson. Throop was a man of big ideas. He designed and built one of the fastest sailing schooners that ever floated on the lake, and his steamer the *Ontario*, also his design, was the finest passenger ship of her time.

One day at the village post office, Captain Throop spoke in greeting to his good friend and neighbor Samuel Cuyler, who in turn asked, "Have you heard of the new law? If a slave runs away it's our duty to return him to his master."

Throop answered, "If a man has enough grit to run away and gets as far as Pultneyville, I'll be danged if I'll send him back south."

"Well that's what I think too-I and others. How would you like to join us? With your ship, you could take our "passengers" on the last leg of their trip to Canada."

Throop had worked hard since he was twelve years old and by now he was well off. He owned interests in two ships and had a fine stone house by the lake. He thought how things might have been if he had not been free to steer his own course through life. There had been setbacks. But there had also been opportunity, and when it came along, he had been free to seize it. He felt fortunate to have done what he wanted. He had sailed the lake on his own ship and had become wealthy doing it. So he said yes.

A day later when the captain again came out of the post office, Cuyler greeted him and then he asked, "Will you be making the run with the *Ontario* to Rochester tomorrow?"

Throop nodded.

"Then we'll have a cargo for you," said his friend with a quick wink.

Throop glanced at a stranger across the street. The man was leaning on the bridge rail studying the several schooners tied up in the creek. He hadn't expected any fugitives to arrive in Pultneyville so soon. But he answered, "Very well. My boat runs for passengers."

The stranger looking over the harbor was a bounty hunter in search of runaway slaves. If he had heard the conversation he gave no sign, and Throop went on his way back home.

As he walked down Washington Street, Throop wondered how he would get his "cargo" aboard the *Ontario*. He could close one or two fugitives up in trunks or crates and have them carried aboard. But too many large boxes might make the slave catchers suspicious, for Throop's steamer normally did not load much cargo in Pultneyville. Nor could he walk the runaways aboard openly. Cuyler could perhaps distract one bounty hunter, but Throop knew at least three southerners were hanging around the town right now, and that at least one would be watching all the departing ships. Clearly they suspected some "passengers" were about to arrive in Pultneyville on the underground railroad. The slave catchers would collect a large reward for each runaway returned to the south, and anyone caught helping an escaped slave could be fined. It was even possible that the courts could seize his vessel for breaking the law and auction it off.

As he considered ways to outwit the bounty hunters, a wagon load of firewood approached. The teamster, Will Murton, pulled up his mules and said, "Captain Throop I have your wood for the steamer here. This is the first load. Do you want it stacked on the pier?

Throop glanced out at the lake, noting the clear sky and gentle west wind. There would be no bad blows or heavy waves from the east tonight. He said, "Yes, that will be fine." Then he had a sudden thought. "Hold on a moment, Will. I'd like you to do something a little different with our fuel this time."

Throop looked around for nearby strangers, and then stepped close to the wagon seat and in a low voice gave Will some odd directions as to how to stack the wood on the pier. Then he walked on to his home.

There were seven of them, Peter Butler, his wife Mary, Peter's father, and four other men, all field hands and all from a North Carolina plantation. They'd come north through Philadelphia to New York City and then up the Hudson to Albany where they were given passage west on the Erie Canal aboard Black Joe's boat. Black Joe was a free black man. He owned his own canal boat, and in the past he had smuggled dozens of runaways from Albany aboard it. He had put the group ashore in Palmyra, a day's journey from Pultneyville and the runaways had then come north to Williamson concealed under a wagon load of hay. Here, they spent a day at another "station" on the underground railroad before traveling afoot during darkness with a guide leading them the last five miles to Cuyler's house by the lake.

It was now late afternoon, and Cuyler and Peter Butler stood on the porch surveying the lake and the little harbor to the west. They were also watching a large steamer, bold of bow and graceful of line, now slowing as she neared the harbor pier. The slap of her paddle wheel blades striking the water and the grand sounding hoot of her steam whistle as she backed down to come alongside the pier carried clearly to them over the quiet harbor.

"There's your boat," said Cuyler. "After dark you'll go aboard. The captain will take you to Rochester and you'll be transferred to a Canadian-bound steamer there. For now though, we'd best stay inside. The fewer people see you the better. We have at least three bounty hunters in town, and I'm sorry to say a few locals would also like a reward for turning in runaways."

Darkness comes slowly in mid-summer on Lake Ontario. It was nearly 11 o'clock before the front door of Cuyler's house opened, and the fugitives filed out into the quiet night. Peter had told his wife to follow close with Father at her back. Peter led them quickly across the road and into the dark shadow of the warehouse on the pier's end. Here they pressed against the wall a few yards from the pile of cordwood for the ship's boilers that lay stacked down the length of the pier. The wood had been piled in two long lines about four feet high with a narrow lane between them just as Cuyler had told him it would be. Beyond lay the sleek white ship waiting to take them to freedom, her hull pale in the starlight. The lake lay still and hushed as if it were holding its breath, and the voices of a small group of men on the pier next to the steamer carried clearly to the runaways.

Peter looked up at the North Star near the bowl of the Drinking Gourd. They had followed that star for many days on their journey to Canada and freedom. Now the *Ontario* lay directly beneath it. He uttered a quick whispered prayer and then bent down to slip into the wood pile, followed by the rest of the group. As he disappeared into the shadowed lane, the unexpected sound of a banjo playing the song 'Dixie' came to his ears.

At the other end of the pier stood three southerners talking with Captain Throop who leaned on the railing beside his wheelhouse above them. Cuyler strolled up hands in pockets just as one of the southerners called out, "Play another- do you know Jimmy Crack Corn?"

Throop picked up his instrument and said, "Sing with me if you will. Sam here says I have a voice to shame a frog."

Peter was nearly to the end of the wood pile. He crouched in its shadow wondering how they could get by the bounty hunters. The three slave catchers stood barely fifty feet away when he heard Mary gasp. A sudden loud clunk of a falling stick of firewood hitting the dock sounded behind him. Peter's stomach knotted in fear. He froze with bent knees in the darkness. A rat bolted across his feet, raced up onto the top of the woodpile beside him, and scampered away.

"What's that?" the tall man beside Cuyler asked as he turned to stare towards the wood pile. Peter's legs ached as he tried to stay still. His skin crawled as he imagined the slave catcher's harsh grip and the weight of the shackles upon his legs.

Cuyler also turned and sounded casual as he said, "I didn't hear anything."

Then he gestured towards a small movement in the water, the V shaped wake left by a muskrat swimming by.

"There. It was that little swimmer perhaps." He turned back to face the men. "Gents, I came to tell you a card game is in the making up at the Pigs Ear. If you can take yourself away from our Captain's sweet serenade, you'd be welcome to join us." As he spoke, he jingled a handful of coins in his pocket.

The tall slave catcher's eyes followed the muskrat. Then he looked back at Cuyler and said, "Reckon there's no action here tonight. Let's see what cards you Yanks can deal us."

They moved off as Throop struck a chord from the banjo strings once and then began strumming a lively tune. When Peter still crouched on trembling legs, as motionless as the firewood next to him heard "Picayune Butler is Going Away" he reached for Mary beside him who took his hand and squeezed it in silent celebration. When the song ended, he straightened up and stepped forth followed by his family and the four men. All the runaways walked boldly up the gang plank for freedom.

Throop's shadowed figure awaited them at the head of the gangway. The captain reached out to shake Peter's hand as he came up to the deck. "You're almost there. One more short passage and your journey's done. Now follow me

157

this way."

The next morning, after her fuel wood had been loaded, the *Ontario* cleared Pultneyville bound west. Once free of the harbor, Throop left the wheelhouse and went down to his cabin where he had hidden Peter's family. He invited them up on deck telling them, "You're safe now. You can have the run of the ship until we reach Rochester. There we'll put you aboard my friend's boat for Canada. Andrew the Steward will take you down for breakfast now."

But Peter lingered behind for a moment. "Why do you do this, all you 'conductors'?"

Throop looked out over his ship's bow at the now calm waters ahead. Then he turned to meet Peter's steady gaze.

"I can't speak for Samuel or the other captains or Black Joe. Only myself. I was twelve when my father died. I turned to and went to work, for I had a mother and brother and two sisters to support. By the time I was twenty I had built my schooner *Sophia*, a thirty tonner. I lost her my first season through my own poor judgment. But people gave me another chance. My old master took me back at his shipyard and gave me work. I paid off my debts and began anew."

Throop paused and leaned on the railing to gaze down at the water foaming close alongside the *Ontario*. He lifted his eyes to the horizon and continued.

"I have been very fortunate. There have been trials. I have always regretted my failure to secure investors for my screw driven steamer. I know my design was superior to the Ericsson propeller. But I have also worked with good people and I was exceedingly fortunate to have had the opportunity to design and build my *Ontario*, the finest steamer on all the lake."

Throop straightened and again met Peter's steady gaze. "It's only right that others should have the same chances that I had. In the path of life there are many thorns as well as flowers. But man should be free to take that path wherever it leads."

Peter nodded. "We are grateful."

"Well, enough lofty talk. You should join your family for some food."

"Yes sir. But can I ask one last question?"

"Assuredly."

"Why does your ship have a big eye painted on her side?"

"I caused that to be placed there. It is the Eye of Providence-under whose protection all men must mutually pledge to guard one another's lives, fortunes, and honor. Both afloat and ashore, we can do no less."

158

A few notes on slaves and Lake Ontario to go with Mattie's tale

As Twink realizes, one person's actions can change history. Especially if they write a really good book. Some historians have credited Harriet Beecher Stowe's novel *Uncle Tom's Cabin* as being an important factor in stirring up emotions and support for the Civil War. There is a tale, perhaps not true, that when she met with President Lincoln he said, "So this is the little lady that started the big war."

Harriet Beecher Stowe was a teacher living in Maine with her preacher husband when she wrote her book *Uncle Tom's Cabin, Life Among The Lowly*. Her story about brave black people and cruel slave owners was the best selling 19th century novel in the world and was translated into many languages. According to *Wikipedia,* the only book then selling more copies in America was the Bible.

Stowe wrote her story after the 1850 Fugitive Slave Act was passed. This law required people in the north to aid in the capture and return of runaway slaves. It stirred up the passions of many southerners and northerners alike as each region tried to assert its rights and impose its laws upon the other's citizens. Stowe was partly inspired by a memoir by Josiah Henson, a runaway slave who traveled to Canada crossing the Niagara River to freedom. Here he "shook the lion's paw" as contemporary accounts put it, referring to the protection slaves received on the north shore of Lake Ontario and Erie under British law. Henson's home is still standing near a town called Dresden in Ontario. One of his descendants traveled with Peary to the pole.

We have no idea how many slaves passed through Great Lakes ports on their way to freedom in the north. Few written records of the underground railroad exist, and accounts are difficult to verify. It seems likely that thousands crossed Lake Ontario on their way to Canada. Oswego, where Gerrit Smith, a prominent and wealthy abolitionist from the town of Peterboro near Utica had interests in shipping and harbor front properties, was a gateway to freedom for many slaves. Port Ontario and Pultneyville were also ports with known sympathetic ship captains and ship owners who helped many runaways. My own current home port of Fair Haven also apparently saw some activity. There are letters and hints in oral tradition of local runaways being smuggled aboard vessels from Little Sodus Bay. One ship from here variously identified as either a sloop or schooner was named the *Wide Awake* (also the name of the then active radical abolitionist wing of the Republican Party).

Another point of departure was Sodus Point. A settlement of several dozen free blacks lived on the banks of Maxwell Creek, a few miles west of this small lake port. Undoubtedly, they sheltered runaways and helped them on their way as did the family of whites living in the cobblestone house that still stands here beside Lake Road. Local legend has it that the drumlin hill just west of Maxwell Creek (now known as Freedom Hill) was a landmark used by mariners who picked up runaways off the beach there. The Niagara Falls area was also a major crossing for runaways, with lesser numbers coming up through Ohio and crossing Lake Erie.

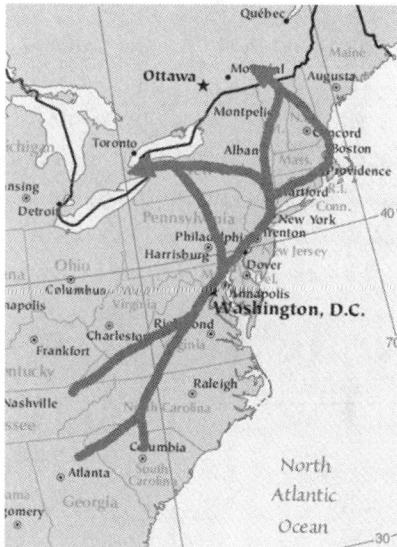

Some of the main underground railroad land routes shown above

Harriet Tubman is one of the most famous "conductors" of the underground railroad. Some say she helped three hundred or more people to reach freedom. She lived for several years in St. Catherines, a Canadian port at the west end of Lake Ontario where many runaways first landed. She eventually settled for good in Auburn about thirty miles south of Lake Ontario, and her house there today is a museum with displays on her life and work. Besides being a guide on the underground railroad, she later served as an armed scout, a spy, and a nurse during the Civil War and was eventually awarded a tiny pension for her service to the Union. As a black woman in a time when all women's rights and freedoms were severely limited, her exploits and courage seem little short of incredible.

She is probably the best known of the black conductors, but other free blacks, some of them sailors or canal boatmen, also helped runaways get to Canada. In the 1830s and 1840s central New York's "burned over district", so called because of the red hot fever of religion and reform that swept the area, made the region fertile ground for abolitionists. Harriet Beecher Stowe's brother Thomas came to Elmira to serve as pastor to a church sympathetic to the abolitionist cause. Some of the most active whites in the effort to help runaways were of the Quaker faith.

A number of runaways settled in St. Catherines, Ontario, then as now, an important shipbuilding center and port on Lake Ontario. St. Catherines was the terminal for the east end of the Welland Canal, and a considerable concentration of marine service businesses grew up there providing work for some of the escaped slaves. Others went on to inland locations. Some settled and became successful Canadian citizens. Some eventually returned to America. Life in Canada was not particularly easy for many of the runaways. An interesting account of an escaped slave's experiences in New York and in Canada is the book *Twenty-two Years a Slave Forty Years a Freeman* by Austin Steward published in 1857. The entire text has been placed on line by the University of North Carolina.

Steward lived briefly on the shore of Sodus Bay when his white owner tried to carve a southern plantation style farm there from the virgin forest. He escaped around 1813, but lived in New York State for some time before going to Canada around 1830 where he stayed about six years before coming back to Rochester.

During Captain Throop's time on the lake, blacks worked aboard ships in various tasks. It's been estimated that perhaps as many as 25% of the sailors serving aboard naval vessels on the Lakes during the 1812 war were blacks, and some of them likely remained in the area after the war and continued to follow the water. Underground railroad history suggests that more than one black sailor or steamer crew might have quietly served as a "conductor". The character operating a canal boat in the Throop story is imaginary but based on a historical canal boat owner. And solid evidence supports the story that Throop and Cuyler were active parts of the underground railroad.

We shall probably never know of the countless acts of heroism and altruism by both black and white people that were performed in the face of an evil institution that prevails to this day in various places around the world. They believed in a cause and they acted defying what they considered to be an unjust law.

Climate Change and the Great Lakes

When Twink has her flying dream in chapter two, she looks down first upon the dried up bed of the once vast Aral Sea. Then she visits the southwestern U.S., a rapidly growing region that desires more water than it has. Could the Great Lakes be drained in a human lifetime by water withdrawals? It seems possible.

Some say all the water on earth originated with comets striking our young planet's surface. Others believe it escaped from our molten planet's core as steam. Whatever its origins, water has been cycling around our earth ever since. For all practical purposes, our current planetary supply can be neither created nor destroyed. It can, of course, be redistributed (and polluted) by humans. And humans have been moving water around ever since our ancestors invented agriculture. We now have the ability to shift truly mind boggling amounts of water from place to place and we often do so with little consideration of the longer term consequences.

The Great Lakes represent 95% of the surface freshwater in the U.S. Yet, only about one percent of their volume is renewed annually. Remove more than that and a permanent drop in levels results. As pressures on the aquifers and reservoirs that supply other areas of the country increase and water supplies decrease, it seems all but inevitable that policy makers and entrepreneurs will seek Great Lakes waters to grow food and lawns and to wash cars and flush away wastes in areas of the country outside the Great Lakes watershed. Already some towns and cities are withdrawing water and discharging it through sewage systems into different watersheds. One study claims that the level of Lake Erie has permanently dropped five inches due to withdrawals.

Irrigation to grow forage crops, biofuels, and grain for meat and poultry production and for the foods that we eat, such as the winter lettuce and tomatoes that garnish our salads, is America's biggest user of water. It was irrigation that sucked the Aral Sea in central Asia nearly dry, and it's irrigation that has dropped aquifers ninety feet in the western U.S. And it looks like the need for irrigation in the U.S. is going to increase considerably in decades to come.

There are several reasons for this. Two of the biggies are global climate change and increased demands on the planet's ability to produce food for humans. There are more humans, and thanks to globalization that has spread the wealth of modern day capitalism around to a lot more countries including the most populous one on earth, China, more of those humans want to eat meat. This has greatly increased the amount of land needed to grow food. It takes about 2,500 gallons of water to produce a pound of beef. Increasingly, the available water to irrigate with is being used up or is too polluted to use.

Then there's the projected impacts of climate change. Nearly all the models of climate change and the Great Lakes predict drops in lake levels even with *no* increase of withdrawals for human use. Some predict up to a 40% reduction in outflow through the St. Lawrence by the end of the 21st century! As the climate in the Great Lakes region warms up, more water will evaporate from the lakes and be lost from their drainage basin. This will be especially apparent in the winter. On Lakes Erie, Ontario, and Michigan, less ice cover will allow more water loss from the system in the form of lake effect snow. Much of the lake effect snow on my own home lake of Ontario falls on either Tug Hill or south of it and so leaves the Great Lakes watershed via the Mohawk and Hudson River drainages. A lot of Lake Erie's winter snow ends up heading down into the Chesapeake Bay or the Ohio River.

Rising summer temperatures will also reduce soil moisture and increase droughts within the Great Lakes basin which will dry up stream flows into the lakes. Streams will also dry seasonally more often because of reduced ground water supplies. One cause for lesser recharge of aquifers is a change in the way water falls to the ground. Both land use changes and climate change are at work here.

In the past, precipitation in the winter fell as snow and built up into a snow pack that usually melted gradually in the spring and soaked into the soils of forests that were rich in humus and water holding organic matter. Spring melt water was also held in sponge-like wetlands and beaver ponds and seasonal swamps and swales. All these sources nourished tributary streams.

Global warming models predict more water will fall as rain in sudden heavy winter storms. And these days, that water is more likely to hit a road, a roof, a short grass lawn, or a bare farm field from which some commodity crop like corn or soybeans has been harvested. Such a rain has no time to soak and filter through soil to recharge aquifers. Rather it runs off quickly, often taking a good deal of soil with it.

The precise relationship of groundwater to the water in the Great Lakes is as yet not well understood, but those in the know increasingly suspect that adequate groundwater supplies are pretty important to the overall well being of the lakes. The impacts of warming and lower water levels are being felt first and most strongly in the nearshore shallows of the lakes and in their adjacent sheltered bays and wetlands. These areas are also the most productive parts of the lakes in terms of biological activity. It's here that the highest numbers of aquatic insect larvae, crayfish, and other invertebrates along with a variety of warm water fishes flourish. These sunlit shallows are where plants grow and provide food and shelter to many warm water fishes. A number of the lake's open water fishes also depend on the shallows because they move seasonally inshore to spawn in these nursery areas. Lowering lake levels could shift some wetlands offshore where they would re- establish. But in many locations the embayments and marshes so vital to the lakes' web of life and to its hydrology will simply vanish. Other streams that presently flow year around with clear cool water where trout and young salmon can feed on abundant aquatic insect larvae will warm up and become sluggish and weed choked or will simply dry up completely.

There is also growing suspicion that climate change is one of several factors leading to the increased frequency and severity of botulism outbreaks in the Great Lakes. The bacteria that causes these outbreaks grows most rapidly in decayed material during warmer periods. (See page 189 for more about botulism).

It now appears that global warming will impact almost every part of North America. In the far west snow packs will diminish as winter rains will increase. The rains will run off quickly and less water will be captured and then gradually released by melting for later use. Rising sea levels will cause saltwater intrusions of aquifers and reduce the fresh water available to Southern California from the Sacramento River Delta. California is an area of rising population which makes water conservation there even more difficult. Currently individual household usage has leveled off in southern California, yet in 2007 San Diego used more water than ever before because of an increase in households.

In the heartland where so much of our grains are grown for animal feed or biofuel, winter rains pounding on bare soil will increase erosion, and the runoff of water laced with fertilizers and pesticides. Higher summer temperatures will bring about more drought and need for irrigation. Similar summer dry spells are predicted for the southeast.

As many people before me have predicted, it seems all but inevitable that our thirsty neighbors to the south and west will look towards the seemingly limitless freshwater seas of the Great Lakes and demand water from them. Indeed, there are already considerable volumes of water being withdrawn and not replaced. In Michigan power plants on the lake used over 8 million gallons of water a day in 2004. This is more than the 7.6 million gallons a day diverted by the Chicago Sanitary canal into the Mississippi River drainage.

The Buffalo based environmental group Great Lakes United estimates that an additional diversion of 6.5 million gallons per day would drop the lake levels about half a foot. In 1981 The Army Corps funded a study that estimated the annual cost to power generators and commercial shipping by such a drop would run 45 million dollars a year.

The Aral Sea, a shallow slightly brackish body of water in south central Asia, was filled with water in the late Pleistocene. In 1960 it was the fourth largest lake in the world by surface area and was on average about 16 meters deep. (Lake Erie's average depth is 19 meters.) By 1987 because of withdrawals for irrigation, its surface area had decreased by 47% and its average depth was about 9 meters while its salinity had tripled. The many square miles of dried lake bottom are covered with deposits of various mineral salts generously laced with pesticides and fertilizers contained in past runoff from the cotton fields. These poisoned sediments readily blow in damaging dust storms for hundreds of miles. These salts are toxic to crops (and to animals and people) and have been detected in fallout 600 miles away from the lake. Because of the salt deposits, re-vegetation of the lake bottom has been slow.

Even the weather has been affected by the shrinkage of the lake. The growing season is shorter, temperature ranges are more extreme, and summers are hotter. Groundwater levels have dropped causing wells to dry, and the once productive fishery that employed thousands in fishing, fishery support, and processing industries in the 1950's has vanished. The costs of this ecological disaster have probably never been accurately measured. In recent years, there have been some measures made to divert water back into the northern part of the Aral Sea, and a recovery seems to be underway in the Kazakhstan controlled part of the sea. But Uzbekistan seems more interested in prospecting for oil on the dry salt flats of the southern portion, and the lake as a whole remains far from the productive life-filled body of water it once was.

Lake watchers have been worrying about the diversion of Great Lakes water to other regions and countries for decades. However, as the concept of climate change seems increasingly real to increasing numbers of people, it is adding urgency to the overall sense that policies to protect the Great Lakes from withdrawals need to be beefed up. A peer reviewed study by Scripps Institute, the world famous oceanographic group, published in 2008 projected probabilities for the depletion of water in the big Colorado River reservoirs like Lake Mead which southern California depends on. It predicted a 50% chance that within 13 years the water levels would be too low for gravity to send the water on to California. Within 15 years, that huge reservoir could be desert dry, leaving the region to depend on far more chancy and less stable seasonal flows of water. As the fountains dry up and the hydro powered lights go off in Las Vegas, does anyone hear that giant sucking sound? It's that straw in Lake Superior sending water south.

Efforts have been made to strengthen the legal standing of the Great Lakes states and Canadian provinces in their effort to control their water. The North American Free Trade Agreement (NAFTA) to increase trade between Canada, Mexico and the U.S. and subsequent other global trade agreements have lent urgency to this effort. There have been instances where the World Trade Organization's (WTO) agreements have overridden national and local control of resources in the past. In 2002, for example, 'dolphin safe tuna' was challenged by Mexico as being an impediment to trade. This prompted the Bush Administration to change the label standard so tuna caught by purse seines set on dolphins could be called 'dolphin safe'. In another case in 2006, European countries attempting to protect food safety by blocking genetically modified food from the U.S. were found to be violating trade agreements.

The Great Lakes Charter, a non-binding agreement that states 5 million gallon or more per day diversions approved by Great Lakes states and the two provinces was approved by U.S. and Canadian leaders in 1985. It was written after a plan to suck water westward was seriously proposed, and also after Ontario approved a scheme (that was never implemented) to ship fresh water out of the lakes via tankers.

More recently the Great Lakes Compact was approved by the provincial

166

leaders of Quebec and Ontario and by the legislatures of all the Great Lakes states. But some legal experts say it is still not clear who owns the water in the lakes or if the Compact can truly protect them. The resources under the water, such as oil and gas, have well-defined owners, but the water itself appears to be "in the public trust". At this time, governors of states have a clear legal right to protect any of their states' natural resources that are held in trust for the public. But, the lawyers say, that apparent ownership might be challenged and successfully overturned under WTO trading agreements. Our best chance to withstand those legal challenges is to come up with a policy that clearly and consistently seeks to protect and restore the Great Lakes from abuses and withdrawals by water users *within* the watershed of the lakes. Otherwise, if Syracuse or Chicago can take water from Lake Ontario or Lake Michigan for drinking and are then allowed to discharge the sewage into another drainage system, so, too, can China or Oman purchase and withdraw water from the lakes.

Though the Great Lakes Compact is a step in the right direction, comprehensive consistent policy that protects the Great Lakes that could also stand up to a legal challenge under the WTO treaties has yet to be put in place. Several environmental groups including Great Lakes United and the Waterkeeper Alliance are trying to push the creation of such a plan. If a comprehensive and sound policy were adopted, Allegra Cangelosi, a senior policy analyst for the Northeast Midwest Institute, writes on the group's website, then "our region... could show... the world what a sustainable water management regime looks like". Such an example would create greater water security for everyone if they followed our example.

Will we learn from repeated failures and disasters in water management like the Aswan dam, the Aral sea, the ancient Anasazi collapse and others? Or will we continue to make the same mistakes over and over? I guess if I were a Las Vegas bookie I'd put money on "stay the course". Drink 'er dry. Still, as Jared Diamond points out in his book *Collapse: How Societies Choose to Fail Or Succeed,* mismanagement of natural resources is not a given. He cites several examples of societies that did manage to establish sustainable living policies. Haiti and the Dominican Republic, who share the two halves of the island of Hispaniola in the Caribbean, nicely illustrate his point. Perhaps there is enough political will in North America to avert a repeat of the Aral Sea. Time will tell. And it won't be long before it does.

The *Vandalia*, A Lake Ontario First

The screw propeller has been called one of the most important inventions of maritime history. Like many revolutionary inventions, it evolved through time with dozens of people working on the idea, one of whom was H.N. Throop of Pultneyville. Throop built and launched an undecked two ton boat in 1832 that was powered by a screw propeller of his own design. Regrettably for his personal fortunes, he was unable to interest any investors in the idea and so could not complete the lengthy process of getting a patent on it. Eight years later, a chance encounter between an Oswego businessman and the Swedish engineer John Ericsson in New York City where the latter was making deals with the U.S. Navy, led to its introduction to the Great Lakes.

People knew about screws moving water since at least the time of Archimedes, and Robert Fulton made reference to a 'spiral oar' in his writings. The Revolutionary War submarine, the *Turtle* used such a water auger in its unsuccessful attack on the British, and by 1785 the idea had been patented by a British inventor. He never did anything with it, so its development was left to other engineers and inventors including Throop and Ericsson.

Much of Ericsson's early sales effort was directed towards the military. He promoted the advantages of the submerged screw propeller over the exposed and fragile sidewheel paddles for warships. He is remembered as being the designer of the Civil War iron clad the *Monitor,* often credited with being the first 'modern' U.S. warship. However, it was the limitations of canals in both Britain and the U.S. that gave Ericsson his first big break in the world of commerce.

The compact screw propellers had several advantages over the side mounted paddle wheels used by lake steamers. They were mounted aft and under the boat's stern so they were out of the way when entering a narrow canal lock, and they worked better in rough water. When a paddle wheel powered steamer rolled and pitched, the paddle blades often came out of the water. In storms on the Great Lakes, such steamers floundered in rough weather and sometimes even broke their drive shafts because of the strains on their machinery. They then drifted helpless before the wind and sometimes were driven ashore and wrecked.

The screw propeller was also more efficient than the paddle wheel because the screw blades were always submerged, unlike the paddle wheel's blades which drove the ship forward only during a small part of their revolution. More efficiency and less fuel consumption made the ships cheaper to operate.

The machinery to drive a screw propeller was also more compact than that of the side wheelers, so there was more room in the hold for cargo. However, side wheelers could operate in shallower water, and so they hung on for many years on the western rivers before the days of dredged channels.

Lake Ontario business men like Captain Van Cleve of Oswego also immediately saw that a screw propelled ship could be built with more beam than a side wheeler so it could carry more west bound cargo through the narrow locks of the Welland Canal. That's why a group of Oswego investors were the first to put the screw propeller into commercial use on the lakes. They had an engine and boiler put into a small wooden ship built on the lines of a typical canal sized schooner. They gave her two six foot propellers and shafts, a fifty horsepower steam plant, and named her *Vandalia* after the then capital of Illinois. She was rigged as a sloop and set her sails whenever the wind favored her course to help her along and save fuel.

The *Vandalia* was launched late in the 1841 season and promptly set off on a demonstration/sea trial run up to the west end of the lake. As part of her trials, she went as far as St. Catherines on the Welland Canal where she was well received. The local paper reported that "she steers...delightfully, the movement of the screws assisting rather than retarding the action of the rudder." Heading home from her maiden run, she encountered some November weather and gave a good account of herself as a competent sea boat. Her skipper declared that he thought her the safest vessel he had ever sailed in, able to stay off a lee shore in rough weather thanks to her engine and propellers.

Soon she had several successful sister "propellers" in the Oswego to Chicago trade, much to the chagrin of Buffalo's boosters who had dubbed the *Vandalia* The Oswego Humbug. At that time there was a fierce rivalry between the two cities. The Oswego newspaper enthused that the Ericcson propeller would work wonders for the city's economy, adding fifty percent to the value of property in Oswego.

Though the *Vandalia* and her sisters did operate profitably carrying freight and passengers west to the prairies, they were not able to compensate fully for the limitations of geography and the Welland Canal, a persistent bottleneck to western trade for many years with its physical size and tolls. Buffalo, at the western end of the Erie Canal was ultimately victorious in the race between the two ports for the profitable grain trade.

Historic Sackets Harbor

When *Ariel* and I first visited Sackets Harbor in 1980, the expansion of Fort Drum and the rapid "gentrification" of the village and its waterfront that followed, fueled by a hefty injection of U.S. taxpayer money via military and civilian contractors, lay in the future. This revival was in keeping with the town's history. Military money has always kept Sackets on the map. It never lived up to the potential as a commercial center that Augustus Sacket, the land speculator who founded it in 1801, had hoped for. Water power and railroads largely bypassed it, and after the navy pulled out in 1874, it subsisted quietly as a small lake port and summer resort. There was a commercial shipyard for many years on the site of the old navy yard, thanks to the harbor's deep water, and the army kept a considerable presence there until well past World War One.

Today, however, the old barracks I described in 1980 as forlorn and abandoned, are now part of an upscale housing development. As of this writing there was still a commercial facility serving recreational sailors, the Navy Point Marina in the harbor, so at least cruisers can still stop over and access town. There's more choice of restaurants, too, than in 1980.

Excerpt from *Ariel's World* printed in 1995

Sackets is one of only a handful of villages on the lake along the U.S. shore. (Most New York settlement took place along two important transport corridors a few miles inland, the Erie Canal and Ridge Road, a prehistoric beach berm left by glacial Lake Iroquois). The reason for Sackets' existence, its deep water harbor, also won the village a secure niche in the history of our nation.

For over a century Sackets was home to a military force of one sort or another, and many stone and brick memories in the form of buildings from its garrison days remain. Everywhere you look today are reminders of the past, and several good historic exhibits and museums memorialize the blood and sweat expended here in the name of national sovereignty. I spent a day reading museum and battlefield plaques, wandering through the abandoned grounds of the old military post, and studying museum exhibits and monuments.

Sackets saw war time incidents of courage, valor, and ingenuity, as well as a generous share of absurdity and tragedy. The great cable carry, when a hundred men marched a two and a half ton anchor cable from Stony Creek to

170

Sackets, was an example of the first category of action. The two battles of Sackets Harbor fall into the second.

Sackets Harbor was once a major garrison post and briefly was the most important naval station and shipbuilding center in the country. At one time a third of our entire infant navy's personnel, some 5000 men, were stationed here, and 3000 workers labored in the shipyards. And one of the war's first actions also took place at Sackets, a comic opera affair that, it seems to me, is a splendid example of how all wars should be fought.

A fair sunny morning of gentle warm breezes on July 19, 1812, saw the British "battlefleet", a few smallish warships, slowly approaching the outpost. They hoped to strike a decisive blow at America's only deep water base on Lake Ontario. If able to knock it out, they would then have undisputed control and command of the lake. Since these waters were a vital transport pathway to the western battle fronts, keeping command of Sackets was crucial to the American cause.

At that time the base had just one warship the brig *Oneida* built at Oswego a short time before. She was too slow to escape the approaching British fleet, so the post commander anchored her near shore and unloaded several of her guns to improvise a shore battery just north of town. From here they could rake the entrance of Black River Bay and hopefully keep the British out.

Here, too, stood a tiny "fort" and defending it the only large cannon then at Sackets, a long 32 dubbed by the farmer-militia men "the Old Sow". According to historian Arthur Pound's book on Lake Ontario, this ancient gun had been shipped to the colonies in 1689, surrendered to Ethan Allen at Fort Ticonderoga during the Revolution, and later hauled across the hills and mountains by ox team to Sackets. It was no easy task back then, to get anything to Sackets. The British held the St. Lawrence River so all military supplies and arms had to come from the East Coast via the Hudson, Mohawk, and the very tenuous and shallow Wood Creek connection. One historian has said it then cost two thousand dollars to ship a four hundred dollar cannon to Sackets.

Given such a long thin-stretched supply line and the tremendous transport difficulties, it's not surprising that there was no shot on hand for the thirty two pounder. The only cannon balls in town that day were 24 pounders all far too small for the Old Sow's wide maw. The militia scoured the village for patriotic rugs and attempted to make their cannon balls fit by wrapping them in strips of fabric before stuffing them down the barrel of the long thirty two. Not too surprisingly, the carpeted cannon balls fell short of the enemy ships.

Meanwhile, the British opened fire, and for the next two hours the forces exchanged volleys with little apparent effect. Finally, however, the British warship *Royal George*, fired a thirty two pound ball that made it ashore. A militia crew rushed to it, dug it up, and hurried it back to the Old Sow. They loaded and carefully sighted the old gun on the flagship. The cannon went off with a roar and a cloud of smoke and the lucky ball tore away the *Royal George's* mizzen mast and injured several of her crew (or so says one account.) The British abruptly lost interest in pummeling the embryonic American base. They broke out sail and headed back to Kingston.

After reading the battlefield plaque detailing this action, I looked over the windswept grassy field trying to imagine that long ago summer day. I pictured the little group of gunners in homespun, powder blackened faces jubilant as they shouted victory after the retreating enemy. Perhaps the British ships braced up their yards sharp against the freshening afternoon breeze that so often blows into Sackets on summer days, and perhaps their clouds of canvas merged with a light haze on the horizon that afternoon as they sailed away. Little did the militia know then, that single shot may well have been the most important of the entire war. Had the British persisted and won against the weak American defenses, the War of 1812 might have begun and ended that year with a British victory, and *Ariel* and I might be Canadians. Only a few weeks after the Old Sow spoke at Sackets, Fort Detroit fell to the British who then had control of all the upper lakes. Only Erie and Ontario remained up for grabs.

As summer of 1812 wore into fall, the Americans held on to Sackets, and the U.S. military machine began gearing up. Isaac Chaucey arrived to take command in October, and shipwright and naval architect Henry Eckford came up from the East Coast to build a warship fleet. Eckford must have been a superb organizer, for once he got his yard going, he cranked out ships at a staggering rate, on average of one every six weeks! His first, the 24 gun *Madison*, was built in forty five working days. Later, after a bit of practice, his crews turned out a hundred ton schooner in three weeks. With no power tools.

The wood for building these vessels was close at hand, oak for keel, frames, and for the thick heavy hull planks, pine for decks and cabin work, and light weight cedar for upper works. Everything else, though, had to be fabricated on the East Coast and then laboriously carted and floated to Sackets. It took much longer to rig and arm the vessels than it did to build them.

There was at this time, almost nothing in the way of saw mills, foundries, roads or other infrastructure around Sackets, only dense and as yet almost untouched forest. Logs were felled and cut into planks entirely by hand. After a major timber for a keel was selected and cut, a gang of fifty to a hundred men would converge upon it with their adzes to square it off where it lay. The timber, still wet with sap was then hauled to the yard the next day and set up on the keel blocks for framing.

Of course, such ships rotted almost as fast as they were built. They were throwaways, created only for the Lake Ontario military theater and useless anywhere else because the rapids on the St. Lawrence blocked them from moving off the lake. As owner of my own wooden vessel, all I could think in reading of this was "what a waste of virgin timber!" But war has always been an exceedingly wasteful business.

Just west of the museum lies a grassy lawn where the second battle of Sackets was fought. It took place in May 1813 shortly after the burning of York (Toronto). It was this American action that resulted in a retaliation by the British against Washington and that famous bombardment of Fort Henry near Baltimore whose rockets' red glare inspired Francis Scott Key's anthem to Old Glory.

But back on Lake Ontario, the second battle of Sackets was not glorious. It was bloody, though, with over a thousand men killed or wounded. The British got a considerable force ashore who fought their way towards the naval yard and its priceless stores. They got so close that the Americans fired their own supplies not wanting them to fall into enemy hands. All appeared lost as the reinforcing militia men fired one volley and then fled. But General Brown managed to rally the scampering irregulars, and with them and a small company of soldiers he succeeded in halting the British advance. Brown then gathered another group of militia and counter attacked the British rear. Instead of standing his ground, the British general thought he was being surrounded and cut off by a greatly superior force. Not wishing to be slaughtered, he ordered retreat and a mad rush ensued leaving dead and wounded behind.

The so called War of 1812 dragged on after that for still another year with many more casualties, especially in the winter when bacteria and viruses rather than bayonets and musket balls felled the men. The ship *Madison* buried a fifth of her crew in those bitter short days, and dozens of the wood cutting crew died of the effects of harsh unrelenting cold, hard labor, and poor nutrition. But building went on at frantic speed and, at last, culminated at Sackets with the hull of a massive three decked ship of the line, the *New*

Orleans. At three thousand tons and designed to carry 120 guns, she was the biggest wooden ship ever built on Lake Ontario. And Eckford's men had her ready for the caulking gang in ninety days! But "Old Never Wet" as she came to be called, was not launched, for by then the war was finally over.

As Chauncey told Twink, the massive hulk of the *New Orleans* sat for many decades upon the shore of Sacket's Harbor, covered by a huge 'ship house'. Finally in 1884 she was broken up. But as the workers set to sawing off a piece of her on a February morning, the hulk struck back. She shifted on the blocks and began to slide, moving about ten feet. Several men fell from ladders and from the hulk itself. A news story recalls "John Oats, aged 29 years, an unmarried man, was killed. One of the falling timbers containing a square two-inch bolt, fell across the body piercing the bowels and coming out of the back, and a large spike was driven into his head, death was instantaneous." And so occurred the last casualty of the War of 1812, 70 years after the war's end.

After the War of 1812, the Sackets military post remained for many decades, though in post Civil War days its importance waned. By 1900 history had passed it by, and only a handful of men remained here. When the base commandant died, his widow was appointed in his place. Mrs. Metcalf's duties consisted mainly of seeing that the grounds got mowed and the flag was raised and lowered each day. Nonetheless, she had the distinction of being our country's first female base commander.

In 1955 the risk of another war with Canada appeared slight, so the base was finally closed down. At the time of *Ariel's* first visit in 1980, little had been done since then. I took a walk through the abandoned post in the afternoon, following a broken weed grown sidewalk through waist high grasses to the one time parade ground. Here someone had mowed the lawn around the old stone barracks. I passed along their silent row once so full of life and activity. It was a ghost town. The forgotten base was a strange sad monument to war. Some roofs had fallen in, some walls of mortar and stone had crumbled, though many of the buildings still stood as straight and true as the day careful masons had laid them up in 1816.

I peered in a shattered window screened by cobwebs and saw a gutted interior stripped by vandals. Sinks torn loose and left on the floor, bricks lying about after being thrown through the window panes--such senseless destruction only heightened the somber mood of the ruins. No bugles, shiny insignia, sharp uniforms, ceaseless drills, or barked commands here now, just a platoon of pigeons wheeling overhead on clattering wings, while across the

174

windswept grounds came the harsh cries and commands of crows riding the strong westerly wind.

I returned to *Ariel* feeling strongly the impermanence of all those things for which wars are fought. Sooner or later, buildings, boats, and all else we fashion with such care and pride and defend with such vigor fall into ruin and rubble. Less tangible, and sometimes more lasting are the things of the spirit, but only for as long as history remembers them.

Great Lakes Weather

The Great Lakes are so big that they make their own weather. And, as Chauncey told Twink, fall and winter is when that weather is most impressive. There's a reason why so many of the shipwrecks took place in November on the lakes back in the days of steam and sail. All of the lakes create fall rain squalls and water spouts, and heavy winter snows. In the fall the still warm waters of the Great Lakes can actually feed energy into passing storm systems to intensify them just as hurricanes draw energy from tropical oceans. The fast strengthening gales of November that can attain hurricane strength and whip up giant "rogue" waves of 40 feet or more, have been the end of many a ship. The Great Gale of November 1913, the subject of several books, is an example. This single storm killed more than two hundred people and cost the shipping industry perhaps a hundred million in today's dollars.

Lake Ontario's "Perfect Storm" of 1880 that I wrote of in *Passages On Inland Waters* was another deadly fall storm. One shipwreck witness recalled that he never saw such a wind. The protected waters of Wellers Bay near Presquile were covered with blowing spindrift six feet high. A schooner at anchor there lost one of her sails that quickly flogged to bits. Pieces of it later turned up caught on fence rails miles away.

Throughout the winter under the right conditions localized but intense blizzards and whiteouts with snowfall rates of four to five inches an hour can occur along the lee sides of all the lakes. Each lake has its usual "snow belt" that moves around according to wind direction. The upper peninsula of Michigan can get snow from more than one lake, and sometimes the snow from the lakes can be carried over a hundred miles inland. Lake Erie snows have reached down into Maryland, and the author's upstate New York driveway has at various times managed to get snow from Lake Erie, and Lake Huron as well as from Lake Ontario (not simultaneously, though.)

Buffalo and Syracuse lie within the areas of frequent lake effect snows from Lakes Erie and Ontario respectively. In 2002 Buffalo got 80 inches of snow in a six day dump off Erie, while Syracuse averages over a hundred inches per year. In 1993 one storm dumped three feet on Syracuse in 24 hours. Syracuse frequently beats out Buffalo for season totals because shallow Lake Erie usually freezes over by late winter. This cuts off the moisture supply that is the source of the snow.

A short drive north of Syracuse lies the Tug Hill plateau where many U.S. snowfall records have been set. This upland area on the west edge of the Adirondacks has experienced season totals in excess of 400 inches while a single 24 hour period saw 77 inches land on the little town of Montague here. I think that works out to something like six inches an hour! Another Tug Hill location piled up 39 feet of snow in the winter of 1976-77. I had some Tug Hill folks out for a boat ride a few years ago in July who told me they still had a pile of snow in the shade under their patio the month before.

Tug Hill is elevated, rising to around 2100 feet on its eastern edge. This, along with its location squarely at the east end of Lake Ontario where prevailing west winds sweep the full length of the lake picking up moisture enroute, gives it the distinction of having the heaviest snows east of the Rockies. Below is an excerpt from *Ariel's World,* published in 1995, concerning snow on 'the hill';

At the east end of Lake Ontario lies an area of sparsely populated elevated land called the Tug Hill Plateau which has evolved a sort of seasonal snow culture. Tug Hill, home to the state's snowplowing school for highway crews, has some of the toughest winters anywhere in the Northeast. It is today a land of second and third growth spruce and sugar maple forests, rocky fields, and empty weathered gray farm houses. Some dairying still goes on here, but most of the farmers have sought out the Black River Valley just to the east and left the hard scrabble hill to revert to its precolonial condition. As you drive about in the summer, you'll observe almost every little road side garage in the area has a sign out announcing snow mobiles repaired here. Several ski slopes have been carved out of Tug Hill's eastern slope, and they seldom need snow making machinery. Each winter hundreds of snowmobilers converge on the area, second only to the Adirondacks in popularity for the sport. They ride the miles of old logging roads and country lanes. And each fall locals place stripped saplings and sticks by country mail boxes and village fire hydrants and guardrails to help the plow crews avoid them. Once when driving here after a snow I noticed a home owner clearing his drive not with pick up truck plow or small tractor but by bulldozer. Snow means business here. But let a native tell the story.

He is Matt Macierowski, a long time amateur weatherman and volunteer National Weather Service observer who took up residence just outside Barnes Corners. He came to this bleak land of his own free will. He wanted to study snow and he certainly picked the right place. In 1977 he measured over 370 inches of white stuff in his backyard.

My interest in lake weather grew as I experienced some of the summer phenomena with *Ariel,* so I decided an article on lake snow was in order. The best place to get information was surely from the Tug Hill Observer himself, so one late winter day when the twelve foot high snow banks were beginning to hemorrhage water even up on Tug Hill, I braved the weather to venture up for an interview. Macierowski, formerly of southern Connecticut, had come to the area perhaps 25 years ago and built his own house up on a hill with panoramic views in every direction. Here he could sit by the hour watching the weather as fascinated by it as any small boat sailor. Somehow he also commuted daily for many years in those winters to Watertown. He told me he took all his vacation as "snow days".

Since my interview in 1990, health problems forced him to give up the rugged life on "The Hill", but I'll always remember the enthusiasm that lit his face when he talked about his favorite subject.

Macierowski was a real snow nut, had a local reputation for it, and even self published a book about his studies of lake effect snow. In it he wrote "because of its vast water surface area, condensation in the form of thunderstorms violent snow squalls and blizzards occur over Lake Ontario every fall and winter on a large scale. These savage well-organized lake effect storms commonly result in snow fall at a rate of two to four inches an HOUR." Macierowski adds thunder and lighting can accompany these winter squalls, something I've seen and heard myself several times in the last five years. He once recorded a snow fall of five inches an hour, and in one seventeen hour period in 1975 saw 54 inches fall, not too far from the total seasonal snowfall some years on the lake's south or northwest shore!

During my interview, Macierowski pointed out that lake effect snows rarely occur without a ten to twenty degree temperature difference between lake and air. By early March the lake's surface has cooled to near freezing, while the average air temperature is slowly but surely rising again with lengthening days, so lake effect snows become rarer. They can occur as late as April, though, and a couple years ago I recall twenty inches of lake effect in mid-March near Rochester.

Along about the end of February residents of the lake's south shore begin to see the sun again after a three month hiatus. For most of the winter when they don't get snow here, they get clouds. In December 1985 as I searched the sky for Halley's Comet, I recall two partially clear nights all month. In the winter of 1992-1993 we had seventeen weekends in a row with precipitation. Not until the last weekend in February did the streak break. But in March lake clouds become less frequent, and the average percent of sunny days goes from 30% to 50% in Rochester, about the same as that for inland areas.

Though many folks along the lake, myself among them, despise lake generated gloom, both clouds and the water itself moderate the area's winter cold considerably. On a clear bitter cold night radiational cooling can drop inland temperatures ten or twenty degrees below what they dip to near the shore. Temperatures are moderated here because the clouds help prevent heat from radiating into space at night. Water is also exceptionally good at storing heat, so the lake acts like a giant hot water bottle, slow to yield the energy stored up on hot summer afternoons. This further moderates the most frigid weather near shore during the winter. Of course, this is one reason for the area's intensive fruit farming industry. Fragile cherry and peach trees and buds of all varieties are less likely to suffer from a severe freeze if close to the lake.

I enjoy spring flowers but am no lover of winter lake snow. Sailing after all, is my passion. But a lake effect snow delights all but the most winter weary. The flakes are large and fluffy, and on calm days they drift slowly down in big clumps making for postcard perfect winter scenes. I've seen blobs as big as a 25 cent piece floating down and individual flakes are easily visible if you look closely at a surface. When they settle so gently from the gray sky, they land as perfectly formed and intact crystalline stars.

Such snow caps twigs with six to eight inches of airy fluff and even door knobs wear a snow cover four inches thick. Shoveling snow like that is like pitching goose down. But gradually, as it begins to pile up, moving even fluffy stuff around becomes a decided chore. On the Tug Hill Plateau, highway crews use big rotary plows to cut through ten and fifteen foot packed powder drifts that sometimes clog roads. Shoveling your roof is a regular chore there, too, lest accumulated snow cave it in.

Because lake effect snow is low in moisture and relatively light in weight, it also blows around at a great rate if a wind accompanies it. The flour fine stuff makes for intense white outs, fast drifting, and bad driving.

In the famous Tug Hill blizzard of 1977 Macierowski wrote of fifteen to twenty foot drifts driven by sixty-five mile an hour wind. The packed powder was so hard you could easily walk atop drifts, he recalled. President Carter declared a state of emergency in the area as Macierowski wrote "As the formidable digging out task began, I realized that I hadn't been out of my home for fourteen days." Many houses had drifts around them reaching to roof tops and at least one dairy barn collapsed from its laden roof. Macierowski had to dig down four feet to hit the top of his drifted in car at the foot of his driveway!

What makes lake effect snow even more dramatic (and maddening) is its extremely localized character. That 1977 blizzard that buried Buffalo and Adams at the east ends of Lakes Erie and Ontario totally missed south shore Rochester. While one town is experiencing white outs and snow at up to four inches an hour, scarcely five miles away the sun may be shining in a clear blue sky. One Christmas day I watched twenty six inches pile up on *Ariel's* cover. Barely ten miles to the west, my sister, enjoying a crisp sparkling sunny winter day, called to find out why we hadn't arrived for Christmas turkey yet.

To read more:

http://en.wikipedia.org/wiki/Great_Lakes_Storm_of_1913 Wikipedia entry on the "white hurricane" of the upper lakes

Passages On Inland Waters Chapter 3 The Great Gale of 1880 published by Susan P, Gateley, 2004 isbn 0-9646149-2-8

Did a comet kill the schooner *Annandale*?

When Twinkle Toes and the *Ariel* were sent off course by Charity Shoal, they weren't the first boat to go astray here. A hundred and five years before Ariel's trip, the schooner scow *Annandale* bound from Oswego to Kingston with a load of coal stranded in fog on Charity Shoal. It was calm, the crew got off, and a few days later the old ship broke up on the rocks in a blow. Did she have something in common with the North American Mammoth?

As the human race continues its massive experiment with fossil fuel induced climate change, the notion that climate can shift suddenly and catastrophically has gained traction within the scientific community. Studies of tree rings, fossil pollen, ice cores, and even written records from ancient villages have documented several such rapid changes like the 'little ice age' which is thought to have driven the Vikings from their colonies in Greenland as well as other older but no less abrupt shifts.

A few decades ago a cooling event called the Younger Dryas was recognized by scientists. It happened around 12,900 years ago and ironically, the theory went, the melting of the glaciers in North America caused a sudden release of water from the interior of the continent through the Great Lakes basin which, in turn, shut down the Gulf Stream. This caused Europe to go into the deep freeze. The same event might have also impacted the early human inhabitants of North America and some of the animals they depended on for food.

Still, controversy remained as to the cause of the thousand year cool down, and the archaeologists had never managed a really convincing explanation of why the Clovis people of North America suddenly experienced a catastrophic population decline along with over a hundred species of land mammals ranging from camels to saber tooth cats. Most of the animals that died out were larger species, weighing over a hundred pounds of so. Some of them, like the horse and camel, survived in the old world, but died out in the new. What had been the exact cause of this large scale extinction? Did highly efficient and meat hungry paleo-Indian hunters kill them all off? Did the fleas, dogs, lice, or other organisms traveling with the humans bring some virulent new disease from the old world that transmitted to and then devastated native animal populations? While nobody knew for sure which theory or combination of causes was correct, there was increasing suspicion that the Younger Dryas cooling event had something to do with it. So there was a lot of interest in the theory of a comet strike as the trigger for the big chill when it was presented at a scientific conference in Mexico in 2007.

There is growing evidence that a large comet exploded over Canada north of the Great Lakes about 12,900 years ago and that fiery fragments rained down onto a large area of North America. The theory goes that the after affects of the comet's strike could have plunged the continent back into a mini ice age causing the extinctions of a number of large animals like the mammoth and the giant ground sloth. And many of the ice age humans may also have been victims.

At that conference, Dr. James Kennatt told his audience that surveys of Clovis sites found that the highest concentration of extra terrestrial materials such as iridium, particular isotopes of helium, and unique forms of carbon, occurred in the Great Lakes area. The major part of the comet might have impacted over the glacier itself (which is why no big meteor crater has been found north of the lakes in Canada). This then might have caused a massive sudden melting and break up of a large part of the ice sheet, leading to the sudden release of water as ice dams in the St. Lawrence Valley gave way. Other comet fragments appear to have hit far to the south where forested areas caught fire sending massive amounts of smoke and soot into the air causing world wide cooling. These combined impacts may have launched the Younger Dryas event and with it a massive extinction of larger North American land animals.

An interesting piece of the puzzle is the presence of numerous small depressions that are elliptical in shape and often now form shallow wetlands from New Jersey to Florida. They all seem oriented in a way that indicates a possible rain of fragments striking from the northwest.

Last year, while I was doing a beach walk with some folks, one asked me if I had heard of a meteor crater in Lake Ontario. I looked blank and said no. But more recently a chance encounter with a geologist led me to a spectacular detailed map of the bottom of Lake Ontario, courtesy of NOAA, on the Internet. This showed where the crater question came from. Charity Shoal, an oddly circular reef almost like a coral atoll under water, lies near where the shipping lane turns to head up into the St. Lawrence northeast of Main Duck. And it may be of extra terrestrial origin. Could Charity Shoal have a connection with the demise of the North American Mammoth?

In 1999 the *Journal of Great Lakes Research* ran an article documenting the presence of a "small rimmed depression" in Lake Ontario that they proposed might have been caused by a meteorite. Supporting the theory was the long standing knowledge of a magnetic anomaly (marked on my well used paper charts of the area) which is typical of impact events. The article went on to say several time periods for the event were possible including Pleistocene or Holocene. If indeed it was from those more recent times, that would match the era of the Younger Dryas cooling event.

As far as I can find no definitive study of the shoal has been made that has turned up any extra terrestrial "markers" such as iridium granules, shocked quartz, or what the scientists call 'nano diamonds'. But it's not that easy to sample rocks that are 50 feet under water and filled with hard clay sediment. I wonder if any scuba divers are checking out its geology?

Charity Shoal has been the death of several unfortunate Lake Ontario vessels. One part of the raised circular rim is only a few feet below the lake's surface. A diving site lists the schooners *Annandale* and *Maria Annette* along with the *Lucinda* as known victims accessible to divers today. Maybe while they're down there studying the ships, they could look around at the geology as well. Charity Shoal incidentally takes its name from one of the first English schooners built on the lake who found it, died on it, and gave it her name.

Who would have thought that a comet could perhaps have been responsible for sinking several ships on Lake Ontario 12,900 years after its own demise? It's a curious world out there.

Below is a link to a paper published in 2007 on the possible link between a comet strike and the Younger Dryas event.

http://www.pnas.org/cgi/reprint/0706977104v1

Two Nations and the Great Lakes

Despite the first impression that Twink and her companions had upon viewing Canada's peaceful Point Traverse Harbor, in truth the Canadian population on Lake Ontario considerably outnumbers that of New York State's shoreline. Most of Canada, the second largest country in the world by land area, is a vast, cold, and sparsely populated place, and most of its 31 million people live within a hundred miles of the southern border. A substantial portion of those reside between Windsor and Montreal in urban or suburban areas, so the north shore of Lake Ontario lies within Canada's most densely populated "megalopolis".

Canada's largest city, Toronto, stands on Lake Ontario. The population of the city and its surrounding rapidly expanding suburbs totals five million. The western end of the lake, the so-called golden horseshoe, is the lake's most urbanized and industrialized shore and is home to another three million or so Canadians. One of the world's largest research institutions devoted to studying freshwater The Canadian Centre for Inland Waters is also located within this region in Burlington, Ontario at the lake's west end.

Ontario with its wealth and industry is the most populous and politically influential Canadian province. Because Ontario borders all the Great Lakes, the lakes tend to have a somewhat higher national profile within the looser confederacy of Canada than in the U.S. where many different geographic jurisdictions border them and compete for influence within the D.C beltway. Even New York State, despite having shoreline on two of the Great Lakes, focuses much of its attention (and funding) on the Hudson and other waterways thanks to a population distribution and regional politics dominated by downstate and New York City.

Luckily for the Great Lakes, there have been at least sporadic efforts by the two countries that share them to cooperate in the management and remediation of pollution here. Back in 1905 the forerunner of the bi-national agency known as the International Joint Commission (commonly called the IJC), was created. In 1909 a treaty to jointly manage lake levels for hydro-power was signed by the U.S. and Canada which gave the agency legal standing. As the need to deal with water pollution became obvious, the IJC's mandate was expanded. In the 1950's additional regulatory groups, the Great Lakes Fishery Commission, established to manage the region's fisheries and control the sea lamprey and the Great Lakes Commission, charged with oversight of water quality and pollution issues, were created.

Canada has its own problems with the politics of pollution and the environment. The generous angler incident in Point Traverse Harbor witnessed by the cats is in contrast to the views of many Canadian sportsmen who dislike fish eating birds just as much as Americans do. They have lobbied for cormorant destruction just as they have in the U.S. Indeed, almost everyone on both sides of the lakes seems to have little kind to say about the cormorant which has made a spectacular recovery on Lake Ontario after toxic chemicals nearly caused its extinction here in the 1960s. Even bird watchers complain that the big black fish eaters overrun islands and destroy nesting habitat used by less common fish eating birds.

One clear difference between the two nations, at least on Lake Ontario, has been a notably greater commitment to public access to the shore for land lubbers and boaters alike in Canada. Many of the little towns and villages on the Canadian shore still have a public town dock. Perhaps a lingering memory of a time when general commerce and economic activity involved more use of the lake than it does today helps keep the docks and launch ramps public. In the U.S. there has been little effort to stop a general land grab by developers along the lake shore. There are also a number of waterfront parks and conservations areas on the Canadian shore of Lake Ontario including the important bird sanctuary on Point Traverse where Twinkie made landfall.

Unfortunately, for those mariners who would follow in *Ariel's* wake, the number of people actively using the lakes as boaters or fishermen is in decline. As use declines, so, too, may interest in the lakes' welfare. Without interest in using the Great Lakes, access to them is likely to further dwindle. It then becomes politically more palatable to further privatize the water and waterfront for a narrow set of uses on both sides of the border.

Eel Update for Lake Ontario

Fifteen years ago eels were incredibly abundant in Lake Ontario and elsewhere in North America. About two weeks into my new career of fisheries grad student back in 1974, a large eel was one of the first fish I encountered while sampling a pond in western Massachusetts. During my stint on the Chesapeake Bay in the late 1970s, eels supported a large and lucrative commercial fishery, and young "snot snakes", as we called them, were almost aways a major part of our bottom trawl survey samples. In the 1980s when I was sailing *Ariel* around the lake, they supported a thriving fishery and were at that time one of the most valued species for commercial landings on the lake. One biologist estimates that before they were extensively exploited, they made up a half of the entire fish biomass of the lake's inshore waters.

Eels have long been sought after as food. Early accounts by the Jesuits published in *The Relations* describe individuals spearing a thousand eels in a night in the inland waters of central New York. Their oily flesh made them valued for smoking and salting, and eels were an important source of protein for First Nation peoples and for early settlers alike. Commercial landing statistics go back to the 1880s, but they were extensively fished long before that.

When Twink took her first cruise with me aboard *Ariel,* the eel population in Lake Ontario had started to crash. Counts of young eels climbing the fish ladder at the Moses Saunders Dam dropped from 25,000 a day in the 1970s to 230 a day in 2005. The dramatic hundredfold drop in Lake Ontario occurred even as a decline in eel numbers was being seen all up and down the east coast of the U.S. and in Europe.

What's really kind of scary about the eel population crash is that Lake Ontario has in the past contributed a significant portion of the species' total spawning stock. Nearly all the eels in the lake, as Ellen correctly told Twink, are large females. Perhaps a fifth to a third of the *entire* North American eel population's spawning stock comes from Lake Ontario. So if our eels are in trouble, everybody's eels are in trouble. The situation has gotten so dire, that there was a serious effort made recently by U.S. conservationists to list the American eel as endangered. Canada now considers it a "species of special concern". Interestingly, European eels, (considered a different species) are also declining in numbers as are the Pacific eels of Asia.

Surveys of the literature posted on the World Wide Web suggest, as is so often the case, it isn't just one thing that's causing the decline of the eels in

Lake Ontario and elsewhere. So it may not be all that easy to stop the losses. Certainly the power dams on the St. Lawrence bear some of the blame. An estimated forty percent of the large females that run down the river and pass through the turbine chambers are killed. Dams also block the young eels from migrating upstream to fresh waters. Though there are ladders for them in the St. Lawrence, many smaller dams on tributary streams and rivers that once supported eels have been recently re-activated to produce power and don't have fish ladders.

Along with the toll taken by dams, fishing has contributed to the declines. Over harvesting of the eel in Europe is pretty much well established as part of recent history. Numbers there have dropped 99 %, and a March 2007 *Toronto Globe and Mail* news article stated that illegally caught tiny glass eels were going for 1000 Euros a kilo. That would give the poor blue fin tuna in the Japanese sushi market a run for their money.

It's a bit hard to 'manage' the eel fishery given their offshore spawning and a general lack of information on them, but it's a good bet they've been overfished in much of North America, too. Some scientists even think global climate change is shifting ocean currents and changing near surface sea temperatures which is affecting their survival. And the eel is a long lived and oily fish, and so is quite vulnerable to accumulating oil soluble toxins like the PCB's which could well stress and weaken the fish making them more subject to disease and parasites. Toxins could also be passed on to the eggs impacting fertility.

What can be done? Cleaning up the environment and removing barriers like the dams might help, but don't count on it happening next week. The St. Lawrence River dams produce some of the cheapest power on the continent. They won't be dynamited anytime soon. Cutting fishing down would help. But even that's easier said than done because so many different countries and jurisdictions have eel fisheries. Working out agreements on harvest limits can take a long time. By then there might be no more eels left to manage. At least in Lake Ontario, Canada has shut down the commercial fishery and other groups are working together to manage eels in a more sustainable way.

When all else fails, the fishery folk are apt to try stocking. Sometimes it works. The current Great Lakes sport fishery is largely sustained by hatchery raised salmon. Ontario and Quebec have both tried planting young eels. It remains to be seen how successful this will be.

As of 2008, research was underway to try to determine if toxins are playing a role in the eel's Lake Ontario decline. Eels are long-lived and may stay in

Lake Ontario for twenty years or more before heading downstream This gives them lots of exposure to chemicals in the environment. A Queens University research project in Kingston was examining some toxin concentrations and their possible effect on eel fertility. If some streams were cleaner than others, it would make more sense to stock the young eels there. Other research on the eel's complex life may also shed light on what can be done to protect remaining eels.

One of the most challenging things about trying to help eels is that they integrate so many aspects of the environment during their wide ranging lives. Conditions in the open ocean, streams, pollution, physical barriers, degradation of lakes and ponds, even the harvest of Sargassum weed in the ocean (which might also be scooping up tens of thousands of tiny eels) could, and probably in some cases are, making life difficult for the hardy eel. Because they stitch together so many aspects of our globe's web of life, it's worth paying special attention to their world wide declines.

If something as tough and ubiquitous as an eel is now being considered a species at risk, I'd say we're getting a pretty clear message here. As Twink says, we might be next.

Endocrine Disruptors in the Great Lakes

Within the last ten years concern over the impact of very low amounts of man made chemicals in concentrations of a few parts per trillion on human and animal health has risen markedly. Back in 1996, Theo Colborne and others published a general interest book titled *Our Stolen Future*. The book promptly stirred up considerable (and continuing) controversy as chemical manufacturers disputed its conclusions and brought wider attention to an important area of study. Recent advances in analytical equipment now make it possible to detect amounts of chemicals far below what was possible 20 or 30 years ago, and has led to more understanding of the problem of so-called 'sub-lethal' effects of chemicals in our environment.

Dozens of man-made chemicals employed in various manufacturing processes including flame retardants used in construction materials and carpets, compounds used to soften plastic, and by- products and waste materials from plastic manufacture along with several heavy metals and a number of pharmaceutical drugs can scramble the subtle hormone balances and chemical interactions of the body's endocrine system. Like the pesticides of the 1960s and the PCBs that were banned in the 1970s, these things are ubiquitous and world wide and are carried by winds and ocean currents from pole to pole.

The endocrine system that they disrupt is made up of the various glands and hormone messengers that control growth, sexual development, the proper function of the immune system, and behavior. Its smooth function is essential to life and reproduction.

Cadmium, arsenic, lead, mercury, certain PCB's, dioxins and furans, and uranium can mimic the action of the female hormone estrogen. A number of pharmaceuticals including birth control products that affect estrogen levels, are also present in our water, having gotten there either through being excreted with human wastes or by improper disposal down the toilet. Some animals are very sensitive to very low levels of these compounds and metals. In lab studies, mice exposed to levels of uranium leached from mine tailings that were well below the government's standards for safe drinking water showed physical changes to their reproductive systems and evidence of abnormally early sexual maturity.

Studies of actual effects of endocrine disruptors on populations of animals in the wild are tricky. The doses are low, effects vary with the timing of exposure during animal development, and the potential for interaction with other chemicals in the environment is considerable. Different species of animals also react very differently. Some creatures are a hundred times more sensitive to a particular chemical than others. It's a bit like trying to tease out the effects of long term low levels of exposure to radiation from all the other things a person is exposed to during his or her life. It's difficult to do, so "smoking gun" proof of direct linkages is not easy to come by as the chemical and drug industries are quick to point out.

But there's plenty of evidence that real effects do exist. They range from hermaphroditic fish to reduced penis sizes in Florida alligators. Unfortunately for human health effects, hormone mimics seem to have the greatest impacts on creatures such as polar bears that, like people, feed higher on the food chain and so take in more chemicals. Despite industry claims to the contrary, there's more than enough evidence to prompt the International Joint Commission of the Great Lakes to state *"We do not know what all of the effects of human exposure will be over many years... For the Commission, however, there is sufficient evidence now to infer a real risk of serious impacts in humans. Increasingly, human data support this conclusion."*

On the shores of the St. Claire River near Sarnia, Ontario, the Aamjiwaang Indian reservation, beset with chemicals from a wide variety of nearby petrochemical manufacturing plants, has a population of children increasingly skewed towards female. Prior to the 1990s the small town of Chippewa residents had approximately 100 girls to every 105 boys, just like everyone else. But around 1993 the number of girls born began to increase. In 2006 the community was seeing two girl births for every boy born.

Other probable Great Lakes region impacts of hormone mimics and disruptors include enlarged thyroid glands among top level predator salmon and abnormal behavior observed among colonial nesting birds. Nesting terns and herring gulls have been seen engaging in odd pairing behaviors. In some cases two females paired up and tried to nest. Or male birds seemed to have taken up polygamy, as they were found hanging out with two females. In such pairings, one female was subordinate and had markedly less success at hatching or raising chicks. Researchers suggest this could be another example of skewed sex ratios with the birds trying to compensate by doubling up with the available males. A sampling of the birds showed testes of most males also contained ovarian tissue.

A few years ago, Great Lakes hatcheries began experiencing up to 90% losses of fry from something they called early mortality syndrome (EMS). Eventually EMS was traced to a thiamine (B vitamin) deficiency that researchers linked with an enzyme present in alewives, the main food of lake trout. A very similar problem also appeared in Scandinavian salmon hatcheries in the 1990s where they called it M74. As yet, no direct link between hormone mimics and early mortality syndrome has been made, but research continues with some attention being given to the possible role of chemicals and or thyroid dysfunction interacting with the diet of the trout to cause the deficiency. At least one study of brown trout in the Gulf of Bothnia off Finland suggested a possible linkage between "early mortality syndrome" and dioxin like compounds.

Synergistic effects where low levels of chemical pollution interact with naturally occurring pathogens are difficult to study. But there are indications from a number of studies that very small amounts of these substances can and do affect the immune system and other aspects of an animal's metabolism. In the 1990s lobsters started showing up in traps in Long Island Sound and southern New England with ulcerated shells. By 1996 30% of the population in the region has 'shell rot'. The rot is caused by a normally benign bacteria.

Recent research has found high levels of known estrogen mimics called alkylphenols in the affected lobsters. These compounds are used in the manufacture of paint, food cans, pipes, rubber, and plastic. Studies also showed considerable amounts of the chemicals in near shore ocean sediments. The suspicion is that the alkylphenols, by-products of manufacturing and the breakdown of synthetic materials, are entering the lobsters' world through waste treatment plants which are not set up to remove such chemicals. Perhaps by affecting the moulting cycle which is controlled by hormones and/or other lobster physiology, they promote the development of the harmful bacterial ulcers.

Lab studies of Caspian terns from the Great Lakes have shown reduced immune system responses in birds with higher levels of PCBs and dioxins in their bodies. Less contaminated terns were on average longer lived, suggesting disease could also be taking a toll on the birds from more polluted areas.

Downstream from the lakes in the lower St. Lawrence River remains a remnant population of beluga whales. The beluga whales feed on small fish and live in waters draining from the industrialized polluted heartland of North America. They also feed on eels that are moving downstream to the Sargasso. Eels from Lake Ontario contain high levels of PCBs. The whales show high rates of cancer and other diseases and disorders including thyroid lesions and evidence of weakened immune systems when compared to populations of whales in more remote arctic regions.

One begins to wonder if perhaps it is no coincidence that we now are seeing so many fish diseases becoming widespread in the lakes. Spring viremia of carp, vhsv, whirling disease, assorted parasites-- as with botulism outbreaks, it may well be that several things are working together here to cause the alarming increase in fish kills here in Lake Ontario.

For more information see the book *Our Stolen Future - Are We Threatening Our Fertility, Intelligence and Survival*? by Dr. Theo Colborn, Dr. John Peterson Myers and Dianne Dumanoski published in 1996.

Recent Botulism Outbreaks

Botulism, a substance produced by a common soil bacteria called *Clostridium botulina*, is an extremely deadly poison. It acts on the nervous system and causes paralysis and death. Humans typically die of suffocation. Fish eating birds like gulls or terns or ducks that are affected typically sit on the water or on shore with their heads flopped to one side. As they can't hold their heads up, they usually drown. Because of this, when it was first observed on lakes in the western U.S. about a century ago, the 'disease' was called limberneck.

We had a bad outbreak of this on Lake Ontario in 2006, an unusually wet rainy summer. While sailing, I noticed several terns and gulls during the summer floating on the water with the flopped over head of paralysis. Then that fall hundreds if not thousands of migrating loons died along the shore, also victims of the toxin.

There are a number of genetic variants or "strains" of *C. botulina.* The type A strain produces the toxin used for Botox cosmetic makeovers, though after reading about this stuff, I'll take wrinkles any day. These are also the bacteria that can kill people who don't process their home canned low acid foods like string beans or meat carefully. Pickled beets with plenty of vinegar for me! In the Great Lakes the outbreaks of poisoning have usually involved the type E strain of the bacteria, although the type C strain has also killed near shore ducks on the Great Lakes in the past.

The toxin is said to be the most lethal natural biological agent known to man. It's right up there with plutonium. If you could somehow distribute it evenly among all the victims, a single gram could kill a million people. It's 600 million times more toxic than sodium cyanide. One maggot containing the toxin producing bacteria in its gut can kill a duck. It does not seem to affect invertebrates such as zebra mussels, insect larvae, or freshwater scuds, however, all of which reside in the Great Lakes. These and other creatures have been found to contain the toxin. Many of these "carriers" are important foods for fish and birds and so can pass the poison on up the food chain.

Despite a few misguided efforts to employ *C. botulina* in germ warfare (The Japanese are said to have used it against China during World War II) and by terrorist groups to poison other humans with it, no waterborne outbreaks that have killed humans are known, though the bacteria can live in water for several days. The toxin is quickly broken down by heat, light, and chlorination, so treated drinking water won't contain bacteria or the toxin produced by them.

There have apparently been a few cases of humans being poisoned after eating smoked and or salted fish that contained type E bacteria and toxin and that had not been cooked at high enough temperatures to destroy the toxin. So anglers take note. Don't eat it if it acted sick. Fish eating birds who, alas, must eat their fish uncooked, can easily absorb a lethal dose of botulism toxin from their prey which can harbor the bacteria in its gut.

Unfortunately for fish eating birds, botulism outbreaks seem to be increasing not only in the Great Lakes, but also world wide. One recent major

North American outbreak is said to have destroyed 5 million ducks. On the Great Lakes, a very conservative estimate is that 75,000 birds have died since the first big outbreaks were recognized in 1999. The first lake to suffer from them was Lake Erie. In 2002 an estimated 25,000 fish eating birds died on Lake Erie alone. In 2006, the first big die off I saw, I counted dozens of loons along with grebes, mergansers, and other birds, in a short stretch of shoreline near Little Sodus Bay.

One of the unfortunate aspects of botulism poisoning is that it can kill a very great variety of animals. Over fifty different species of birds have been killed by outbreaks, and everything from turtles and mud puppies to sturgeon and bass are susceptible under the right conditions.

The *C. botulina* bacteria don't always produce the poison, and scientists are still unraveling the puzzle as to exactly what causes these deadly outbreaks. Botulism toxin production depends on the genetic strain of the bacteria, infection of the host bacteria of some strains by a virus called a phage, and environmental conditions including temperature, the type of food available to the bacteria, and salinity and pH. The bacteria can only grow where no oxygen is present, and they produce the toxin when they have access to a protein rich food source.

Dissolved oxygen levels are lower in warmer water, and decay organisms work faster then, so warmer conditions late in the summer are more likely to lead to botulism production. Many outbreaks have been observed on the Great Lakes in the summer and fall.

In research labs around the lakes there's considerable energy going into trying to figure out just what conditions trigger the terribly lethal conditions that have left our beaches littered with dead loons and other fish eating birds. One researcher I talked with said there is a strong and widespread suspicion that global warming and higher water temperatures may have a lot to do with it along with the zebra and quagga mussel. The mussels may have changed the lake in some way that now leads to more frequent outbreaks. The type E strain of Botulism bacteria has been present on the lakes and is known to have caused an outbreak of poisoning among birds back in 1966 on Lake Michigan when masses of rotting algae and dead alewives created conditions favorable to its production. But outbreaks now seem to be occurring almost every year on Lakes Michigan, Erie, and Ontario, hence the belief that something has changed in the Great Lakes environment.

The zebra mussel and its near relative, the deep water quagga mussel, may have physically altered the Great Lakes environment by their sheer numbers in some way. One hypothesis suggests that mussel beds create additional habitat for the bacteria that causes botulism. Mussels may also filter the bacteria out of the water and concentrate them and the toxin within their bodies. Then, when the mussels are eaten by fish such as the round goby, or a freshwater drum, the toxins are acquired by the fish. Poisoned dying fish swim erratically and probably make themselves obvious to and easy prey for a fish eater, so they may be selectively preyed on.

Zebra and quagga mussels also filter the lakes' water for food. Lab studies suggest that a single mussel can probably filter a liter a day, and there are now so many billions of these little shellfish that they are capable of filtering much of the lakes' total volumes in a relatively short time. The result is water far clearer than at any time in the recent past. On Lake Ontario I've seen the bottom over forty feet down from my boat, and recreational divers report visibilities of up to a hundred feet now. This clear water allows sunlight to penetrate more deeply. The near shore lake waters, unfortunately, also have a lot more fertilizing nutrients than they did two hundred years ago, so now more filamentous attached algae can grow at deeper levels than since the start of European settlement here. When the algae begins to die off later in the summer due to lower light levels, its decay creates ideal widespread anaerobic conditions, 'dead zones' if you will, necessary for botulism toxin production.

In 2006 we had an extremely wet and rainy summer so a lot of run off containing fertilizers made it into the lake that year. The next year was a lot drier, with less run off. That fall, the die off was far less severe. This seems to support the theory that excessive fertilizers from human activity, zebra mussel clarified water, lots of algae growth and its rotting equals botulism and lots of dead birds. One writer referred to it as the lakes' version of the dead zones now plaguing more and more areas of coastal saltwater.

There seems little hope for reducing or eliminating botulism in the lakes anytime soon. The bacteria are ubiquitous, found in soils and sediments almost everywhere. We've been trying to clean up excess phosphates and nitrates in the Great Lakes for forty years, but as the generous growth of filamentous algae along the shore of Lake Ontario each summer testifies, sewage, farm field, and lawn care fertilizers, and other so called non point sources are still damaging Great Lakes water quality especially near shore. In fact with the advent of factory farming that produces huge amounts of manure in small spaces, the problem might even be getting worse.

Botulism has been around for far longer than we have, and if it weren't for all the other stresses that we've piled on the Great Lakes birds and fish, they could possibly tolerate the periodic losses. Some of our more common water fowl and the hardy gulls may be able to withstand the impacts of this latest development. A few scavenger birds like the turkey vulture are even highly resistant to the toxin. But given the amount of habitat destruction by human action, competition from invasive exotic species, and now, the probable impact of land use change and climate change on the lakes, it is hard to be optimistic about the outlook for less common fish eaters like the loon or the graceful terns that have livened our skies for so long.

Viral Hemorrhagic Septicemia Virus (VHSV)

The first indication of more trouble ahead for Great Lakes fishes from a 'new' virus came in 2005 when a huge die off of fresh water drum described as being "several hundred tons" occurred in the Bay of Quinte. The fish kill was the first confirmed outbreak here of the viral disease known as VHSV (viral hemorrhagic septicemia virus). However, when archived samples of frozen muskellunge collected from Lake St. Clair in 2003 were analyzed, the virus showed up there as well. Viral hemorrhagic septicemia is deadly and highly contagious to fish but does not affect humans.

By 2006 the virus was known to have reached Lake Huron where it was found in Chinook salmon and whitefish. It's been reported from Lake Erie and Lake Michigan as well. As of late 2007, VHSV had also been reported from several inland locations in New York State. Ominously for our fish and for the large recreational fishing business on the lakes, estimated to generate 4 billion dollars in economic activity annually, the virus has been called the most serious and deadly viral disease yet found in hatchery raised freshwater rainbow trout in Europe. Many organizations consider it among the most important viral diseases of fish. Not all species of fish are equally vulnerable to the strain of virus in the Great Lakes, but some of our native species are quite sensitive.

Historically, the VHS virus was mostly seen in marine species of fish and in trout hatcheries in Europe, and it's not known how it first entered the Great Lakes. It's possible that it arrived in water or in a fish transported from salt water via a freighter's ballast tank. Some strains of the virus including the one in the Great Lakes can live for several weeks in cool water. In one study VHSV lasted a year. Some scientists think that VHSV was transported to the Pacific's fish populations via shipping. It's widely thought that it is mainly transmitted by fish movements including natural migrations or by some sort of transport of living fish by humans or other forces.

Genetic studies of the virus found in the Great Lakes suggest that the virus could have originally been a marine form found off the Atlantic Maritimes of Canada. If so, that lends a certain plausibility to the theory that it was introduced to the lakes via ballast water, since ships entering the lakes are supposed to do a ballast water "exchange" some distance offshore before entering the St. Lawrence. The ships pick up salt water on the theory that salt water organisms are less likely to pose a danger to the Great Lakes ecosystem. Perhaps the exchange also picked up a fish or some water containing VHSV. Researchers say we'll probably never know how it got into the Great Lakes. They also say we don't know for sure how it is spread from one fish to another, although an article posted on a website for the culture of ornamental koi fish states contact with urine and sexual fluids are one mode of transmission. The virus has also been found on the surface of eggs from infected fish. We do know it is quite contagious.

A wide variety of fish including some important recreational game fishes are vulnerable to the virus which causes internal bleeding. Organ failure and death often follows. Some dead fish appear normal and show no obvious signs of the disease. Some fish can survive the virus to act as carriers while themselves showing little signs of the disease. Most fish kills have occurred in the Great Lakes when the water was between 40 and 60 degrees. VHSV can travel to new populations of fish though exposure to an infected fish. If anglers dumped unused infected bait minnows in a pond or lake after a day of fishing, this could spread the virus. It's possible that it can also be spread by the water in boat live wells. These possible means of spreading it have prompted a major effort by fishery management people to educate anglers about the dangers of the disease.

Unfortunately, the yellow perch, a fish sought by both anglers and commercial netters, appears to be vulnerable as is its bigger cousin the walleye. The much sought after salmon and trout seem to be among the less susceptible fishes, but the muskellunge, a prized trophy species, is quite susceptible and appears to have been hard hit in the St. Lawrence.

Sick fish may swim in circles or hang listless just below the surface. Sometimes the fish look sick and may have reddish blotches or lesions on their skin or reddening in or around the eyes. But they also may appear normal to the casual observer. If it isn't already there as of this writing in early 2008, the disease is expected to spread throughout all the Great Lakes, including eventually Lake Superior.

To date, VHSV has been found only in wild fish populations in the Great Lakes. Because of its potential virulence to so many kinds of fish, the Federal Animal and Plant Health agency (APHIS) has issued a number of directives and guidelines aimed at keeping it out of fish farm and hatchery populations. In the past in the U.S. and in other countries, a number of fish diseases and sick fish that were moved around by anglers, hatcheries, and bait farm operations have helped spread new diseases to wild populations of fish, so this 'new' virus is of considerable concern to fishery managers who now are taking a number of precautions to test and monitor for it. There has also been considerable effort on the part of various state agencies concerned with fishery management directed at educating anglers about the dangers of spreading the disease through bait minnows, residual water in live wells, and other means. But nothing much can be done to stop its spread within wild populations as fish move about the lakes.

The outlook for the virus and our fish is uncertain. As Pearl suggests in her visit with Twink, about the best we can hope for is that the fish of Lake Ontario may eventually develop some resistance to the virus through exposure and subsequent survival. The VHS bug, like human flu, is a type of virus that mutates rapidly. One scientist wrote that "We have not yet seen any genetic diversity of many VHSV isolates from the Great Lakes Basin. [a possible indicator of it's relatively recently arrival here aboard a single ship] This is surprising..." Perhaps it will gradually become less deadly to its Great Lakes hosts through such mutations. But it may be a rough few years for the lake's fishes until that happens. We can hope it'll happen soon!

There are a number of websites with articles on alien species of plants and animals in the Lakes. One is located at GLIN's website
http://www.great-lakes.net/envt/flora-fauna/invasive/invasive.html

Another is the EPA labs site at:
http://www.epa.gov/glnpo/invasive/index.html

For more on VHS virus check the Wikipedia entry at:
http://en.wikipedia.org/wiki/Viral_hemorrhagic_septicemia

Waterfront Land and Swan Conflicts

When Twink has a run in with a mute swan at Kingston, she learns first hand the territoriality that some waterfront land owners feel towards their views and private beaches. And unfriendly territorial land owners are not unique to the Great Lakes. A Canadian cruiser observed in an email to a friend recently that there has been a 'creeping' sense of ownership of the water and/or the land under the water out in front of the cottagers' property on a number of smaller inland lakes. In Florida where many towns have placed restrictions on anchoring, a boat owner deliberately violated the municipal law in 2007 so he could take the matter to court and challenge it. He won his case, and the state of Florida subsequently strengthened legal protection of anchoring rights for cruisers. But the assault on freedom to navigate (and anchor out) continues.

There are several reasons for losses of navigational rights. One is a growing problem of abandoned derelict boats left at anchor or on moorings in places like California and Florida. They present a particular hazard to other boats and waterfront property during hurricanes, and waterfront home owners complain about junked boats ruining their view. Some waterfront owners even consider perfectly functional cruisers anchored for the night near their homes as being objectionable. With the rapid increase in waterfront home building in recent years, the conflicts are intensifying on fresh and salt water alike.

A general "gentrification" of working and commercial waterfronts is also adding to pressures on cruisers who anchor out and on the businesses that serve them. From Maine to Florida, commercial waterfront businesses such as boatyards and marinas are being taxed out of existence and their prime land converted to condos and other waterfront residential use. Many of the parks, convention halls, casinos, and other buildings and businesses taking over old decayed city waterfronts don't need water to operate or exist. They simply are taking advantage of the view or the general ambiance of being by the water.

Access conflicts are also intensifying for those non-boaters who would walk the shore. Once when the waterfront was commercial and most of the open beach and shoreline was wild, few land owners objected to a pedestrian's passage along the water's edge. But with the coming of condos and mansions that's begun to change. There's a long tradition going back to Roman law known as the public trust doctrine that seeks to protect access to the water and shore for navigation, commerce, and fishing for food. But protecting the beach for sun bathers and beach combers and others who seek pleasure or spiritual renewal by the water is a bit more problematic these days.

In my own state in a Hudson River shoreline dispute, The United States District Court for the Eastern District of New York found that the State of New York owns the land between the high and low water marks (the

196

"foreshore") unless specifically granted otherwise by the state. The court also found that waterfront property owners only have a right to "reasonable access" to the adjacent navigable waterway, reasonable access being defined on a case by case basis. Defining mean high water gets a bit tricky, but most people would agree that at least some portion of the beach would generally fall below it. I go by the terminal berm. I figure that's where the waves most recently reached so if I'm below it, I'm on public land. I haven't tested my definition on any angry home owners yet, but maybe it'll sound convincing when I do run into one.

But recently a county court ruled in favor of a group of Lake Erie waterfront land owners who claimed their rights extended to the water's edge. Other Great Lakes states like Michigan define the public shore as being to the ordinary high water mark. According to a fishing website, in Wisconsin the Ordinary High Water Mark (OHWM) is described as "the point on the bank or shore where the water is present often enough so that the lake or stream bed begins to look different from the upland. Specifically, the OHWM is the point on the bank or shore up to which the water, by its presence, wave action or flow, leaves a distinct mark on the shore or bank. The mark may be indicated by erosion, destruction of or change in vegetation or other easily recognizable characteristics."

It would seem then, that edge walkers be they human or feline, should in theory at least still have a right to walk the beach. But, as another website devoted to waterfront access notes, "laws are meaningless without someone to activate them."

Territorial Swans

Twinkle Toes' territorial nemesis the mute swan, a spectacular and showy bird, one of the largest and heaviest waterfowl on the lakes, is a breath taking sight as it flies past low over the water on singing wings. But it is also a conspicuous example of an invasive alien species that in many areas is causing damage and disruption to native wildlife. And the birds are every bit as pushy as the incident suggests. Twink and I really were assaulted by a swan in Toronto, and we are far from alone in our dislike of the big birds.

The adult mute can be distinguished at close range from our less common native Great Lakes swans by its orange bill. The mute swan first arrived in the U.S. as an ornamental bird stocked in New England and downstate estate ponds. Though most of those birds were valued and had their wings clipped, by 1912 a few had escaped and gone native along the lower Hudson and on Long Island.

They have since thrived and multiplied there and on the Chesapeake where from a population of 5 in 1961 there are now 4000 birds in one area alone. Their population in the Northeast and on the Great Lakes has been increasing at up to 20% or more a year. Twenty years ago, they were rare on the U.S. side of Lake Ontario. Now every bay has at least one pair, and in 2006 there were over a hundred on Irondequoit Bay alone.

The mute swan is big and aggressive and so can push aside any native waterfowl in its way. They tend a territory up to 15 acres in size and sometimes are so aggressive as to prevent any other marsh birds such as the beleaguered black tern or so called common loon from breeding within that territory. They have been known to kill Canada geese and herons, and as noted in part one, they also won't hesitate to attack a human in a dinghy that has a cat aboard. Near my home port there 's a swan on Sodus Bay who particularly despises (and attacks) personal water craft aka Sea-doos and the like. Swans typically will try to drown the intruder who has entered their territory. A video posted on You Tube shows a swan doing its best to pull a woman into the water by hauling on her long dress presumably with drowning her in mind. I have read of a close escape by an older woman in Europe who was knocked down by a swan, and of a swan attack that capsized a canoe and caused a human death. The British used to eat swans. Maybe we should encourage the practice here, as with few natural predators, the birds are increasing rapidly in number on the Great Lakes.

Swans are also viewed as harmful to the lake's near shore ecology because of their destruction of aquatic rooted vegetation. Though to some swimmers and boaters, like myself, rooted aquatic weeds are a nuisance and a bother, these plants are an essential part of the ecosystem. They provide food for many native waterfowl and also play a key role in the shallow water environment. Dozens, if not hundreds, of different small invertebrates and aquatic insect larvae depend on weeds and in turn serve as fish food. Some fish need vegetation in order to reproduce, and other fish use weeds for food or cover both as juveniles and adults.

Swans pull up six to eight pounds of weeds a day to eat. As they forage, they rip up an additional amount of vegetation, up to three times what they eat. A busy flock of swans can have a large impact on weed beds, water clarity, and other parts of the food web.

When the weeds disappear, the water becomes more turbid. Frequently more blooms of toxic blue green algae and less food and cover for fish occur and there is less food for other animals ranging from tree swallows to moose. So called weeds also help prevent erosion of banks by damping wave action and by helping hold the substrate together. As populations of fish decline, so does angler interest and activity and for resort areas such as my homeport of Fair Haven, NY, this would not be a welcome side effect of swan residency. I once lived on the northern Chesapeake on a small bay that was filled with permanently muddy turbid brown water. An old timer told me that before the property owners went after the weeds with herbicides in the 1960s, the water had been clear and the blue crab population far higher than at the time I lived there.

Mute swans are, without doubt, charismatic and beautiful. Their public image has made them popular and has complicated efforts to control their populations. Unfortunately, they are also extremely aggressive. You need to be a pushy aggressive bird to live in a human dominated world, but the other Great Lakes natives who already have plenty of problems with habitat loss, toxic fish, and chemical pollution, don't need one more source of stress from mute swans.

Farley Mowat Canadian Conservationist and Author

Farley Mowat was born by the waters of the Bay of Quinte in Belleville in 1921, and according to one Internet website, has published 38 books and made his living as a writer since 1949 (no easy task!) The *Wikipedia* website states his books have been published in 52 languages and have sold over 14 million copies and quotes him as saying that in his writing "my chief concern is that of men and other animals living under conditions of natural adversity." He has written of northern First Nation and Inuit peoples and of native Siberians and ancient Viking explorers. He has also written of seafarers and salvage tug men, war (he was a young army officer in Italy in World War II in Italy), and he has written of man's war on nature in several books, among them the heavily researched (and extremely depressing!) *Sea of Slaughter.*

His best selling *Never Cry Wolf* was made into a popular movie and his humorous *The Boat Who Wouldn't Float* is required reading for the owners of elderly wooden Canadian built schooners. Mowat's writing, as Harry tells Twink, did indeed help inspire the founder of Sea Shepherd. Mowat served as an honorary chair of the Sea Shepherd Society which named one of their ships after him. He has never been shy about stirring up a bit of controversy. It is, after all, a good way to help sell books, and during the Reagan years he was denied entry into the U.S. for a speaking engagement because of it. One Internet article states that his books "either inspire admiration or anger". He has lived in Port Hope, the little Lake Ontario shoreline city with the mildly radioactive harbor near Cobourg, for many years.

His father Angus, described by one reviewer as being a soldier, sailor, bee keeper, and librarian (and also an army vet --of WWI), wrote several novels. Never as widely read as his son, he nonetheless enjoyed mild success with them. Two of his novels *Then I'll Look Up* and *The Carrying Place* have Lake Ontario settings. I enjoyed the first because of its realistic rendering of the days of commercial sail and schoonermen on Lake Ontario. Angus Mowat lived on Lake Ontario's shores for many years and enjoyed cruising the Bay of Quinte in his old age. I've been told his last little yacht is the Mackinaw boat now on display at the Kingston Maritime Museum. His son acquired a taste for sailing in part aboard the family yacht *Scotch Bonnet* sailing on Lake Ontario. Later Farley moved to the Maritimes where he acquired a Newfoundland built schooner not unlike *Sara B*. He has written a number of books for younger readers.

Although Skipper Sue has read many of Mowat's books, she never did meet up with him.

For more reading:
Born Naked, is a memoir that tells a bit about Mowat's younger days on the Bay of Quinte and elsewhere where he explored the world of nature.

Also a must read is his book about Mutt, the dog he spent those years with- *The Dog Who Wouldn't Be*
Both are described as being 'young adult' books but the stories appeal to readers of all ages.

Aliens Among Us

Illegal aliens both afloat and ashore were a hot topic at the time of this writing in early 2008. The ones that Richard got all steamed up about didn't come from Mexico or Central America with fake ID cards, but, like the human immigrants, they are stirring up plenty of animosity as they pursue their own survival in our neighborhood. Many ecologists now rank invasive species as second only to habitat destruction as a threat to local plants and animals.

200

There are presently more than 180 known non native plants and animals living in the Great Lakes system with new ones showing up about every six months or so. Some of them go on to become very successful, growing like weeds and crowding out native species. Almost as soon as the Europeans arrived, they began modifying the Great Lakes environment. As they did so, they made it harder for the natives to survive, and the altered lakes and their watersheds became more hospitable to nonnative plants and animals. Some of the newcomers like the zebra mussel also physically changed the lakes, making them even more vulnerable to further invasions.

Alien species got into the lakes in a variety of ways. Some, like the sea lamprey, have followed man-made channels and canals. Some were deliberately or accidentally planted by people who dumped bait buckets or who thought they could 'improve' their favorite fishing hole by adding a new fish. And a lot of them hitched a ride on or inside a ship or boat.

Today the Great Lakes are among the most modified large ecosystems anywhere in the world. Like the road shoulder on a summer day, they're a weedy mix of exotics and plantings by humans with a handful of natives hanging on. In many instances the natives are being increasingly marginalized by the pushy newcomers. A number of Great Lakes natives are now extinct, the blue pike, several of the ciscoes, and a number of native clam and mussel species among them.

Lake Ontario and the rest of the lakes were especially vulnerable to change because as ecosystems go, they were not particularly resilient or robust even before European settlement. After the glacier retreated, the lakes assumed their present form and their compliment of assorted animals and plants just 6000 years ago. That's a long time by human history's measure, but very brief indeed by nature's clock. Such recently created ecosystems tend to be less complex and so less resistant to change than communities that have evolved together for many hundreds of thousands of years.

The rapid and intensive exploitation of the lakes' fishes by humans followed by a population explosion of the sea lamprey in the upper lakes made short work of the open water fish community made up of lake trout, whitefish, and the various lake herrings and ciscoes. Then a succession of accidental and intentional introductions of exotic prey and predator fish assured a permanent transformation of that same community. Some sources say the sea lamprey was an invader that arrived here via the Erie Canal. Others claim that, like the Atlantic salmon, it was left in Lake Ontario from a time when the lake's basin was filled with sea water.

Whatever the story, there's no doubt that the sea lamprey used the Welland Canal to become an alien invader in the upper lakes, and its impact there was swift and devastating. Commercial and recreational fisheries worth millions of dollars were wrecked in a few years time as sea lampreys killed off the remaining large trout and other sport fish.

Smelt and alewife, either intentionally or accidentally introduced by humans, moved in to the various lakes to fill ecological niches or "jobs" that had been vacated by over fished native chubs, ciscoes, and bloaters. Besides directly competing with native planktivores, the alewife in particular also eat the eggs and larvae of the native open water fishes. The newcomers did their best to fill the vacancies they found waiting in the various lakes' depths. By the 1950s when I was exploring the shoreline as a child, the lower lakes were awash in alewives, and smelt runs abounded in Lake Ontario streams. The lamprey, along with over-fishing, had pretty well eliminated the lake's top level predator fishes.

Sea lamprey control began in the 1960s using a species selective chemical in the streams where lamprey larvae live for a number of years before transforming into parasitic adults. Then fishery managers stocked the lakes with several species of fast growing west coast salmon. The hungry salmon gobbled up the excess of alewives and created a trophy fishery that quickly became immensely popular. Sportsmen journeyed from Pennsylvania, New Jersey, and Massachusetts to fish Lake Ontario for forty pound "kings". A veritable fleet of small charter boats and weekend captains came into being to serve them, and the sport fishery generated millions of dollars of economic activity each year on Lake Ontario alone.

Ironically, the anglers were pursuing fish officially deemed by both U.S. and Canadian authorities to be contaminated and unfit for consumption by children or pregnant women. But that didn't seem to discourage anyone very much. And it did seem for a time that things were improving. Even the contaminants in the lakes dropped, though after about 1980 the rate of decline seemed to slow or level off and recently some contaminants in some fish species appear to be increasing again. Some of the fish consumption advisories for certain types and sizes of fish have also been relaxed, though many remain in place.

But the invaders kept coming.

And the pace of invasions picked up markedly after the Seaway System opened in 1959. Ironically, as the major ports in Europe, like the U.S., began cleaning up the worst of their pollution, more animals could now survive in the cleaner harbors to be taken in with the ship ballast water. A number of creatures ranging from cholera bacteria to gobies have been accidentally introduced into the Great Lakes through the dumping of ship ballast, a practice that increased after the Seaway opened. As more larger ships moved through the system more quickly, more critters survived the trip inside the ballast tanks. Before long dozens of strange plankton and larger creatures were being discovered in the lakes. Some ecologists suspect the newcomers are also now finding it easier to establish in the lakes. As a general rule, new immigrant "weeds" do best in recently disturbed ecological systems with many "vacancies" in their web of life. You'll see, for example, new plants growing along a hedgerow or a driveway before they make their way into the less disturbed forest. By the 1950s the Great Lakes were a deeply disturbed ecosystem, having lost a number of native species. They were ripe for invasion, and the newcomers were more able to establish a foothold here.

The zebra mussel and its deep water relative the quagga, were first noticed in 1988 near Detroit. They quickly engineered a huge shift in the Great Lakes' food webs and energy flows, moving energy from the open lakes to their bottoms. We still don't fully understand the ultimate impact of this on the lake's open water fishes. Zebra mussels may also have contributed to the increase in botulism outbreaks in the Great Lakes and are suspected of causing the sharp declines in the population of lesser scaup, ducks that over winter on Lake Ontario in large numbers to feed on zebra mussels. It's believed that the filter feeding mussels concentrate selenium, a by-product of coal burning and foundry operations. Possibly the ducks accumulate enough selenium from their food to impair their reproduction. Populations of lesser scaup in North America have dropped up to 50% over the last decade or so.

The filter feeding zebra mussel has had lake wide impacts on the one celled floating algae that make up the base of the food chain. Research suggests that some algae types, like the toxic blue greens, may have increased in abundance since the mussels' arrival. The zebra mussel and its close relative the quagga are also prime suspects in the basin wide population crash of a small bottom dwelling shrimp-like amphipod called *Diporeia,* a key food item for the lake's offshore fishes.

Because of its huge impacts on the Great Lakes, the zebra mussel has been described as the 'poster child' for the general problem of invasive species in an increasingly globalized world. A U.S. Geological Survey website credits the little shellfish with helping kick off a new field of ecological study "invasion biology". Before its arrival in the Great Lakes, most of our study of exotics and aliens was concentrated on agricultural pests and diseases.

Diporeia is (was?) a vital link in the Great Lakes food chain serving as high quality fat rich food for small bottom dwellers like the sculpin and for young whitefish and lake trout. It was once extremely abundant. Up to 20,000 animals per square meter formerly lived in the lake depths. The zebra mussel with its hard shell, is a less nutritious substitute as fish food. The feeling among researchers is that *Diporeia's* decline is a profound and serious loss that will impact the entire Great Lakes' ecosystem. (see page 208 for more on *Diporeia's* decline.)

Around the time the zebra mussel showed up, two small fish also arrived in the lakes via ballast water, the round goby and the ruffe. The goby has spread with incredible speed through Lake Ontario since first being sighted here in 1995. In 2006 I saw my first one in the shallows on the south shore. The following spring virtually every large rock in the shallows by my canoe launch site had a goby sitting on it. The voracious and aggressive little goby gobbles up the eggs of a number of other inshore fishes and like the mute swan, chases less pushy natives out of prime habitat. The goby has the potential to seriously re-arrange the inshore fish community. Perhaps even the hardy bowfin and bullhead will have trouble competing with it. Gobies feed offshore, too, down to 300 feet or more, and are able to feed in complete darkness thanks to a special lateral line adaptation which makes them extremely effective competitors with other bottom feeders. And if they survive the goby, our native fishes have the silver and big head carp to contend with. These two fish have virtually re-made the Mississippi into a carp pond. Now they are knocking at Lake Michigan's back door via the Chicago River with only one man made barrier between them and us. (see page 206 for more on carp)

The effects of the zebra and quagga mussel invasion continue to ripple through the system twenty years later. Some have even questioned if we can afford to continue operating the St. Lawrence Seaway.

A study by professor John Taylor of Grand Valley State University in Michigan made news a couple years ago when Dr. Taylor asserted that the St. Lawrence Seaway only saves about 55 million dollars a year in transportation costs, while the cost of clearing water intakes of zebra mussels alone runs 200 million a year. Although some have questioned his methodology, the study has considerable credibility. Since the 1970s as containerized shipping took hold, freighters have grown too big for the Welland and St. Lawrence locks, and use of the Seaway by salt water ships has declined. Today much of the Great Lakes ship traffic moves within or between the lakes. Only about 7 % comes from over seas. But that small percentage of tonnage has had a huge biological impact.

In 2004 the Seaway handled less than 4% of the grain exported from the U.S. Some of the reason Seaway traffic has declined has to do with shifting trade patterns. Previously grain sales to Europe were more important to the Midwest. Now much of our grain goes to Asia and there's no reason to send it out the Seaway. Instead it goes by rail to the west coast ports.

Part of the interest in the Taylor study probably comes from a looming repair bill for the Seaway's locks. Within the next few years, the Seaway will need extensive and costly refurbishing if it is to remain efficient and competitive. The St. Lawrence locks were designed to last about 50 years. They began operating in 1959. A few people are now beginning to challenge the idea that it's worth the cost to refurbish and then operate the Seaway if it continues to bring destructive biological invaders into the lakes. One proposal being kicked around is to return to the more regional nature of pre-Seaway shipping which would reduce the pace of the illegal immigration here. In this scheme, the shipping would mostly be within and between the lakes. Cargoes coming from over seas might be transhipped at Montreal as they historically were before the Seaway. Though it would add to transportation costs of goods, it might reduce the constant introduction of new exotic animals and plants which are now devastating the Great Lakes ecosystems while still allowing the growth of "short haul" shipping as an alternative to more energy intensive trucks and roads.

In late spring 2007 I began seeing unusual numbers of dead fish of many different species floating in the open lake shortly after my sailing season began. That's about six months after a devastating new fish disease called viral hemorrhagic septicemia, VHSV for short, began making news. Though its route of entry into Lake Ontario isn't certain, ship ballast is a suspect. (see page 193 for more on VHS virus)

There are some people with a lot more knowledge of what's happening in the Great Lakes today than I've got, who think we are perhaps approaching a 'tipping point" or what some have called an impending ecosystem collapse here. This is a hypothesized state of stress at which the Great Lakes' web of life really starts to seriously unravel. After last summer's fish kills and the ongoing mortality of fish-eating birds as seen on the beach near my house this fall, I wonder if they might be right.Will Lake Ontario and the other lakes end up much like our road shoulders? Will both be communities filled with tough adaptable hardy 'weeds' a lot of which aren't going to be real attractive to sportsmen or very tasty to eat? Possibly. But they will be survivors out there, able to co-exist with humans. Time will tell.

Carp And Carp Diseases

The "Chinese" carp that Richard rants about, first showed up in the Mississippi River in the 1980s after flooding washed them out of catfish ponds. The fish farmers had put several species of Asian carp in their ponds in the south to clean up algae. Once the carp got into the river, they exploded in number. They also began moving north up the river towards Chicago and Lake Michigan

Two species of special concern to Great Lakes fishery folk are the silver and the closely related big head carp. The big head grows to 80 to 100 pounds, the silver to 40 pounds. Both are so fast growing that within a year they're too big for almost anything else to eat them. And they feed very low on the food chain so they under cut most of the lakes' native fishes. The silver and big head probably compete with zebra mussels to some extent as, like the mussels, they feed on tiny planktonic plants. The carp can also shift to zooplankton. Either way, they would divert energy away from the Great Lakes' native food web, or what's left of it anyway. They also would compete directly with virtually all our larval and juvenile native fishes at least in inshore waters.

The silver carp has generated a lot of media coverage for being a 'flying fish' of sorts. When startled by a fast moving motor boat or Jet Ski watercraft, it jumps high into the air and a number of boaters have been injured by being smacked in the face by a twenty pound carp. One source says they can jump ten feet up. A government document on the carp invasion notes that "Water skiing on the Missouri River is now exceedingly dangerous..."

A lot of fishery folks figure if (when) these two carp species enter the lakes, they will completely take over as dominant fish as they have in the Mississippi. There are now stretches of that river where 90 % of the total fish biomass is made up of silver and big head carp.

Some people might observe that since these are important food fish in China, maybe having a lake full of carp is not such a bad thing. Maybe we'll have a commercial fishery again. But if we end up with just carp and nothing else, as many fear we will, we'll also have an even more simplified system than we have now. And simple ecosystems are prone to extreme instability and crashes. If the carp took over the warm inshore waters of the Great Lakes to the extent that they have overrun the Mississippi, a virus like VHS or spring

206

viremia could perhaps wipe out much of the lake's fish life in a season.

The present Great Lakes sport fishery is said to annually bring in 4 to 4.5 billion dollars to the region. It's doubtful that people would be as willing to spend hundreds of dollars to catch carp. They might support a commercial fishery, but as a fisherman selling them to a freezer plant on the Mississippi suggested, we might need to call them something like Rochester whitefish or Oswego Sole first.

Right now an electric weir is keeping them out of the south end of Lake Michigan. At least as long as the juice stays on. (The Chicago Sanitary canal connects Lake Michigan to the Mississippi drainage.) It seems inevitable that sooner or later the big head and silver carp will find their way in to the lakes. They have already popped up in isolated ponds, having gotten there by way of bait buckets. Juvenile Asian carp look like bait minnows, and anglers sometimes dump their bait in the water after they quit fishing. According to a U.S. Geological Survey website a big head carp has been taken off Cedar Point in Lake Erie.

A few years ago I saw live big head carp for sale in a store Toronto's Chinatown (though a fisheries website states that their sale as live fish is now prohibited in Canada). And there's been at least one report of a big head carp found in a Toronto fountain. Some folks like to let fish go. I guess it's a good luck good karma thing kind of like letting white doves or plastic balloons fly away. But if a pair of them get into one of the lakes, it won't be good karma for the rest of the surviving natives there.

Spring Viremia of Carp

The virus disease called spring viremia was first recognized and described in Europe in 1971. It first appeared in the U.S. In 2002 in a koi hatchery in North Carolina but not before a lot of the infected ornamental koi carp had been shipped all over taking the virus with them. The virus was probably in Lake Michigan by 2003.

Like VHSV, also a viral disease, viremia is highly contagious and also is most often seen at water temperatures below 18 degrees C (about 65 degrees F). In cooler water, carp are more vulnerable to disease as they are stressed by the cold. Spawning carp are also vulnerable to the disease as they are stressed by both the changes in water temperature and by the energy demands of spawning. It hits juvenile fish especially hard with up to 70% mortality, and also attacks the silver and big head carp. In 2006 Canadian researchers

207

confirmed the the virus was present in Hamilton harbor's carp.

Another large die off of carp occurred in late spring 2007 on Lake Scugog an hour's drive north of Toronto that may have been viremia. We first started noticing unusual numbers of dead carp lying around when we visited Main Duck's carp paradise up by the lighthouse around 2006. Perhaps they, too, were impacted?

In spring 2007 the virus was detected in carp in the upper Mississippi River, after a carp die off prompted a federal Fish and Wildlife Service investigation. Maybe the virus will help keep the big head and silver populations in check there?

Disappearing *Diporeia*

The sudden disappearance of the deep water shrimp-like amphipod *Diporeia* has been called one of the most dramatic and enigmatic changes to occur within the Great Lakes biological community of the last few decades. The collapse of this key part of the Great Lakes food web was first noticed in southwestern Lake Ontario in 1992. Since then populations have declined in all the other lakes except for Superior where recent studies suggest numbers are variable but with no clear trend.

The little brown 'scud' or side swimmer that you may see if you pull up some water weeds from the shallows and swish them around in a tray, is similar to the related deep water amphipods called *Diporeia*. These small crustaceans live on or just below the surface of soft ooze and sediment in the dark cold depths of all the lakes. They feed on one-celled algae and bacteria that settle to the bottom and often burrow through the mud to find food. A lot of their food is provided by the annual spring "bloom" of tiny floating plants called diatoms. After the diatoms eventually sink to the bottom, they are recycled by bacteria, protozoa, and the deep water amphipods. Diatoms are a particularly nutritious and fat rich food source for *Diporeia*.

The little animals are about a half-inch long as adults and are themselves a high quality food for fish as up to 30% percent of their body weight may consist of fats. Historically, they were extremely abundant and were a vital part in the food web, linking small fish in the lake's depths with the production of food at its surface. Up to 70% of the biomass at the bottom of the lakes was estimated to consist of these amphipods.

The commercially important lake whitefish depended heavily on deep water amphipods for food. *Diporeia* was also eaten by alewives and to a lesser extent by smelt which, in turn, are the main food for other larger fish including the trophy salmon and trout in the lakes. So its loss means a loss of food for the sport fishes of the open lake. The deep water quagga mussel (a close relative of the zebra mussel) has replaced the amphipods in many areas and is a far less nutritious food for fishes with its indigestible shells and lesser fat content. Even the hardy little round goby, a known mussel eater, seems to prefer mysid shrimps and other foods to mussels if it can catch them.

In places where *Diporeia* has crashed, fish populations have shown stress, weight loss, and population declines. Since *Diporeia's* decline, the alewife, so important to the open water salmonid fishery as a bait fish, is apparently even more scrawny than it was previously. In one study that measured the calories present in alewives, researchers estimated that Chinook salmon would have to swim after and catch 22% more alewives to gain the same weight as they had before the amphipod's disappearance. In Lake Ontario, a drop in the number of young bottom feeding lake trout may be linked to the decline of their food. And in Lake Erie, smelt stocks that once supported one of the last commercial fisheries on the lake have dropped, probably at least in part because of the vanishing amphipods.

Diporeia populations first began plummeting throughout the lower lakes in the early 1990s just about the time the zebra mussel and its deepwater relative the quagga mussel were becoming abundant. Never abundant in Lake Erie's shallows, they're now nonexistent in samples. At one site that had been monitored in Lake Ontario for many years, their numbers which had averaged around 8000 per square meter for the preceding ten years dropped to a few hundred per meter in just two years. Many researchers believe there is a connection between the mussels' arrival and *Diporeia's* disappearance, yet the amphipods have managed to survive and apparently co-exist with mussels in some places such as Cayuga Lake. At least so far.

At the time of this writing, nobody seemed to know for certain why Great Lakes *Diporeia* populations have crashed. Theories range from direct competition from zebra and quagga mussels to UV impacts on the nutritional value of the algae they eat. A common theory, at least initially, was that the mussels were filtering out the small one celled algae that the amphipods had relied upon. If this were true, it should be possible to see some indication of starvation among the amphipods. However, when studies looked at their fat content and the number of eggs produced by *Diporeia* sampled from an area in Lake Michigan where they were declining, no obvious evidence of food stress was seen. Periodic sampling from this location did show that few newly hatched *Diporeia* were surviving to become adults. The animals slowly disappeared from the site over three to four years. Maybe the fast growing young weren't able to find enough to eat, but it seemed odd that the adults sampled showed no apparent food related stresses.

One theory suggests perhaps the mussels produce a waste product that damages the viability of the amphipods in some way. Lab studies have shown lower survival of individual *Diporeia* when they were exposed to mussels or to material that the mussels have been attached to. Yet both these bottom dwellers seem to be co-existing in several of the Finger Lakes.

Perhaps a synergistic interaction of factors has caused the population drop. *Diporeia* are known to be sensitive to a number of toxic chemicals present in Great Lakes sediments. These might make them more vulnerable to parasites or disease or otherwise make them less able to compete with the invading mussels.

However, some studies also have shown declines in some areas of other bottom dwelling animals such as midge larvae, worms and small fingernail clams in some parts of the lakes. Possibly the declines coincide with massive increase in the mussel populations or a build up of a pollutant. Something is going on out there. We may never know what has changed in those mysterious dark depths. But the profundal zone of the lower Great Lakes has changed profoundly.

Yet amidst the gloomy depths of Lake Ontario a glimmer of hope remains. Recent surveys along the lake's southern shore have hinted that the quagga mussel has not been increasing in number as rapidly as previously. A survey made in 2006 even documented declines in quagga mussel numbers at some sampling stations. When an alien species enters a new and favorable environment it frequently explodes in abundance. Its population peaks and then often drops to a lower more stable level leaving a bit of room for the natives it displaced. Though it's a little early yet to say for sure, it may be that this will occur here with the invading zebra and quagga mussels. It's doubtful that the exotic mussels ever vanish, but perhaps possibly there will remain a few deep areas of the Great Lakes where pockets of the native amphipods will be able to persist. Then if the opportunity ever arose, they might someday be able to repopulate at least some portions of the Lakes deeper areas.

Read more here:
http://www.epa.gov/solec/sogl2007/0123_Diporeia.pdf
an excerpt from the 2007 State Of The Lakes (SOLEC) report on line.

Ship Ballast

While Richard's rant about invaders correctly describes the route of entry for the zebra mussel, since that arrival, new regulations have been put in place to reduce (though not yet completely eliminate) the number of unwanted aliens arriving in Lake Ontario.

Ships have been carrying unwanted passengers around the world for thousands of years. Rats, cockroaches, and countless weed seeds are a few examples from past centuries of ship borne invaders. In the last few decades ship ballast water discharges have spread hundreds of creatures around the world. Salps, crabs, flounders, and bacteria are finding new homes and causing big problems for natives of coastal waters. It's estimated about ten billion tons of ballast water are shifted around the globe each year. Small jelly fish called ctenophores from the Chesapeake are now disrupting food webs and devastating fisheries in the Caspian Sea, the home land of the zebra mussel, even as the Great Lakes have been devastated by invaders from various locations. Over 140 creatures have traveled here in ship ballast tanks and established populations. These creatures have hit the already stressed ecosystems of the lakes hard. The zebra mussel alone, is estimated to cost the nation's economy 5 billion dollars a year, a figure I suspect is quite conservative when all the indirect effects like botulism in the Great Lakes are considered.

Because the ecological communities of coastal salt water and inland freshwater alike have been so devastated by creatures dumped with ballast water and because human pathogens like cholera have showed up in U.S. waters thanks to ship ballast, the marine transport business and its regulators have taken steps to reduce the transfer of plants, animals and bacteria. Ships now exchange water well offshore before entering the lakes or when feasible, they sail with no ballast on board as "nobobs".

It is no simple task, however. Ballast exchanges take time and cost shippers money. They can cause stresses on the ship's hull if not done properly, and even the residue of sludge in the tanks can amount to several tons and may contain bacteria and other organisms. So shippers are working hard to develop and install technology to treat ballast water and tanks to sanitize them.

Ship owners are also trying to develop more efficient ways to exchange and flush the water used for ballast. An international law mandates that all ships install a treatment system by 2016, while legislation in Congress is pushing for a 2013 implementation date. However, the chemicals like chlorine used in some of these systems can also be damaging to life in the lakes as well as to the ship's steel tanks, so UV light, filters, and other measures are being researched and tested. One cruise ship line has been using a Norwegian made combination filter and UV light treatment system for a number of years with good results.

The problem of ballast water invaders has been so severe it has even been suggested a total embargo on all ballast water be declared for the Great Lakes. Under this plan, salt water cargoes would be transferred to lake based ships at Montreal. However, this measure would not be of any help to salt water communities facing marine invaders. Stay tuned as to how quickly (if at all) innovation, technology and sensible regulation can fix this problem.

Community Builders

Though there is a great deal of bad news out there, as Sid and Pearl tell Twink, there are also brave-hearted people all over the world trying to move our society towards a more sustainable level of activity. Some of them like Canada's David Suzuki and Farley Mowat and former U.S. Politician Al Gore are well known and have written books that have been read widely. Others are less well known but no less dedicated. Since this is Skipper Sue's notebook it's probably not a coincidence that she decided to write about a couple of female environmental activists.

There is a profound connection between our human health and our society's well being and that of our environment--something the women (and men) mentioned here know intuitively and scientifically. The breakdown of the environment all too often leads to a breakdown of society. Take Somalia for example. Off the Somalia coast where piracy has flourished for ten years or more, the past overfishing by large ships from distant countries along with illegal dumping of toxic wastes largely stripped the native coastal fishermen of their livelihood. Some of them turned to piracy, and the lure of easy ransom money soon recruited more impoverished and bitter young men. And the encroaching desert (thought to be a result of climate change), that led to conflicts among Somalia's nomads and farmers, then caused the disintegration of the country's government and subsequent raids by foreign ships on the inshore tuna stocks.

Rosalie Bertell, originally from Buffalo, is now a Gray Nun of the sacred heart who lives on the shore of Lake Ontario. She holds a PhD in biometrics and has studied environmental epidemiology for forty years. She has worked to protect people from industrial and military chemical and radiological pollutants and currently works with a Toronto nonprofit group called the International Institute of Concern for Public Health. For decades she has tried to point out to politicians and the powerful men running big corporations the connection between our own health and that of our planet's ecosystem.

Bertell's transformation from researcher and math professor to activist began in earnest when she helped a small group of women get a moratorium on the construction of a nuclear plant in Niagara County next to farms raising food for a baby food factory. Her employer, the Roswell Park Cancer Institute, let her know in no uncertain terms that lobbying against the nuclear industry that was supplying much of their research money was inappropriate behavior. So she quit. After a year long retreat, she emerged from a monastery determined to defend the earth and its less powerful people through activism and science. She has been recognized as an expert of international reputation in the study of low levels of radiation and impacts on human health.

In 1984 a chemical plant in India began to leak a poisonous gas that killed an unknown number of people. At least another 100,000 were to develop cancer, suffer miscarriages, become blind, and suffer from other health problems. Bertell directed the international commission that investigated the disaster. About that time she also founded the International Institute of Concern for Public Health. She worked on behalf of the people living near Chernobyl whose land and food and water were contaminated, and she worked for justice for the people of the Pacific islands who had been damaged by open air testing of nuclear bombs.

As the years went by, Bertell became increasingly disillusioned about the military's role in the destruction of our environment. In a 1986 radio show talk she spoke of military might and the rule of militarism concluding ..." we are capable of running the world on a different basis than that. It has happened before in history that we have turned aside from behaviors and it can happen again. And it *will* happen again."

In her most recent book published in 2001 *Planet Earth:The Latest Weapon Of War,* a Critical Study into the Military and the Environment, she wrote of our beautiful planet "It deserves our best efforts. Enjoy it, love it, and save it."

The International Institute of Concern for Public Health website is at www.iichp.org

Paul Watson was born in Toronto and lived by Lake Ontario until he was six years old when his family moved to the New Brunswick coast where he then resided until 1964. After his father died, he ended up back in Toronto for a few years before the call of the sea led him to join the Canadian Coast Guard. He also worked aboard Norwegian, British and Swedish freighters.

He helped start Greenpeace in 1969 and was involved in that group's protests of nuclear bomb testing in the Aleutian islands. He was also involved with early campaigns by that group to halt the killing of whales and, off Newfoundland, the slaughter of fur seals. (I assume this was where he and Farley Mowatt, who was also opposed to the seal hunt, may have first found common ground.) They have worked together for over 25 years according to an article by Watson posted November 2008 on Mowat's most recent book "Otherwise". Watson, like Skipper Sue, was an early admirer of Mowat's writings.

In the 1970's Watson split with Greenpeace feeling that more needed to be done to protect marine life and founded the Sea Shepherd Conservation Society. The group is considerably more aggressive than Greenpeace in its efforts and has been labeled ecoterrorist for its sabotage efforts against whalers and other ships pursuing unsustainable fishery practices.

Watson's own interpretation of the law justifies his actions which include several sinkings of ships engaging in unlawful fishing practices. He's been controversial and colorful, but the *Wikipedia* entry on the group states that outcries notwithstanding, none of the fishermen targeted by the group have been killed. This is more than we can say for the countless mutilated sharks and slaughtered seals and whales Watson is trying to defend.

Because of the frequent accusations of piracy from people targeted by the group, Watson's Sea Shepherd ships now fly a jolly roger flag. After their ships' were pulled by Belize and Britain from their registries, Watson's 'navy' was granted the flag of the Kanawake Mohawk nation in 2007. However, *Wikipedia* says they're now under Dutch registry.

For more about Watson's gutsy campaign at sea with his "Neptune's Navy" of feisty little ships and gutsy crews and his very savvy and effective PR campaign ashore on behalf of whales, sharks, and other voiceless inhabitants of the sea visit the group's extremely interesting website at http://www.seashepherd.org/

David Suzuki, considerably less colorful but no less committed to the environment than Paul Watson, is a Canadian PhD geneticist who has made a successful career out of communicating scientific concepts and environmental messages to mass audiences through books, radio and TV media. He has published 43 books and several TV series including The Secret Of Life and A Planet For The Taking that were seen by millions.

Suzuki was born to Japanese parents on the west coast of Canada. But like so many other Japanese families his was interned during World War II and his father was sent off to a labor camp. After the war the Suzuki family was forcibly moved to Ontario Province. David grew up in London Ontario, but attended college and graduate school in the U.S. before becoming a professor of genetics at the University of British Columbia in Vancouver where he still lives.

In recent years Suzuki, like so many scientists, has become increasingly focused on global climate change and the dire need to change course in our dealings with the planet. He, like Al Gore, has done his best to foster that "major perceptual shift" that he calls for through lectures and speeches, writing and other media. A visit to the David Suzuki Foundation website reveals some of the environmental priorities the group is addressing, one current one being a revived call to export freshwater from Canada to dry and needy places.

The Foundation rightly points out that trading and selling our water is a good way to lose legal control over it. Exporting fresh water is expensive and yields few jobs compared to shipping goods and produce that require water for their production. And the impact of exporting water from the Great Lakes on the ecology of those waters would not be good. Less than one percent of the Great Lakes' waters is annually renewed. Take more than that out, and their levels will drop permanently. While lake front home owners might enjoy this, lower lake levels would be very bad for wetlands and for many nonhuman Lakes inhabitants.

Suzuki has written a number of books for younger readers about science and ecology among them *There's a Barnyard In My Bedroom* and *Salmon Forest* both of which are eloquent and delightful explorations of the connections between ourselves and the larger community of life. He has also written books for adults including *The Sacred Balance*.

A Note About the Cats and the Boats

"Riddle" is a mix of fiction and fact, and readers will have to decide for themselves which is what. But Twink, Dusty, and Miss Piggy did really go to Canada (several times) with me, and *Sara B* and *Ariel* were both real boats sailed by the author.

The cats joined me as crew after their cat-sitter, my mother, passed on. From 1991 until 1996, I cruised with cats (and fleas) aboard *Ariel*. Miss Piggy, as portrayed in the story, was indeed a 'fraidy cat. Once while anchored in Picton Harbor a passing motor boat startled her and she fell overboard. Piggy also had a very tender tummy and was more prone to sea sickness than Dusty and Twink. I don't think I ever saw tough little Twinkle Toes get sick. She was truly a lion hearted cat, as bold as her black and white coloration. Twink had yellow-green eyes and a sleek silky black coat except for her tummy, toes, chest, and chin of snow white. Her white whiskers stood in sharp contrast to her dark face.

Piggy was a large brown tabby with long hair and aqua eyes. I thought with her furred feet and elegant long ear whiskers that a Maine Coon Cat might have climbed into her family tree at some point. She was a nervous sailor. Once she hid herself back alongside the motor for a whole day. I was certain she'd gone overboard, for I had searched every corner of my 23 foot boat. Or so I thought. Piggy really did seem to be one of those cats that senses things people don't. I never saw her in my mother's downstairs bedroom until the last day my mother spent at her home. It seemed as if Piggy stood vigil that night on the back of the sofa, seeing something I didn't, a few days before death came calling in a hospital room.

Dusty, the dearest sweetest cat anyone could ever have known, was a motley little gray and buff short hair of the color pattern known as "dilute tortoise" by the cat fancy trade. A friend of mine thought she was a very odd color-he called it lavender. Dusty was a very young mother, and after having Twink and three other kittens, she was spayed. (Fixed doesn't seem quite the right term, after all we were taking something away from her!) Despite the lack of further future mother capacity, she loved her grown daughter as much as from day one when Twink was a newborn. I never saw her slap Piggy either.

Dusty also despised the boat and jumped or possibly fell overboard and swam ashore on three different occasions. But each time when I got ashore in the dinghy, she was lurking nearby and went back willingly with me. Because I worried about hazards ashore, I tried to keep track of my kitty crew. I rarely gave them shore leave unless the surroundings were quiet and known to be dog free. Rather, I would buckle a little harness on the cat and take her for a walk on a leash. Twink tolerated the indignity of walking on a leash (and even managed to catch a mouse once while on a walk). She stalked along and tried to pretend the leash didn't exist. Piggy and Dusty were insulted by the whole process. Piggy would slouch and drag her feet but with lots of persuasion would maybe walk a hundred feet. Dusty would just sit down. Dusty, a normally mellow sweet tempered cat, thought walks on a tether were totally inappropriate. I soon gave up on it with her.

In my effort to keep track of my kitties and keep them safe (?) aboard, I anchored out whenever possible. I had seen other cats from yachts wandering ashore unsupervised. I once had a young Siamese stroll aboard while we were tied up in Kingston. Cats love to explore hidden places on a yacht and it would be pretty easy to take off with somebody's cat on your boat and never be aware of it.

Some of the plot incidents are imaginary, but in my opinion totally plausible. Twink and I really were assaulted by a swan once. We were both scared out of our wits by it. And while the encounters with Richard, Pearl, Harry, and Sid are fiction, Main Duck's dockmaster snake has been a fixture of my cruises there for quite a few years as have the big snappers, some of whom panhandle food from the boaters. I never got lost in the fog in the shipping lane, but Charity Shoal could and probably did affect the compass headings of many a boat in the past. And Skipper Sue wasn't always as diligent about steering a close compass course as she might have been in the days before auto-helms.

The *Ariel* was a William Crosby design, a 23 footer called Osprey, whose plans were published in *The Rudder* magazine. She was built by a professor (and later dean) at the forestry college of Syracuse University. He knew his boat building woods and used top quality material in his little v-bottom hard chine hull knockabout including black locust for the keel and stem, white oak frames, and cedar planking. *Ariel's* plans were published in in 1939, but her builder, William Harlow, didn't get her finished until about 1947. *Ariel* was one of thousands of little homebuilt boats created from plans published in boating magazines of the day.

A lot has changed in the world of pleasure boats since 1895 when the first popular do-it-yourself boat plan was published, but one thing has been constant, the appeal of building your own. Thomas Fleming Day, editor of *The Rudder*, boosted circulation of his newly launched publication with a feature on How To Build A One Rater. Today *Make Magazine* offers on its website instructions for How To Build Cozy Boat (a low budget lashed together frame and cloth skin double ender.) This summer I met an eighty plus year old who 15 years before had started building his Tahiti ketch. He'd had the plans for at least twenty years before that. But he got 'er done.

Alas, through the years yachtsmen have often looked down their noses at the humble homemade boat, and most historians of the pastime of messing with boats have failed to give them their due. However, in my view homemade boats provide a window from which to view a wider world of changing family values, economic activity, and even global environmental shifts. You sure don't see many boat plans today specifying clear old growth Sitka spruce or white cedar, for example, as was common in 1930. Plywood or "hem-fir" from Home Depot or perhaps pressure treated pine are as likely to be the woods of choice today.

Backyard built boats during the first decades of the 20th century helped make yachting affordable for the middle class and spread sailing to places like Manitoba and Des Moines where it had never been seen. By doing it themselves, thousands of people otherwise beached by limited liquidity, could afford to get afloat.

Between 1900 and 1940 the rapid growth of backyard boat builder numbers was fueled by a steady supply of How To magazine articles and by a passion for tinkering in the home workshop. The optimistic "can do" spirit of the times saw backyard Edisons and tinkerers putting together airplanes, radio sets, and lots and lots of boats.

By the roaring 20s and the less lively Depression era 30s, hundreds of designs had been published for home builders. One of the more enduring was John Hanna's husky double ended ketch, the Tahiti. Dozens of kit boat builders also supplied amateur carpenters with a short cut to getting afloat. A typical "frame kit" consisted of full sized patterns and frames and of a ready made stem and back bone timbers, often with rabbets and bevels already cut. A frame kit for a nineteen foot Lightning sloop from Delta Manufacturing cost thirty eight dollars in 1940.

Many smaller one design sailboats such as the Snipe, Lightning, Comet, and Penguin, and a fair number of outboard powered speedboats and hydroplanes were built from kits. The beveled and sanded frames and floors, deck beams, mast step, and pre-assembled centerboard trunk allowed most buyers to put their boat together in a winter of weekends in the garage. Kits were excellent short cuts because they allowed first time builders to skip finding a large flat surface for the exacting tedium of lofting each frame and major timber.

Plywood gave post World War II do-it-yourselfers a big boost. A housing boom gobbled up vast amounts of prime quality wood and drove up prices for good lumber, adding to plywood's appeal. Top quality boat building lumber does not come from fast growing plantation trees. It takes at least 75 or a 100 years to grow a good boat board. So plywood was quickly adapted by amateur builders as well as by some production shops. Thousands of lapstrake plywood runabouts still survive from the last days of mass produced wooden boats.

Views are mixed as to whether it's reasonable or smart to use plantation grown pressure treated southern pine that is readily available in the local lumber yard for boat building and repairs. It's being done though. Even some professional shops are repairing work boats with pressure treated pine. In 2008 we experimented with lumberyard "pt" pine (sometimes known as southern teak) ourselves on *Sara B's* bottom.

Plywood enhanced a trend toward v-bottom sailboat designs for backyard boat builders in the 1950s. While some amateurs could and did build graceful round bottomed boats, many more opted for hard chine boats like *Ariel*. Such hulls avoided much, if not all, steam bending and eliminated waste in crafting a one off boat because the molds became part of the hull. It was also simpler to plank these flat sided boats. Then came fiberglass. A few people continued to build, but their numbers dwindled. Today with so many cheap fixer upper fiberglass boats around, a home built woodie is a distinct rarity. Yet, they still get built. We had one, a little gaff rigged cutter with a strip planked hull sailing on Fair Haven last year that was launched about seven years ago by its owner. And you still see a fair number of steel and some ferro cement home built boats when cruising Lake Ontario's Canadian waters.

Connoisseurs of wooden craft who seek out beautifully maintained wooden Alden's and Herreshoff's today are apt to scorn slab sided yachts like my *Ariel* as homely, but to my eyes she was a simple boat of wholesome line designed for beer budget builders. She was stiff, forgiving, and conservative, just what I wanted for sailing the lake alone. I suspect *Ariel*, like some of Crosby's other designs for back yard construction, was intended to keep the amateur builder-beginner sailor out of trouble as he learned to cruise.

In my little *Ariel* and her fast disappearing home built sisters, I also see the optimistic spirit of the hardy men and women who homesteaded, built their cabins, and made their fortunes in a new land. Today, the thread of manual skill and craftsmanship passed from father to son has been broken in many families. But thanks to the legacy of books and mouldering old magazines in attics, that thread can be re-created.

Unlike *Ariel, Sara B* the schooner, another of my boat associates, was professionally built, sort of. We were told that she originated in a Nova Scotia shop as an apprentice training project. As one old salt pointed out, that meant there was plenty of manpower available, and presumably few corners were cut in her layout and construction. *Sara B* was considerably bigger than *Ariel* at 12 tons displacement and 38 foot on deck and 47 foot overall. There were no magazine how-to plans for her hull. Rather, her designer, a boat builder named Ray Stevens, probably followed the old custom of carving out a half hull and then lofting the lines from that.

I obtained a detailed history of *Ariel's* restoration from the man I bought her from. He had found her in the back row of an Oneida Lake marina and purchased her just before she ended up in a July 4 parking lot bonfire. Through him, I also was able to correspond with *Ariel's* by then elderly builder for a year or two before he passed on. But *Sara B's* past remains obscure. We were told by the man we bought her from that she was finished up for a buyer in the mid 1950s and then motored up the St. Lawrence with her masts on deck against prevailing winds and currents to the canal connection to Lake Champlain then south to New York City and Long Island where she was given her inside lead ballast and otherwise finished up. Here she resided until we bought her on eBay in 2004 and exiled her to freshwater on Lake Ontario.

Though built as a yacht, *Sara B's* lines are "true to type" replicating those of the working Tancook schooners as noted by her designer on the single piece of paper documentation that came with her, a faded sail plan. We know little else about her, and I sometimes wonder if any of the apprentices who built her hull are still alive up in Nova Scotia. It would be interesting to meet one of them if they were.

In 1994 Wayne O'Leary, grandson of a Tancook Island boat builder, published a book titled *The Tancook Schooners.* Within a few months of buying *Sara B*, we had found a copy for our home library. In it the author states these little inshore fishing vessels were a mainstay of the coastal fishery from about 1910 to the 1930s. They were able to work twenty to thirty miles off shore using gill nets and trot lines for cod mackerel and herring and were also used to carry cargo in the coastal trade of Nova Scotia. One of the last viable trades for them was freighting cabbages from Tancook Island to the mainland. Many of the schooners were equipped with one or two cylinder 'make and break' gas engines of ten to twelve horsepower.

A number of the graceful little Tancook built schooners caught the eye of visiting yachters cruising the coast and many were either converted from fishing or built specifically as yachts. A classic sea story is that of *The Saga*

Of The Cimba by Richard Maury, a beautifully written account of a long voyage taken in the 1930s with a 35 foot Tancook schooner. A few Tancook boats made their way to Lake Ontario in the 1930s and 40s where they served as pleasure boats. O'Leary states in his book that the Tancook built schooners were "the pre-eminent small craft produced in the Maritimes" in their day. Certainly, I believe they were among the prettiest.

Back in the 1950s people had a rather different notion of what the well equipped pleasure yacht would be outfitted with. Our *Sara B is* downright spartan by modern day standards when the usual yacht has refrigeration, air conditioning, a stereo system, and a microwave. But her lack of amenities is probably in keeping with her background. She is notably lacking in fancy yacht-like features (as *Ariel* had also been). Upon first seeing *Sara B*'s lignum vitae deadeyes, spliced served rigging, wooden blocks, and hand-made iron work, I thought she looked like a little ghost from the past. She looked far older than she actually was.

Sara B was built with white oak framing, white cedar planking, and pine decks. Her caulked seam deck was in rough shape with many leaks and some rot, and after trying for two years to make it watertight, we gave up and tacked painted canvas over it. The little schooner was built in work boat style with rugged scantlings and galvanized steel and iron fittings. Thankfully she was not given a cranky traditional make and break gas auxiliary. Rather her builder installed a British two cylinder Thorneycroft diesel. Her planks were fastened with clinched iron boat nails, and like many a salt water boat before her, the reaction of rusting metal and oak took its toll of her structural integrity. In her time and place of construction, wood and labor were relatively cheap. But fancy bronze hardware and fastenings were not. Boats of her type were typically expected to last about 25 years at most.

As I worked on her bottom each spring, I marveled at the wide twenty foot long white cedar boards that made up her garboard planks and admired the grain of the natural larch crooks that made up the knees that strengthened her hull. The quarter sawn pine strips of her deck wouldn't come cheap either, today. Her two masts were shaped from sturdy solid native Canadian black spruce complete with checks and knots. They were quite different from the more common hollow glued up spars of clear knot free old growth Sitka spruce I'd seen on other yachts. *Sara B's* masts looked an awful lot like small utility poles to us.

Yet, for all her simple down to earth work boat construction, she had her looks. Her lines flowed in one harmonious eye pleasing whole, and under sail with her perfectly proportioned gaff rig, she was as pretty a boat as I've ever seen anywhere. "She's a looker" declared one seven year old upon seeing her. Despite the fact that she soaked up staggering amounts of time and energy and a not inconsiderable sum of money each spring, we were devoted to her and loved her dearly.

As I conclude this project, I look back upon the cats, boats, and people that I knew during my Lake Ontario adventures. I am grateful that I knew them. They made my world more interesting. My three dear old kitties are gone now, but I still live in a cat's house. She hasn't gone sailing yet. And I think she would just as soon continue to keep her feet dry and firmly ashore.

Ariel

Dusty

Piggy

Sara B

Northern water snake

Green frog

Twinkle Toes

Skipper Sue

Dusty and Twink

Other books by Susan Peterson Gateley

Ariadne's Death Heroism and Tragedy On Lake Ontario 96 pages isbn 09646149-4-9 Shipwrecks, rescues, and really close calls on Lake Ontario between 1840 and 2002. Captain Horatio Nelson Throop, the phantom barque, and the heroic beer cooler will keep you turning the pages. **$9.50**

The Edge Walker's Guide to Lake Ontario Beach Combing 160 pages isbn 09646149-3-2 Public beaches, parks, and wildlife management areas along Lake Ontario's shore between Rochester and Watertown. Also information on lake shore geology, marshes, wildlife, and seasonal highlights for hikers, beach combers and canoers- maps, 37 photos, **$17.00**

Passages On Inland Waters isbn 09646149-2-8 144 pages 2004 Jesuit journeys to save souls, a widow's wilderness flight, sailing through Lake Ontario's perfect storm, and a journey on the old Erie Canal are among the varied passages you'll find in this collection of voyages aboard a variety of vessels. **$14.95**

The Edgewalker's Guide to Birding Hot Spots with map. 24 page stapled pamphlet 2007 Describes a dozen great places between Webster and Oswego for bird watching along the lake shore, seasonal highlights and bird observatories. **$3.50**

Mirages Monsters Myths and Mysteries of Lake Ontario 80 pages 2001 Shove off for another exciting voyage of discovery on a great lake with Lake Ontario author Susan Peterson Gateley. Search for monsters, seek out fifty pound salmon, enjoy ghost stories, tales of love, mystery and tragedy **$9.00**

Sweet Waters Of Lake Ontario 127 pages adventure/voyages color cover stories of sailing, fishing, romance, and adventure from forty years of living by and sailing on Lake Ontario **$15.00**

on sale at www.chimneybluff.com or from
S. Gateley, 12025 Delling Rd, Wolcott, NY 14590, 315 594 1906